DISCARD

D1476057

DISCARD

JAPANESE IN MANGALAND
3

Intermediate Level

Marc Bernabe

Translation:
Olinda Cordukes

Cover illustration:
Nuria Peris

Inside illustrations:
Javier Bolado
Gabriel Luque
J.M. Ken Niimura
Barbara Raya
Studio Kōsen

495.68
BER

Pacific Grove Public Library

Marc Bernabe (L'Ametlla del Valles, Barcelona, 1976) is a Japanese-Spanish / Catalan translator and interpreter, working mainly on manga and anime translations. Apart from his translation works, he also specializes in language and Japanese culture didactics for foreigners, with a master's degree by the Osaka University of Foreign Studies. His published works are: *Japanese in MangaLand 1* and *2* (Japan Publications, 2004 and 2005), the Spanish adaptation of James W. Heisig's *Remembering the kanji* series, and other books on Japan and the Japanese language aimed at the Spanish speaking public. http://www.nipoweb.com

Japanese in MangaLand 3
Intermediate Level
By Marc Bernabe

© 2006 by *Marc Bernabe / Represented by NORMA Editorial S.A.*
All rights reserved, including the right to reproduce this book or portions thereof in any form without the written permission of the publisher.
Published and distributed: *Japan Publications Trading Co., Ltd.,*
                   1-2-1 Sarugaku-cho, Chiyoda-ku, Tokyo, Japan.

First printing: *January 2006*

Overseas Distributors
UNITED STATES:
   Kodansha America, Inc. through Oxford University Press,
   198 Madison Avenue, New York, NY 10016.
CANADA:
   Fitzhenry & Whiteside Ltd., 195 Allstate Parkway, Markham,
   Ontario L3R 4T8.
AUSTRALIA and NEW ZEALAND:
   Bookwise International Pty Ltd.,
   174 Cormack Road, Wingfield, South Australia 5013, Australia.
EUROPE, ASIA and JAPAN:
   Japan Publications Trading Co., Ltd., 1-2-1 Sarugaku-cho,
   Chiyoda-ku, Tokyo, 101-0064 Japan.

ISBN-13: 978-4-88996-187-4
ISBN-10: 4-88996-187-9

Printed in Spain

目次　Index

本書の特徴　Introduction

This book is the continuation of *Japanese in MangaLand* 1 and *Japanese in Manga-Land* 2. This means that the lessons here expand on the principles already taught in the previous books of the series: if you have not mastered the previous lessons, the contents herein will not be as useful as they could be. This is especially true for the lessons included in *Japanese in MangaLand* 2, as in this third book there are a lot of cross-references pointing to contents studied in the second book.

Main characteristics

As in the second book, again we will not be using any *rōmaji* here. This is so that you can study without relying constantly on those Roman alphabet "crutches," which may appear to be of great help in the beggining, but in reality, this does not hold true in the long run. The exclusion of the *rōmaji,* combined with the fact that the sentences included here have even more difficult kanji contained within them (always with their reading indicated in *furigana*), proves to create an "atmosphere" similar to which can be found in any manga for young readers, a concept which was thoroughly explained in book 2. If you need more information, please consult that previous work.

Likewise, in this book, we wanted to teach the "real Japanese" used in colloquial conversations as well as in manga. Thus, we have devoted some lessons to topics such as, among many others, casual speech (L.53) or dialects (L.59), which are often found in Japanese comics. However, we have not left the politer Japanese aside altogether, as L.52 (Honorifics) testifies.

The main aim of this method is to hone your already adquired Japanese skills to reach an intermediate level of the written language. Obviously, listening and speaking cannot be dealt with in a written work, therefore, you should try practicing on your on.

The lessons

This book has 15 lessons altogether, numbered from 46 to 60, chronologically following the numeration of the second volume. Of these 15 lessons, 11 are of a "grammatical" type and 4 are a "conversational" type.

GRAMMAR LESSONS, as their name clearly states, deal mainly with grammar issues. In these kind of lessons, you will have complete explanations in English, complemented with many example sentences and claryfing tables that should make comprehension easier. Grammatical patterns are grouped in the lessons according to related subjects. This being a self-taught study manual, we feel this is the most appropiate way to help you relate patterns that are similar in use and meaning, but that have different nuances. Giving a specific example, the expression だけ (only) is usually studied at a very early stage, but, in this book, it is taught in L.58, almost at the end, because it is discussed with other expressions with a similar meaning, such as しか and ばかり, thus constituting a solid block of grammatical constructions.

CONVERSATIONAL LESSONS fill the gap left by the grammar lessons, which strictly concentrate on grammar only. As they revolve around a contextual topic (In the restaurant, Sightseeing), they are useful for learning new vocabulary, practicing previously studied grammatical concepts with lots of example sentences, and even serve as a conversational guide, which is very helpful for possible trips to Japan or conversations with Japanese people. In these lessons, you will find as well a "Cultural Note" section, with insights into different aspects of the Japanese culture and environment.

All lessons, grammar and conversational ones alike, have manga-examples and exercices. The MANGA-EXAMPLES keep the same function they had until now: they will provide specific examples for expressions studied in the theory pages. They will also help you to expand concepts, see some new constructions, and revise constructions seen in previous lessons. Do not to skip them. Finally, the ten simple EXERCISES included in each lesson will help you consolidate your knowledge and check whether you have understood what has just been explained. The correct answers can be found in the first appendix, at the end of the book.

Appendixes

At the end of the book there are three appendixes with very useful extra information:

(1) **Answers to the exercises:** detailed answers to all exercises included in this book.
(2) **Grammar index:** compilation of all the grammatical expressions studied throughout the 60 lessons of the *Japanese in MangaLand* series' three books.
(3) **Vocabulary index:** and index of almost 2,000 words, containing all the vocabulary in this book, as well as all the vocabulary needed to pass levels 4 and 3 of the Japanese-Language Proficiency Test.

In addition to being a useful way to crown the contents of this course, these indexes were specifically conceived as a guide to cover the specifications for levels 4 and 3 of the 日本語能力試験 (Japanese-Language Proficiency Test.)

The Japanese-Language Proficiency Test

The 日本語能力試験 is an internationally recognized test, jointly administered by the official organizations **Japan Educational Exchanges and Services** and **Japan Foundation**, and simultaneously held every year on the first Sunday of December at venues all over the world. This test has become a standard to assess Japanese knowledge of non-native speakers, and it consists of four levels, the most difficult being level 1 and the easiest being level 4. We have created *Japanese in Mangaland* so it contains all the grammatical patterns, kanji and vocabulary required to pass levels 4 (elementary) and 3 (basic).

In the indexes you will find indications which will tell you whether a word or a construction belongs to one level or the other, thereby providing you with all the necessary tools for an in-depth study and to put your knowledge to the test on the next first Sunday in December. Good luck!

Specifications for the Japanese-Language Proficiency Test	
Level 4:	800 words, 100 kanji. The student can read, write, speak, and understand simple texts.
Level 3:	1,500 words, 300 kanji. The student has a sufficient level in Japanese to communicate in everyday life in Japan, and can read, write, speak, and understand texts of a medium-elementary level.
Level 2:	6,000 words, 1,000 kanji. The student can hold with no difficulty conversations with a certain degree of complexity and can read, write, speak, and understand texts of a medium-advanced level.
Level 1:	10,000 words, 2,000 kanji. The student has a command of Japanese at an advanced level in all aspects and has a sufficient level to study at a Japanese university with native students.

On translations

There are many example sentences throughout the book, as well as many manga-examples, with their corresponding word for word translations into English, just like in the first volume. Sometimes, the sentences we offer may "squeak" for not being very natural, since we have chosen more literal translations for an easier understanding of their formation. Trying to create a more natural English translation of every sentence would be a good exercise: it would help you consolidate concepts, make and in-depth analysis of the Japanese sentence, and think about it as a whole rather than a mere group of words and grammatical patterns. Besides, it might help you delve into the world of the translator and to realize the complexity of the work involved.

Acknowledgements

Before going on and entering the actual study, I would like to thank all the people that supported me, in one way or another, to develop *Japanese in MangaLand*, to nurture it and to make it grow to the point in which it has now been translated into seven different languages. First of all, my earnest thanks go to you, the readers, for being there, enjoying the books and, from time to time, sending me comments and encouragement to go on. If you wish to do so too, feel free to write in English through www.nipoweb.com/eng.

More thanks go to my dearest **Verònica Calafell** that, besides supporting me all the way (not an easy task!) during the long and strenuous process of writing these books, contributed to them giving comments to improve it and supervising every aspect. I owe a lot too to the whole teams at **Norma Editorial** and **Japan Publications**, who from the beggining were keen on publishing *Japanese in MangaLand* and helped it become what it has become today. The **Fundació La Caixa** and the **Japan Educational Exchanges and Services (JEES)** gave me the chance, by means of a grant, to learn extensively about Japanese language teaching methodology and resources. This, along with the guidance of professor **Sayo Tsutsui** 筒井佐代, of the Osaka University of Foreign Studies, was directly poured into the production of the books. **Luis Rodríguez** and **Josep Sadurní** revised my work as I wrote, and **Itsue Tanigawa** 谷川依津江 revised the Japanese sections. **James W. Heisig** provided his invaluable technical and moral assistance and help at all times; I consider him my dearest mentor. The artists **Javier Bolado, Gabriel Luque, J.M. Ken Niimura, Bárbara Raya** and **Studio Kōsen** created the manga panels that illustrate the books; last but not least, a big thank you to my efficient translator, **Olinda Cordukes**, and to my dear friend and corrector **Daniel Carmona**, whose precious comments helped improve this book beyond words. Thank you very much to all of you!

Marc Bernabe
July 24th, 2005
Osaka, Japan

略称集 Glossary of abbreviations

Excl.:	Exclamation.
Ger.:	Gerund.
Nom.:	Nominalizer.
Noun Suf.:	Suffix for proper names (people).
Soft.:	Sentence softener.
Suf:	Suffix.
CAP:	Cause Particle. *(why?)* Ex: から
CP:	Company Particle. *(who with?)* Ex: と
DOP:	Direct Object Particle. *(what?)* Ex: を
DP:	Direction Particle. *(where to?)* Ex: へ
EP:	Emphatic Particle. Most end-of-sentence particles state emphasis or add a certain nuance. (L.17, book 1) Ex: ね, よ, ぞ, etc.
IOP:	Indirect Object Particle *(whom?)* Ex: に
IP:	Instrument Particle. *(what with?)* Ex: で
POP:	Possessive Particle. *(whose?)* Ex: の
PP:	Place Particle. *(where?)* Ex: で, に
Q?:	Interrogative particle. Shows that the sentence is a question. Ex: か
SBP:	Subordinate sentence Particle. This particle is used as a link between a subordinate sentence and the main sentence. Ex: と
SP:	Subject Particle. *(who?)* Ex: が
TOP:	Topic Particle. Shows that the preceding word is the topic in the sentence. Ex: は (wa)
TP:	Time Particle. (When?) Ex: に

LESSONS

46 to 60

Lesson 46: Compound sentences (1)

We start this third book with a series of three lessons aimed at introducing several ways to create compound sentences in Japanese. Thanks to the links and structures we will learn, our Japanese will take a considerable step forward qualitywise, allowing us to form quite complex sentences. In this first lesson we will basically study expressions of continuity.

The easiest linking

We already saw in L.35 (book 2) that we can use the *-te* form to link sentences. This may be applied to verbs (寝て起きる *to sleep and wake up*), *-i* adjectives (広くて明るい *roomy and bright*), *-na* adjectives (丈夫で便利な *robust and practical*) and nouns (先生で研究者 *professor and researcher*). This method of linking sentences is very simple as well as useful, since it can have up to five different usages, namely 1) combination of elements, 2) sequence of actions, 3) mode, 4) simultaneous action or state, and 5) cause / reason:

1) 毎朝、牛乳を飲んでパンを食べる *Every morning I drink milk and eat bread.*
2) 早く起きて遠足に行きたい！ *I want to wake up early and go on an excursion!*
3) いちごを使っておいしいケーキを作った *I cooked a delicious cake using strawberries.*
4) 私は映画を見て、彼女は音楽を聞いた *I was watching a movie, and my girlfriend was listening to music.*
5) 博之が帰って広子が安心した *Hiroyuki left and (so) Hiroko was relieved.*

If we want to link negative sentences with the *-te* form (which we didn't see in L.35) we will use the negative conjugation of this *-te* form (〜ないで).

● 塩を使わないでハンバーグを作った *He cooked a hamburger without using salt.*
● 勉強しないで試験に合格した *I passed the exam without studying.*

There is also an equivalent form used to link negative sentences, formed by replacing the ないで of the negative *-te* form with ずに (寝ないで ⇒ 寝ずに, *without sleeping*). The only exception is する: it isn't しずに but せずに. It is used in written and formal registers.

● 塩を使わずにハンバーグを作った *He cooked a hamburger without using salt.*
● 勉強せずに試験に合格した *I passed the exam without studying.*

Another way of linking sentences in the negative

The forms we have just studied, and which are used to link sentences where the first verb is in the negative (〜ないで and 〜ずに), can't be used with the five cases in the affirmative we saw in the first point. To be precise, 〜ない can't be used to express "cause / reason," and we don't use 〜ずに to express "cause / reason" nor "simultaneous action or state," but have no fear, because you needn't know this by heart at this point.

To express "cause / reason," we use the -te form of a verb conjugated in the negative. Ex: 使う (to use) ⇒ negative: 使わない ⇒ negative -te form: 使わなくて. We already saw the conjugations for the -te form of verbs in the negative in the table in L.35 (book 2).

● 博之が帰らなくて広子が心配していた *Hiroyuki didn't return home and (so) Hiroko was worried.*
● 車を買わなくてよかった *I didn't buy the car, (so) I'm happy.*

To link two -i adjectives in the negative (not only "cause / reason," but generally) we also use the -te form of the negative. Ex: 広い (broad) ⇒ negative: 広くない ⇒ -te form of the negative: 広くなくて. In the case of -na adjectives and nouns, we use ではなくて or, in colloquial register, じゃなくて (じゃ is the contraction of では).

● アパートは明るくなくて古いです *The apartment is not bright and is old.*
● 彼女は日本人では(じゃ)なくて、韓国人です *She is not Japanese, she is Korean.*

Simultaneous actions: 〜ながら

To form sentences of the kind "I do x while I'm doing y," that is, sentences expressing simultaneous actions, we use 〜ながら. Usage: Verbal root + 〜ながら. Ex: 使う (to use) ⇒ root: 使い ⇒ we add ながら: 使いながら (while I'm using). Note: 〜ながら is only used with verbs, and the subject (the one who performs the action) must be the same for both verbs (that is, the performed actions) in the sentence.

● 音楽を聞きながら、本を書いている *While I'm listening to music, I write the book.*
● ジョンは笑いながら映画を見ていた *John laughed as he watched the movie.*
● 辞書を引きながら翻訳する *I translate, (while) consulting a dictionary.*
● コーヒーを飲みながら話しましょう *Let's talk, while we drink (have) a coffee.*

In sentences with 〜ながら, there usually is a central action and an incidental action – the verb of the latter takes 〜ながら. – Compare these sentences:

● ご飯を食べながら新聞を読む *While I'm eating, I read the newspaper.* (center: to read)
● 新聞を読みながらご飯を食べる *While I read the newspaper, I eat.* (center: to eat)

A situation remains unchanged: 〜まま

We are now going to see the expression 〜まま, which indicates an action or situation described by the verb, to which this expression has been attached, remains completely unchanged. Usage: 〜まま is used after verbs conjugated in the past tense. Ex. 寝る *(to sleep)* ⇒ past: 寝た ⇒ we add 〜まま: 寝たまま *(he is still asleep / there are no changes in the state of his being asleep)*. This expression is also used with some *-i* adjectives (we don't change anything), *-na* adjectives (we keep な), and nouns (we add の).

● テレビをつけたまま仕事に行ってしまった *I went to work, leaving the TV on.*
● 百合子はドイツへ行ったまま戻らない *Yuriko went to Germany and is not coming back.*
● ずっと学生のままでいたいな *I'd like to be a student for ever.*

If the verb before 〜まま is negative, we don't have to conjugate it in the past tense.

● 鍵をかけないまま家から走り出した *I ran out of the house, without locking the door.*
● 彼は休まないままずっと働いている *He works constantly, without taking a break.*

Non-exhaustive list of actions: 〜たり〜たりする

The next expression is, somehow, the version of や (L.41, book 2) for verbs and adjectives. 〜たり〜たりする is used to express a kind of "non-exhaustive list" of actions or states. That is, we indicate two or more actions or states, and whether "there could be more" is left up in the air. Usage: verbs are conjugated into the past tense and り is added. The last element in the sentence is followed by する. Ex: 買う *(to buy)* ⇒ past: 買った ⇒ we add り (and する if it is the last element): 買ったり(する) *(to buy − and other things)*. *-i* adjectives also go in the past tense, like 高かったり(する) (expensive − and other things). Whereas *-na* adjectives and nouns need the verb "to be" in the *-tari* form (だったり). Ex: 便利だったり(する) *(to be convenient − and other things)* and 先生だったり(する) *(to be a teacher − and other things)*.

● 仕事でインターネットをしたり、ファックスを送ったり、書類を作ったりするよ

  At work, I browse on the Internet, send faxes, write documents (and I do other things).
● 毎朝、コーヒーを飲んだり新聞を読んだりします

  Every morning, I drink coffee, read the newspaper (and I also do other things).

Sometimes 〜たり is used with only one verb or adjective. The connotation is that, even though only one action or state is mentioned, there are more which are not named.

● 鍵をなくしたりしてはいけないね *Don't lose the keys (or something like that), OK?*
● 恋に落ちたりするのは危ない！ *Falling in love (or something similar) is dangerous!*

In the case of: 場合（ばあい）

The word 場合（ばあい）(*case, occasion, circumstance*) can be used to form sentences of the kind "in the case of..." Usage: it can follow verbs and *-i* adjectives conjugated in any form. After *-na* adjectives and nouns it requires の.

- 戦争が起きた場合、逃げてください *In case war is declared, please run away (escape).*
- 雨の場合は体育館で練習しよう *In case of rain, we will train in the gym.*

Not only X, also Y: ～し

Another very useful way of linking sentences is using ～し, which gives the connotation of "not only x, also y." Usage: the usage of ～し is very simple, as it can follow any verb and *-i* adjective conjugated in any form. With *-na* adjectives and nouns, it requires the verb "to be" (です/だ).

- 明日は試験があるし、塾にも行かなければならない

Tomorrow I have an exam and, besides, I must go to cram school.

- この家は広いし、駅が近い *Not only is this house roomy, the station is also close by.*

Sometimes we can find more than one ～し in a sentence, as if forming a list:

- 彼女は頭がいいし、きれいだし、金持ちだし...完璧だな！

She is intelligent, as well as beautiful, as well as rich... She's perfect!

Compound sentences (1): general summary table		
～て	Linking sentences	景色を見て絵をかいてください Look at the landscape and draw a picture, please
～ないで ～ずに	Linking sentences. The first sentence is in the negative	景色を見ないで（見ずに）絵をかくのは難しいです Drawing a picture without looking at the landscape is difficult
～なくて	Linking sentences. The first sentence is in the negative. Expresses cause/reason	彼と会わなくて残念だ It's a pity I won't meet him
～ながら	"While I'm doing x, I do y" (two simultaneous actions)	景色を見ながら絵をかいた While I was looking at the landscape, I drew a picture (Note: the drawing doesn't need to be of the landscape)
～まま	A state or action already done which remains unchanged	私は疲れたままマラソンに参加した I took part in the marathon, being tired as I was
～たり～たりする	Non-exhaustive list of actions	マラソンに参加したり、絵をかいたりするのは楽しいです I enjoy taking part in marathons, drawing pictures... (and so on)
場合（ばあい）	"In the case of..."	雨の場合、マラソンに参加しません In case of rain, I won't take part in the marathon
～し	"Not only x, also y"	マラソンに参加したし、絵もかいた I not only took part in the marathon, I also drew a picture

景色 けしき: landscape｜見る みる: to look｜絵をかく えをかく: to draw a picture｜難しい むずかしい: difficult｜彼 かれ: he｜会う あう: to meet｜疲れる つかれる: to get tired｜残念 ざんねんな: to be a pity｜マラソン: marathon｜参加する さんかする: to take part｜楽 たのしい: enjoyable｜雨 あめ: rain

Conjunctions

So far we have seen expressions we use to create compound sentences. However, at the end of each of the three lessons called "Compound sentences" (this one being the first) we will study some expressions placed at the beginning of a sentence, which are used to link two or more sentences or ideas. In the last lesson in the series (L.49), we will give a summary table with all these conjuctions.

1) For example: 例えば

● 僕は日本料理が大好きです。例えば、寿司や天ぷらや親子丼が好きです

I love Japanese cuisine. I like, for example, sushi, tempura, oyakodon, etc.

● 多くの武道は、例えば空手とか柔道とかが日本から来ている

Many martial arts, like for example karate or judo, come from Japan.

2) By the way: ところで

● 君は２５歳なの？ところで、俺は何歳だと思う？

You are 25? By the way, how old do you think I am?

● 今日は天気がいいな...ところで、何か飲みに行こうか？

The weather is beautiful today, isn't it... By the way, shall we go out for a drink?

3) Besides: それに Note: This expression is almost equivalent to 〜し.

● 明日は試験がある。それに塾にも行かなければならない

Tomorrow I have an exam. And besides, (on top of that) I must go to cram school.

● 今日、彼女と別れた。それにバイクで事故にあった

Today, I split up with my girlfriend. And besides, (to crown it all off) I had a motorcycle accident.

Nominalizing adjectives

Curiously enough, up to now we had not seen one of the simplest characteristics in Japanese grammar: the formation of nouns from -*i* and -*na* adjectives. This is the time to study such a basic and useful point.

<u>-*i* adjectives</u>: We replace the last い with さ.

広い *wide* ⇒ 広さ *width*　　黒い *black* ⇒ 黒さ *blackness*
太い *fat* ⇒ 太さ *fatness*　　明るい *bright* ⇒ 明るさ *brightness*

<u>-*na* adjectives</u>: We replace the last な with さ.

便利な *convenient* ⇒ 便利さ *convenience*　親切な *kind* ⇒ 親切さ *kindness*
きれいな *beautiful* ⇒ きれいさ *beauty*　丈夫な *robust* ⇒ 丈夫さ *robustness*

We have now seen many new constructions in just a few pages, so we'd better relax now with a few manga-examples where we will review what we have seen in the theory section, and we will study one or two slightly different usages of some expressions.

a) Linking a negative sentence to another sentence: *zu ni*

> **Hirose:** 誰<small>だれ</small>も傷<small>きず</small>つけずに生<small>い</small>きてきた人<small>ひと</small>などいない
> *nobody wound put live come person or other not there is*
> **No one has ever lived without hurting anybody.**

J.M. Ken Niimura

Our first manga-example will show us how to link two different sentences when the first one is negative, whether the other one is or not. We have studied in the theory section that this is achieved with the negative *-te* form. In this case, the two ideas to be linked are 誰<small>だれ</small>も傷<small>きず</small>つけない (*not to hurt anybody*) and 生<small>い</small>きてきた人<small>ひと</small> (*person who has lived*).

If we conjugate the first one in the negative *-te* form and we "add" both sentences, we get: 誰<small>だれ</small>も傷<small>きず</small>つけないで生<small>い</small>きてきた人<small>ひと</small> (*person who has lived without hurting anybody*). This kind of linking is #4 (simultaneous action or state) in the list we saw at the beginning of this lesson. However, we have also said that there is a similar alternate construction, used in the formal register. This form, 〜ずに, is the one used in this panel. The speaker is in a tense situation, and he probably chooses 〜ずに to give more "weight" to his statement. The formation of 〜ずに is as simple as replacing the ないで ending in the negative *-te* form of any verb with ずに. Thus, the final sentence is as we see in the example: 誰<small>だれ</small>も傷<small>きず</small>つけずに生<small>い</small>きてきた人<small>ひと</small> (*person who has lived without hurting anybody*).

Notes: There is still another idea linked to this compound sentence: いない (*there isn't*). The word など (in kanji 等) could be translated as *etcetera*. Also, notice the usage of 誰<small>だれ</small>も (nobody, L.37) and of 〜てくる (L.35), and take the opportunity to review these expressions.

b) Everything remains the same: *kono mama*

Kuroda: このままでいたら　みんなに迷惑がかかっちゃうもんな...
this (no changes) be all IOP *nuisance* SP *put (the fact is)* EP*...*
The fact is that if I stay the way I'm now, I'll be a nuisance to you all...

Javier Bolado

Here we have a small and very common variation of ～まま: linking ～まま to the demonstrative pronouns この *(this)*, その *(sono)*, and あの *(ano)* (L.34, book 2). The resultant words could approximately be translated as "as it is."

A typical example (in the supermarket): 袋が要りますか？ *Do you need a bag?* いいえ、このままでいいです *No, it's fine as it is.* This sentence means you will take the product or products "as they are," without the necessity of a bag to carry them.

Note: Notice the contraction ～ちゃう (L.35); the non-contracted version would be 迷惑がかかってしまう *(to cause trouble).* いたら is the conditional (L.56) of いる: *if I stayed.*

c) Non-exhaustive list of actions

Calvin: おれは楽しんだり、笑ったりしちゃいけねえんだ。スーザンは...
I SP *have fun (or something), laugh (or something) do must not. Susan...*
I shouldn't have fun, nor laugh, nor anything. Susan...

Bárbara Raya

Here we have a good example of ～たり～たりする. Remember this is used to form a sort of non-exhaustive "list" of actions or states. Thus, in the sentence 楽しんだり笑ったりする, the main character indicates that "he is having fun and laughing," but he also suggests there are more actions which are not mentioned (that's why we have chosen translating "nor anything"). Notice how the verb する usually closes the "list" (but be careful, as sometimes it is omitted).

Note: ～しちゃいけねえ is the contracted and vulgar version of ～してはいけない (prohibition, L.32). The んだ in the end is a very common softening tag (contraction of のだ), which we studied in the manga-example d) in L.40 (book 2).

d) A slightly different usage of *baai*

> **Fujita:** 責任なすりつけあってる場合じゃないでしょうがあァ！！
> *responsibility recriminate mutually occasion not be true but!!*
> **I don't think this is time to ask for responsibilities, is it?!**

Studio Kōsen

We saw before that the word 場合 is used in constructions indicating "in the case of...". Here we have a somewhat different usage, where the negative inflection of 場合だ *(to be the time)* is used: 場合では(じゃ)ない. This expression, used very often in films or manga (you seldom hear it in real life) means *this is not the time to...* An example: 今は笑っている場合ではない！ *This is not the time to laugh!*

Note: Watch out with the triple compound verb なすりつけあってる (-te form of なすりつけあう). The base is なする *(to extend)*, followed by the suffix 〜つける, which adds the connotation of "pushing, pressing, throwing." なすりつける is translated as *placing the blame on somebody*. Finally, 〜合う makes it a little bit more complicated, adding a connotation of reciprocity, "mutually" (L.44, book 2).

e) Softening sentences: *shi*

> **Man:** ああ スーツも銃も見つかったしな
> *yes suit also gun also find besides EP*
> **Yes... And besides, I have found a suit and a gun.**

We have studied a few pages ago that 〜し is used to link sentences and give them a connotation of "not only x, also y." Here we have an example of this construction, although its usage is slightly different.

In spoken Japanese we very often use 〜し at the end of a sentence to soften a statement or as a simple tag. Sentences like 今日は疲れたしな *Today I'm tired and, (besides)...* or 台湾にも行ったしな *I also went to Taiwan and (besides)...* indicate the speaker wants to express more things in a veiled form, but doesn't, so as not to sound long-winded.

Gabriel Luque

Hence our tentative translation with "besides" at the end of each sentence.

Note: Notice the usage of the end-of-the-sentence particle な (L.17, book 1) in these kind of sentences. It's an informal usage, used sometimes to soften a sentence or to express a wish.

f) Besides

Yūji: それにレッカーはお金かかるからもったいないですよ
besides wrecker top money cost because waste be EP
Besides, the tow truck costs money, and it would be a waste.

Studio Kōsen

Here is an example for それに, one of the three expressions used to link different sentences or ideas which we have studied in this lesson. それに is used in a similar way to our adverbs or adverbial constructions "besides," "apart from that," "to crown it all," "moreover," and so on. In our example, Yūji is going to help someone whose car has broken down on the road. We don't know the previous sentence, but we can suppose, because of the それに, that Yūji had given another reason to offer his help to his interlocutor.

Notes: The *-i* adjective もったいない doesn't have a direct translation into English, but it mainly indicates that something is "a waste," "a pity," or "it's not worth...:" it is generally used with money, time, or other things that can be "spent."

g) Formation of nouns from adjectives

Powell: それがあいつの戦士としての恐ろしさだ！
that SP that guy POP warrior as POP frightfulness be!
Such is his frightfulness as a warrior!

J.M. Ken Niimura

We will conclude the lesson with an example of how to turn an *-i* adjective into a noun. The process is as simple as replacing the last い with さ. Thus, from the *-i* adjective 恐ろしい (*terrible, frightful*) we obtain the noun 恐ろしさ *frightfulness.*

Notes: The literal translation of this sentence would be *that is the frightfulness of that guy as a warrior.* Finally, あいつ is a vulgar term meaning *that guy.*

① Link 浴衣を着る and 外に出ていきたい。
(浴衣: yukata (summer kimono), 着る: to put on, to wear, 外: outside, 出る to go out)

② Do the same as in exercise 1, but this time the sentence 浴衣を着る must be conjugated in the negative. Use both options.

③ Translate the sentence: "This book is not thick and it's light." (book: 本, thick: 厚い, light: 軽い)

④ Tell the difference between: ビールを飲みながら踊ろう and 踊りながらビールを飲もう (ビール: beer, 飲む: to drink, 踊る: to dance)

⑤ Translate into English: エアコンをつけたまま寝てしまった。(エアコン: air conditioning, つける: to turn on, 寝る: to sleep)

⑥ Translate using ～たり: "This summer I swam, walked, rested..." (summer: 夏, to swim: 泳ぐ, to walk: 歩く, to rest: 休む)

⑦ Translate using ～し: "This summer I swam and I walked as well." (summer: 夏, to swim: 泳ぐ, to walk: 歩く)

⑧ Translate into Japanese: "By the way, shall we go out for a tea (or something)?" (To have (drink): 飲む, tea: お茶).

⑨ Turn into nouns the following adjectives: 辛い (spicy, hot), 大切な (important), 元気な (cheerful), and 白い (white).

⑩ Translate into Japanese: "This is no time to dance the flamenco!" (now (this moment): 今, to dance: 踊る, flamenco: フラメンコ)

第(47)課：レストランで

Lesson 47: In the restaurant

Japanese food is famous all over the world... Are you ready to enjoy it? You had better prepare yourself, because we are going to see a lot of food vocabulary, so much that we will have you salivating and smacking your lips by the time you are done with this chapter!

A new world

Indeed, as this title suggests, the gastronomic experience in Japan — or in a Japanese restaurant, of course—, is like entering a new world, as there is a huge amount of ingredients, preparations, sauces, and dishes that immensely differ from what the average Western palate is used to. In this lesson, we will learn how to go shopping for food in Japan, how to use the ever-present fast food restaurants and, of course, how to enjoy the genuine Japanese gastronomy in popular and luxury restaurants all over the *Land of the Rising Sun*.

However, you must prepare yourself to study vocabulary, because there are so many things to learn, we have had to devote up to two pages only to this task. Are you ready for this huge task? Then, let's go!

Buying food

Before you start, we recommend that you review the section "We are going shopping!" in L.42 in *Japanese in MangaLand*, vol. 2, to refresh your memory on basic sentences to go shopping for anything, foodstuffs included.

Now, then, we are ready to fill our pantry. We will start with the simplest step: our first test will be an expedition to a supermarket. Even though they may look very similar to Western ones, Japanese supermarkets will surprise the average Westerner with the enormous quantity of "strange" things you can find in them: from giant radishes 大根 to 豆腐, from take away 寿司 to traditional Japanese sweets, such as 団子 or どら焼き (see vocabulary tables).

In the market or the local shop

Going to the supermarket doesn't involve any "linguistic danger" we can't overcome using the knowledge you have acquired so far. Aside from what you already know (questions such as *will you pay cash?* and so forth, studied in L.42 (book 2) and previous lessons), the cashier may ask you at most:

● スーパーマーケットXのカードを持っていますか? *Do you have the x supermarket card?*

Obtaining your local supermarket card to get points is very typical, and cashiers almost always ask you if you have one.

However, the real acid test entails buying food in the market or at the corner shop run by that little smiling old woman. Make sure to review the counters thoroughly (L.25, book 1) because you will have to use them quite often.

いらっしゃいませ!

Ready to enter the jungle of いらっしゃいませ? This word, which has appeared a few other times already, means something like "welcome," and in all shops throughout Japan (absolutely all of them, restaurants and パチンコ pinball houses included) you can hear rounds of いらっしゃいませ, when a possible client is spotted. Fishmongers, specially, distort the expression to the utmost: things like らっしゃい! are common and typical. The right thing to do when greeted by one of these shouts −very often shop clerks shout themselves hoarse−, is to (oddly enough) ignore it. Even though you might find it embarrassing, you don't need to answer, or even look at the shop clerk.

● これは何ですか? *What is this?* (L.34)
● 北海道特産の大根です *They are "daikon" giant radishes, a speciality from Hokkaidō.*
● その大根を一本ください *I'll have one of those "daikon" radishes, please.* (L.25)
● すみませんが、しいたけはありますか? *Excuse me, do you sell "shiitake" mushrooms?*
● はい、あそこにあります *Yes, they are over there.* (L.34)
● 鶏肉の胸はいくらですか? *How much is the chicken breast?* (L.34)
● 100グラム当たり83円です *It is 83 yen per 100 grams.*

In Japan they use the metric system: グラム *(gram)* and キロ *(kilo)*. But be careful when buying fruit: it is so expensive you don't buy it by the gram or the kilo, but by the unit.

Asking りんごを500グラムください *I'll have 500 grams of apples, please* is unusual. You would normally ask りんごを5個ください *I'll have five apples, please.*

Fast-food outlets

Like almost anywhere in the world, ファストフード chains are a feature in Japan, specially マクドナルド and ケンタッキーフライドチキン. You don't usually have to struggle much if you go to one of these restaurants, because once you can read カタカナ, you will understand most of the items on the menu: ハンバーガー, チキンサンドイッチ and コカコーラ are relatively clear. But take care, as "French fries" are called フライドポテト!

● ご注文はお決まりになりましたか？ *Have you decided on your order?* (L.44/formal: L.52)
● これとあれをお願いします *(Pointing the menu) I'll have this and that, please.* (L.34)
● ハンバーガーとコーラの大をください *A hamburger and a large cola, please.*
● 玉ねぎ抜きでお願いします *Without onion, please.*
● お飲み物は何にしますか？ *What would you like to drink?* (L.34)
● こちらでお召し上がりですか、お持ち帰りですか？ *Will you eat here or is it take-out?* (L.41/52)

However, we recommend that you try indigenous Japanese ファストフード : chains such as 吉野家 or 松屋, with outlets all over the country, offer dishes like 牛丼 or カレーライス, often cheaper than hamburger joints. It is always more interesting than ending at マクドナルド, which you can find in your own backyard. (But, ifyou absolutely must go there, then at least try tomething you can not find back home.)

Meals		
breakfast	朝食	朝ご飯
lunch	昼食	昼ご飯
aft. snack	おやつ	
dinner	夕食	夕ご飯

To the restaurant!

There is no shortage of places to eat in Japan: from small ラーメン, そば or うどん noodle eateries to very luxurious restaurants. Japan is undoubtedly a gourmet country, proof lying in the huge amount of magazines, television programs, and even manga solely devoted to delighting their audiences and readers with sumptuous dishes and recipes.

Finding a place to eat won't be difficult, because most restaurants have a window where they show hyper-real plastic models of the dishes they serve, as well as the price. Thus, it is very easy to decide what to eat, depending on your preferences and your budget. Once you have decided, open the sliding door, be greeted by the loud いらっしゃいませ from the waiters, and sit down or wait to be taken to a table.

● 何名様ですか？ *How many people are you?* | 2人です *Two people.* (L.25)
● ご案内します。こちらです *Follow me (I'll lead you). This way.*

いただきます！

We are now ready to order. Take a good look at the メニュー, and choose whatever you prefer. However, before you actually begin eating, don't forget to say いただきます (L.27).

● 英語のメニューはありますか？ *Do you have an English menu?*

● おすすめ料理は何ですか？ *What dishes do you recommend?*

● 定食はありますか？ *Do you have set menus (main dish with a side of rice and* miso *soup)?*

● ラーメンと餃子をお願いします *I'll have* rāmen *and some* gyōza.

● あれと同じものにします *(Pointing) I want that same thing over there.*

● 外にある「親子丼定食」をください *I want the "oyakodon set" outside (in the window).*

● 日本酒もお願いします *I'll have some sake as well, please.*

● ジュースのお代わりをください *Another juice, please.*

● ごちそう様でした！ *It was delicious! | Thanks for the meal!*

Flavors and sensations	
bitter	苦い
hot	熱い
delicious	おいしい
sweet	甘い
cold	冷たい
spicy hot	辛い
salty	塩辛い
sour	すっぱい
bland	味が薄い

Cooking...	
grilled	鉄板焼き
to roast, fry	焼く
to cook, simmer	煮る
to steam	蒸す
to deep fry (in oil)	揚げる
to boil	ゆでる
to pickle	漬ける
to stir-fry	炒める

Paying

Finally, let's see a few useful sentences when the time to pay comes (review L.42, in book 2, as well):

● お勘定をお願いします *The bill, please.*

● 全部でいくらですか？ *How much is it altogether?*

● 勘定は別々にしてください *We want separate bills.*

● 2000円です *It is 2,000 yen.*

In many restaurants, you pay at the cash register, placed near the entrance. Don't wait for the bill: just stand up, pick up your belongings, head to the register, and one of the ever-alert waiters will rush to the cash register to ring up your bill. An important fact is that in Japan you don't tip, not even in restaurants! When you are given the change, simply keep it if you don't want the waiter to hunt you down in order to give back the money "you forgot."

Saying goodbye with a ごちそう様でした is very good manners. A round of very loud ありがとうございました will accompany you as you exit…

Vocabulary: typical Japanese food

Dishes (日本料理)

炒飯 チャーハン	Chinese style fried rice with egg, vegetables, meat… "Three variety fried rice"
団子 だんご	Typical Japanese sweet. Three rice-flour balls in sweet sauce
どら焼き	Typical Japanese sweet. A small pancake filled with *anko* (see ingredients)
餃子 ぎょうざ	Steamed or fried Chinese dumpling stuffed with meat or vegetables
牛丼 ぎゅうどん	A bowl of rice topped with beef and onion
唐揚げ からあ	Japanese style fried chicken
カレーライス curry rice	Curry rice (Japanese style)
カツ丼 どん	A bowl of rice topped with *tonkatsu* and sauce
味噌汁 みそしる	*Miso* soup
餅 もち	Mashed rice paste
納豆 なっとう	Fermented soybeans
おでん	Winter hotchpotch with *daikon*, *chikuwa* fish paste, meatballs, etc.
お好み焼き このや	"Pancake" on a bed of cabbage, to which anything can be added
おにぎり	Stuffed rice balls (tuna, umeboshi, salmon, *konbu*…)
親子丼 おやこどん	Bowl of rice (丼) with chicken (親, the "father") and egg (子, the "son")
ラーメン	Noodle soup, originally from China, but adapted to Japanese taste
刺身 さしみ	*Sashimi*. Raw fish (dish)
しゃぶしゃぶ	Vegetable and beef stew, with the beef very finely cut and boiled in water
シュウマイ	Steamed meat dumpling, originally from China
そば	Buckwheat noodles served either in hot soup or cold
すき焼き や	Vegetable, meat, and *tofu* stew, cooked by the guests themselves
寿司 すし	*Sushi*. Raw fish on a rice base or rolled in rice and *nori*
たこ焼き や	Flour balls stuffed with octopus, very typical in the Osaka region
天ぷら てん	*Tempura*. Deep-fried battered vegetables and fish
豆腐 とうふ	*Tōfu*. Bean curd
豚カツ とん	Pork, dipped in a crumb batter and deep-fried, served with a special sauce
うどん	Thick wheat noodles, usually served in hot soup
焼き肉 やにく	Meat of different kinds, roasted on a hot plate (done by guests)
焼きそば や	Fried *soba* noodles with a special sauce, vegetables and meat
焼き鳥 やとり	Roasted chicken shish kebabs

Ingredients (日本料理の材料)

あんこ	Sweetened bean paste. Also called a *an*
大根 だいこん	Giant Japanese radish
大豆 だいず	Soy
だし	Soup stock, basic in Japanese cooking, usually made from fish or seaweed
ごま	Sesame
白菜 はくさい	Chinese cabbage
かつおぶし	Dried bonito flakes
昆布 こんぶ	Sea tangle, sea kelp. Giant seaweed
みりん	Cooking sweet sake (rice wine)
味噌 みそ	*Miso*. Fermented paste made from soybeans
のり	*Nori*. Very thin and dry, sweetened seaweed
蓮根 れんこん	Radish. Lotus root
しいたけ	*Shiitake*. Japanese mushroom
醤油 しょうゆ	Soy sauce
竹の子 たけこ	Bamboo shoots
梅干 うめぼし	Pickled dry plum
わかめ	*Wakame*. A type of edible seaweed
わさび	*Wasabi*. Very hot Japanese horseradish

Food vocabulary

Ingredients（ざいりょう）

Vegetables 野菜

cabbage	キャベツ
carrot	にんじん
cucumber	きゅうり
eggplant	なす
garlic	にんにく
green pepper	ピーマン (piment)
lettuce	レタス
onion	玉ねぎ
potato	じゃがいも
pumpkin	かぼちゃ
rice (cooked)	ご飯
rice (raw)	米
salad	サラダ
scallion	にら
tomato	トマト

Meat 肉

beef	牛肉
chicken	鶏肉
ham	ハム
lamb, mutton	羊肉
pork	豚肉
sausage	ソーセージ
steak	ステーキ

Fish 魚

bonito	かつお（鰹）
clam	貝
crab	かに（蟹）
octopus	たこ（蛸）
prawn, shrimp	えび（海老）
salmon	さけ｜しゃけ（鮭）
sardine	いわし（鰯）
squid	いか
tuna	まぐろ（鮪）

Others その他

bread	パン
cake	ケーキ
cheese	チーズ
chocolate	チョコレート
dessert	デザート
egg	卵｜玉子
ice cream	アイスクリーム
omelet	オムレツ
pasta	パスタ
pudding	プリン
soup	スープ
yogourt	ヨーグルト

Utensils（器具；きぐ）

big bowl	丼（どんぶり）
bottle	びん（瓶）
bowl	茶碗
chopstick rest	箸置き
chopsticks	お箸
disposable chopsticks	割りばし
fork	フォーク
frying pan	フライパン
glass	グラス｜コップ (kop)
lunch box	弁当箱
knife	ナイフ
menu	メニュー
napkin	ナプキン
plate	お皿
pot	鍋
small wet towel	おしぼり
spoon	スプーン

Seasoning（ちょうみりょう）

butter	バター
ginger	しょうが
ketchup	ケチャップ
mayonnaise	マヨネーズ
mustard	からし
oil	油
pepper	こしょう
salt	塩
sauce	ソース
sugar	砂糖
vinegar	酢

Drinks（飲み物；のみもの）

alcoholic drk.	お酒
beer	ビール
coffee	コーヒー
black tea	紅茶
green tea	抹茶
juice	ジュース
milk	牛乳
milk coffee	カフェオレ (cafe au lait)
sake	日本酒
soft drink	ジュース
tea	お茶
water	水
wine	ワイン

Fruit（果物；くだもの）

apple	りんご（林檎）
banana	バナナ
cherry	さくらんぼ
grape	ぶどう
kiwi	キウイ
mandarin	みかん
melon	メロン
orange	オレンジ
peach	桃
pear	なし（梨）
strawberry	いちご（苺）
watermelon	すいか

文化編：食卓での作法
Cultural note: Table manners

日本（にほん） is a different country in so many aspects. It is worthwhile knowing some basic table manners so you don't commit any of those typical mistakes characteristic of 外人（がいじん） *(foreigners)*.

We will start with the famous お箸（はし）, used in almost all meals (except with Western dishes, although, curiously enough, seeing someone eating スパゲッティ or パエリア with お箸（はし） is not unusual). Knowing how to use お箸（はし） is essential if you don't want to starve to death in 日本（にほん）, but don't worry: with a little bit of practice one quickly gets used to them.

There are a few taboos with お箸（はし）: sticking them into the ご飯（はん） or into the food −leaving them in vertical position−, and passing food from one diner to another, directly from お箸（はし） to お箸（はし）. Why? Both actions remind one of rituals performed at Japanese funerals and, as you can imagine, are not exactly a sign of a good omen.

Another curiosity has to do with alcohol (mainly ビール), which is consumed in great quantities when there are guests. Never serve yourself: you must wait till someone else does. Raise your グラス and let yourself be served. After which, the right thing to do is for you to serve. Take the びん −better with the label facing upwards−, and make as if you are going to serve: you will see how whoever is sitting with

Soba noodles can be slurped. (Photo: M. Bernabé)

you answers at once raising his / her グラス with a wide smile and a loud ありがとう.

More things: you might be surprised by the fact that all the food in 日本（にほん） comes at once, in small plates. The usual thing is to nibble from one dish to the next one, eating a little bit of everything, sometimes from one or several shared platters from which everybody eats. Besides, it is possible, and even advisable, to noisily slurp スープ and ラーメン, そば or うどん noodles. In fact, they say slurping indicates one is enjoying the dish, and it brings good luck! Last of all, we will mention it isn't bad table manners raising your 茶碗（ちゃわん） of スープ or ご飯（はん） and taking it close to your mouth to eat with more ease. We could go on with more curiosities, but you can start off with these: いただきます！

漫画例　Manga-examples

This lesson is somewhat peculiar because it only has three manga-examples, due to the long vocabulary tables we have offered. It is worthwhile learning those terms well because they are very useful and common in everyday life in Japan. Now, however, let's go to our panels.

a) In the market

Akiko: いらっしゃい いらっしゃい！ 納豆(なっとう)はいかがですか！
Welcome, welcome! Nattō TOP *how about be* Q?!!
Welcome, welcome! How about some *nattō*!?

We start with an everyday scene in any market or shopping area in Japan: a shop clerk trying to attract clients by shouting to each and every passerby about how good her products are. Notice the いらっしゃい, which is just a small distortion of いらっしゃいませ, the greeting used only in business areas (shops of any kind and restaurants). In her next sentence, the clerk usually offers her products asking (nobody in particular, she just fires her question) Xはいかがですか？ (*Do you feel like x?*). Remember いかが is the formal version of どう (*How about...?*, L.34, book 2). In this case, she's offering 納豆(なっとう), extremely smelly and sticky fermented soybeans – very healthy though, or so they say.

To conclude this example, we will show you a little trick that will surely be great for your economy. Supermarkets in Japan usually close at 8 or 9 in the evening, and about half an hour before closing time, the staff starts placing discount stickers on fresh produce. You can save a lot shopping at that time! The stickers read 2割(にわり) (*20% off*), and other derivatives, or even 半額(はんがく) (*half-price*), L.42 (book 1).

In the restaurant レストランで　−27−

b) The profound world of sushi

Client 1:	トロにイカね〜	**Client 2:**	こっちアナゴ追加 <small>ついか</small>
	toro and squid EP		*here eel add*
	One *toro* and one squid!		**I'll have one more eel.**
Client 3:	ビール2本持ってきて〜 <small>にほん も</small>	**Shōji:**	はい！
	beer two bring come		*yes*
	Bring two bottles of beer!		**Coming!**

Gabriel Luque

Here we have a restaurant specializing in sushi, that delicious and typical Japanese delicacy. Let's see now a small sushi "guide" to learn even more vocabulary. There are two basic kinds of sushi: the 巻き寿司 <small>ま ず し</small> and the 握り寿司 <small>にぎ ず し</small>. The first one consists of a roll with the ingredient in the middle, surrounded with rice and closed with *nori* seaweed (巻く <small>ま</small>: *to roll*). The 鉄火巻き <small>てっか ま</small> *(tuna rolls)* are widely known. The second kind is a thin strip of fish, or other ネタ *(topping)*, on a base of pressed rice (握る <small>にぎ</small>: *clasp*). Among those you find in the example, トロ *(fatty flesh of tuna)*, イカ *(squid)*, and アナゴ *(eel)*, there are others like まぐろ *(tuna)*, えび *(prawn)*, しゃけ *(salmon)*, たこ *(octopus)*, 玉子焼き <small>たまご や</small> *(omelet)*, or たい *(sea bream)*, just to name a few.

c) *Katsudon* and *donburi*

Terada:	特製カツドン...でももらおうか <small>とくせい</small>
	special katsudon... or something receive Q?
	Could you bring me… a special *katsudon*?

Studio Kōsen

This example shows us a rather informal way of asking what one wants to eat using the verb もらう (receive, L.28, book 1, and 45 book 2). Notice the usage of でも, studied in L.37 (book 2).

In less "luxurious" restaurants there are small pieces of paper stuck to the walls with the names of the dishes served in the house and their price. In this example, the client looks at the pieces of paper and chooses カツ丼 <small>どん</small> (crumbed pork on a bed of rice), which, moreover, is 特製 <small>とくせい</small> *(special)*. Other dishes on the list include チャーハン *(fried rice)*, 親子丼 <small>おやこ どん</small> *(egg and chicken on rice)*, and 玉子丼 <small>たまご どん</small> *(egg on rice)*. The kanji 丼 (read どん or どんぶり) indicates "bowl of rice on which something is placed."

1. What do the following words mean: 夕ご飯, 熱い, ゆでる, 甘い, 焼く and 炒める?

2. Translate into Japanese the words "chocolate," "water," "cabbage," "tomato," "prawn," and "omelet."

3. Describe in English these typical Japanese dishes: 焼きそば, おにぎり, 親子丼 and 天ぷら.

4. Name and describe at least five ingredients in Japanese cuisine that you can hardly find in the West.

5. You are in the market. Ask the shop clerk for two onions and a lotus root radish *renkon*.

6. You are in a hamburger joint, and the waiter asks you お飲み物は何にしますか? What do you answer?

7. You are at a restaurant and you want to order a "tempura set menu." How do you ask for it?

8. What does the word いらっしゃいませ mean, and when and where is it used?

9. What are the names of the two main kinds of 寿司 and why are they called so?

10. In example c), how much does the dish of fried rice with vegetables and ham cost?

第48課：複文を形成する②

Lesson 48: Compound sentences (2)

Here is the second of three sections we will devote to the formation of compound sentences. This time we will study, among others, expressions of cause / reason, and intention / aim. You should try your best to learn these constructions well: they will be very useful.

Cause / reason: から

We will start seeing expressions of cause / reason, the first of which we already studied in L.41 and briefly in L.34, both in book 2: we are talking about the subordinating conjunction から. In L.41 we offered a global view of the different usages of から: the particle of origin *(from)*, the subordinating conjunction, and the construction 〜てから.

Besides its other meanings, such as "since" or "considering," you will probably remember another usage of から (ie: *because*), used when answering どうして *(why?)*, Usage: After verb or *-i* adjective, nothing is added. *-na* adjectives and nouns require the help of the verb to be (です / だ). The structure is usually "cause / reason ＋ から ＋ consequence."

- どうして帰るの？つまらないから帰る *Why are you leaving? I'm leaving because I'm bored.*
- この本はもう読んだから、あげる *I've already read this book, so I'll give it to you.*
- ジョンはまじめだから合格するだろう *Since John is in earnest, I'm sure he will pass.*
- 彼は先生だったから、これが分かるはずだ *He was a teacher, so he should understand this.*

Cause / reason: ので

ので is a very similar form to から and is used to introduce a cause in an identical position, just as から does: "cause / reason ＋ ので ＋ consequence." Usage: After verb or *-i* adjective, nothing is added. *-na* adjectives and nouns require the help of な in the present tense, but in the past tense this な is replaced with だった.

However, ので <u>cannot</u> be used when answering どうして *(why?)*, and there are other connotations that differentiate its usage from から. The fact is that ので is possibly a "weightier" expression than から: it is used when the speaker is convinced that the reason stated before ので is valid and obvious, and that the listener will agree with him. In principle, using ので is wrong when the first part of the sentence expresses conjecture, invitation, request, personal opinion, or wish. However, there is a tendency nowadays among many Japanese, especially the young, to use ので and から almost without distinction. Still, it is advisable that you bear in mind the slight differences in the meanings between both expressions.

- 昨日は雨が降っていたので行けなかった *I couldn't go, because it was raining yesterday.*
- 頭が痛いので仕事が出来ない *I can't work because I have a headache.*
- この町は安全なので夜によく散歩する *Since this town is safe, I usually take walks at night.*
- 彼はアホなので謝らないよ *Because he is stupid, he won't apologize.*

Aim: ために

Let's now see another useful expression: ために, which is also used to express intention or aim. In other words, it means "for" or "in order to." Usage: After a verb nothing is added, and after a noun we must use の (replaced by だった in the past tense). When expressing intention or aim, this form of ために is not used with adjectives of any kind.

- 車を買うためにいっぱい働きます *I work a lot in order to buy myself a car.*
- 日本人は仕事のために生きているみたいだ *It looks like the Japanese live for work.*
- いい仕事を見つけるために勉強しています *I study in order to find a good job.*
- 彼女のために何でもやれるぞ *I can do anything for my girlfriend.*

However, sometimes ために is used to express cause / reason, just like から or ので. In this case, it can be used with adjectives. -i adjectives don't require anything, while -na adjectives require な. This usage of ために is rather formal and seldom used, but it is worthwhile knowing.

- 風邪を引いたために、家で休んでいた *Because I caught a cold, I rested at home.*
- 家が古いために、修理が必要だ *Because the house is old, it needs repairing.*

Aim: のに

The usage of のに is similar to that of ために, since it expresses aim and can be translated as "for." のに is nothing more than the phrase nominalizer の, which we studied in L.40 (book 2), plus the particle に, which in this case indicates adverbial complement of intention. Usage: This expression is only used after verbs in the infinitive.

- じゃがいもを切るのに包丁を使った *I used a kitchen knife to cut the potato.*
- キムチを作るのに白菜が必要だ *To prepare* kimchi *you need Chinese cabbage.*
- 秋葉原へ行くのに電車が便利だ *To go to Akihabara the train is convenient.*
- ＨＰを作るのに二ヶ月もかかった *It took me two months to make the web page.*

Note: There is another completely different usage of のに which indicates "although," "in spite of." We will study this adversative meaning in the following lesson.

When: 時

Let's leave aside now the expressions of cause / reason and aim / intention, and go on to study other useful constructions in the formation of complex sentences. The first construction we will see is 時, which indicates time or, for a better understanding, "when." <u>Usage</u>: Nothing is added after a verb nor an *-i* adjective. With *-na* adjectives, な is required, while with nouns we must add の. In the past, however, both do without な and の, respectively, and use だった.

- 韓国に行った時、けっこう暑かったです *When I went to Korea it was quite hot.*
- 子どもの時、よく友達と遊んでいた *When I was a boy, I used to play with my friends.*

You can add に to 時, obtaining 時に. The meaning is the same, although 時に is more emphatic and stronger than just 時.

- 試験の時にすごく緊張していたよ *When / at the time of the exam, I was very nervous.*
- 彼が来た時にお姉さんは出かけた *When he came, my elder sister went out.*

While: 間に

間に is used to indicate the interval between two points in time (and is then translated as "while" or "during") or in space (translated as "between"). <u>Usage</u>: The same as 時.

- 日本にいる間に、空手を習いたい *I want to learn karate while I'm in Japan.*
- 夏休みの間、よく勉強しました *I studied very much during the summer holidays.*
- 日本と韓国の間に日本海がある *Between Korea and Japan there is the Sea of Japan.*

Note: In the case of 間に, the action stated in the main sentence happens "within" the time introduced by the sentence ending in 間に. Whereas the expression 間 on its own indicates both actions happen "during" exactly the same time period.

- 週末の間、京都を歩いた *During the weekend (from beginning to end) I walked through Kyoto.*
- 週末の間に京都を歩いた *During the weekend (at some point of time) I walked through Kyoto.*

While: 内^{うち}に

The expression 内に has an almost equivalent meaning to 間^{あいだ}に, and is also translated as "while." In fact, both can be used without distinction in many sentences. Nevertheless, while 間に indicates an interval of time with starting and ending points, which can be measured with a watch, 内に doesn't have that connotation, and merely indicates "time interval not necessarily measurable." <u>Usage</u>: Just like 時^{とき} and 間^{あいだ}に.

- 大学^{だいがく}にいる内^{うち}に勉強^{べんきょう}しなさい *While you are at university, you must study.*
- 雨^{あめ}が降^ふらない内^{うち}に終^おわりましょう *Let's finish while it's not raining (before it rains).*
- 寿司^{すし}を新鮮^{しんせん}な内^{うち}に買^かいましょう *Let's buy sushi while it's fresh.*
- お茶^{ちゃ}を暖^{あたた}かい内^{うち}に飲^のんでください *Drink your tea while it's hot.*

Before and after

The last expressions we will see are used to indicate "before" and "after:" they are, respectively, 前^{まえ}に and 後^{あと}で.

前^{まえ}に <u>Usage</u>: Nothing is added between the verb and 前^{まえ}に. With nouns, の is required. This expression is not used with adjectives.

	Compound sentences (2): general summary table	
～から	Cause / reason. "Since, because, considering"	すしが好きだから、いっぱい食べよう Since I like sushi, I'shall eat a lot.
～ので	Cause / reason. "Since, because, considering"	渋谷は人が多いので、迷いやすいです Since in Shibuya there are a lot of people, it's easy to get lost.
～ために	Aim / intention. "For"	日本へ行くために3年間も働いた In order to go to Japan, I worked up to three years.
～のに	Aim / intention. "For"	すしを作るのに、新鮮な魚がいる To make sushi, you need fresh fish.
～時^{とき}	"When"	渋谷にいる時、いつも迷ってしまう When I'm in Shibuya, I always get lost.
～間^{あいだ}に	Physical or temporal distance between two points. "While, during"	彼が寝ている間に買い物をしに行ってこよう While he's sleeping, I shall go shopping (and come back).
～内^{うち}に	Period during which something remains valid. "While, during"	日本にいる内に北海道へ行きたい While I'm in Japan, I want to go to Hokkaidō.
～前^{まえ}に	"Before"	寝る前に歯を磨きなさい Before going to sleep, brush your teeth.
～後^{あと}で	"After"	買い物に行った後で、魚を食べた After going shopping, I ate fish.

好^すきな: that one likes | いっぱい: a lot | 食^たべる: to eat | しぶや^{渋谷}: Shibuya (district in Tokyo) | 人^{ひと}: people | おおい^多: a lot of まよう^迷: to get lost | にほん^{日本}: Japan | いく^行: to go | さんねんかん^{3年間}: 3 years | はたらく^働: to work | つくる^作: to make | しんせんな^{新鮮}: fresh さかな^魚: fish いつも: always | ねる^寝: to sleep | かいもの^{買物}: shopping | ほっかいどう^{北海道}: Hokkaidō | はをみがく^{歯磨}: to brush one's teeth

● ジムは家に入る前に「おはよう」と言った *Jim said "hello" before entering the house.*

● 昼ごはんの前に君と話したい *I want to talk with you before lunch.*

後で <u>Usage:</u> Verbs preceding 後で must be in the past tense. Nouns require の. **Note:** Sometimes, in informal register, we can do without the で in 後で.

● ビールを飲んだ後(で)げっぷが出た *I burped after drinking the beer.*

● 映画を見た後で公園へ行きました *After watching a movie, I went to the park.*

● 授業の後でゲームセンターに行こうよ *Let's go to the video game arcade after class.*

Conjunctions

Let's now see a few more conjunctions: expressions placed at the beginning of sentences, used as connectors with sentences or concepts previously stated.

1) And (later) / and (then) / and (also): そして

● 昨日は遊園地に行った。そして、おいしい夕食を食べた

I went to an amusement park yesterday. And (later) had a delicious dinner.

● 私はやせたいのでダイエットをしています。そして、運動もしています

Because I want to lose some weight, I'm on a diet. And (also) I'm taking exercise.

2) Then / therefore / later / now: それで

● 岩手県で生まれて、愛知県で育った。それで、埼玉県で結婚した

I was born in the Iwate prefecture and raised in Aichi. Later on, I married in Saitama.

● オレは大学に行けなかった。それで、いい仕事を見つけることが出来なかった

I couldn't go to university. Therefore, I couldn't find a good job.

3) Well / well then / then: それでは (それじゃ)

● もう時間です。それでは、スピーチを始めましょう

It's time now. Well then, I'll start my speech.

4) After that / and then / since then: それから

● 5年前、大学を卒業した。それから、彼と全然会っていないな

I graduated from university five years ago. Since then, I haven't seen him again.

5) Therefore / that's why / consequently / so: だから

● 先週、旅行に行った。だから、今はとても疲れている

I went on a trip last week. That's why I'm tired.

● 社長は無駄にお金を使った。だから、会社が倒産してしまいました

The president squandered money. Consequently, the company went down.

漫画例　Manga-examples

As usual, the manga-examples will help us see in practice how to use the constructions we have just studied. These panels should help you clarify the explanations on the new structures and give you a more concrete idea of their usage.

a) Cause / reason: *no de*

Taku: あんまり腹がへったので、つい無断でたべちゃった。ゆるしてください。
so much stomach SP decrease because, inadvertently without permission. forgive please
I was so hungry I ate it without permission. Please, forgive me.

Gabriel Luque

Let's start with the first example. Someone has eaten the sweet on the table, and the characters are arguing about who's done it. Suddenly, the boy in the panel confesses he is the "guilty" one: he explains the reason in this sentence using ので. Notice how the reason (あんまり腹がへった, *I was very hungry*) precedes the consequence (つい無断でたべちゃった *I ate it without permission*). The verb before ので must be in the simple form. In this case we have 減る, *decrease*, which is part of the set phrase 腹が減る – which literally means *the stomach decreases*, although its real meaning is *to be hungry* (L.27, book 1).

ので is used when the cause or reason expressed by the speaker is rather clear, and it is assumed the listener will accept it as something understandable and obvious. In our example, the connotation of ので is not that strong, and the almost synonymous word から could have been used instead with no problem. Last of all, it is worth mentioning that ので is used in formal situations more often than から: it sounds more "serious."

Notes: あんまり is a distortion of あまり, an expression indicating in this case "so much" which we studied in L.45 (book 2). Notice the contraction たべちゃった, its non-contracted form is 食べてしまった. Take the opportunity to go back to L.35 (book 2) and review this last form.

Compound sentences (2) 複文を形成する②—35—

b) Cause / reason tag at the end of a sentence: *kara*

> **Lin:** もう思い残すことなんか、なんにもないから...
> おも のこ
> *any more regret thing (emph.), nothing there is because…*
> **So, there is nothing else I can regret…**

もう思い残すことなんか、なんにもないから…

J.M. Ken Niimura

After ので, the turn has come for から, also used to indicate cause / reason. In this example, we see から at the end of the sentence, cutting it. It could be the answer to a question with どうして *(why?)*, or a simple explanation about the cause or reason why something is done.

There is another explanation for this last usage: sometimes a sentence is ended with the tag から, ambiguously implying, by way of excuse, that there is a reason for what one is doing, but without putting forward a specific explanation. Sentences like 私、もう帰るから... *I'm* わたし かえ *going now, (so…)* or ちょっと忙しいんだから... *I'm a little* いそが *busy (so…)* are very common. **Notes:** なんにも is the distortion of 何も *(nothing, L.37,* なに *bool 2)*. Review as well the usage of もう *(L.40, book 2).*

c) Idiomatic usage of *dakara*

> **Sayaka:** うん...だから土曜日の映画、行けないの
> どようび えいが い
> *yes… that's why Saturday POP movie, go PE*
> **Yes… I've already told you I can't go to the movies on Saturday.**

At the end of the theory we have seen the version of から at the beginning of a sentence: だから, which is used to state a reason or a cause, as in: 彼 かれ は菜食主義者だ。だから、肉を食べ さいしょくしゅぎしゃ にく た ない *He is a vegetarian. That's why he doesn't eat meat.*

うん…
だから土曜日の映画、行けないの

Studio Kōsen

However, in this example, we find a slightly different usage of だから, which is, nevertheless, very often seen in spoken language: だから is used, at the beginning of a sentence, to show the interlocutor certain "annoyance" or insistence on something. It could be translated as "for goodness sake," "I've already told you…," "but you…"

Note: うん is the informal way of saying "yes," while ううん means "no."

d) Aim: *tame ni*

> **Teruo:** 俺はこのために生まれてきた！
> *I* TOP *this for born come!*
> **I was born for this!!**

Javier Bolado

A few pages ago, we learned that ために means "for" or "in order to:" here is a good example of its usage. The speaker indicates the "aim" for which he was born, using ために. However, he says it with the pronoun この *(this)*, and, therefore, unless we know the context, we can't tell what he's talking about. Since he appears to be playing soccer in the image, we can imagine the original sentence could have been something like 俺はサッカーをするために生まれてきた *(I was born to play soccer)*. Using the kosoado pronouns (L.34) この *(this)*, その *(that)*, and あの *(that over there)* in conjunction with grammatical constructions is very common. We will see another instance in example f).

e) When: *toki*

> **Fletcher:** いや、私が先生と最後に電話で話した時、こうおっしゃっていた
> *no, I* SP *teacher* CP *last telephone* IP *talk when, in this way said*
> **Well, when I last spoke with the teacher on the phone, that's what he said.**

J.M. Ken Niimura

Let's now study how to say "when" in Japanese using 時. As we can see in the example, the process is quite easy: all you need to do is add the word 時 after the sentence with which we want to indicate "when." In the example, the teacher said something 最後に電話で話した時, that is, *when I last spoke with him on the phone*. Try making your own sentences with 時: it is simple and with practice you will master it.

Note: Depending on the inflection of the verb or adjective preceding 時, the meaning changes. If conjugated in the past tense, it refers to something that happened in a previous stage: 昨日、料理をしていた時、彼が来た *Yesterday, when I was cooking, he came.* In the infinitive, it refers to something that we know will inevitably happen in the future or something that usually happens: 私は寝る時、悪夢を見てしまう *When / whenever I sleep, I have bad dreams.* **Note 2:** おっしゃる is a formal synonimous verb of 言う (L.52).

Compound sentences (2) 複文を形成する②–37–

f) Before: *mae ni*

その前にお前の首へし折るぞ

Gabriel Luque

> **Charlie:** その前にお前の首へし折るぞ
> *that before you POP neck break EP*
> **Before that, I'll break your neck.**

Let's now see an example on how to say "before" using the word 前 *(before)*, which we already know. We simply add 前に *(before)* after a sentence, like in the example: 私を殺す前にキスしてね *Kiss me before you kill me.*
The opposite of 前に is 後で, which comes from the word 後 *(after, behind)* and means "after."

As we mentioned in example d), it is common seeing the *kosoado* pronouns この, その, and あの together with grammatical constructions: here we have その前に *(before that).*

More examples: この後で *(after this)*, あのように *(in that way, L.43, book 2)*, そのはずだ *(that is almost certain, L.43, book 2)*, この場合 *(in this case, L.46)*, その内に *(one of these days, L.48)*, このまま *(just as it is, L.46).*

g) Starting a speech: *sore de wa*

> **Kitano:** えーそれでは新しい人事の発表をー
> *err... then new staff POP introduction DOP*
> **Err... Well, let's introduce the new staff and...**

We will conclude this intense but useful lesson with an example of それでは, which, as we see in this panel, is usually used in speeches or introductions as a "sign" that we are about to start talking, like our "now" or "well, then."

それでは is also used when saying goodbye, but in this case, では is contracted into じゃ when speaking: one of the first expressions we saw in L.4 (book 1) was それじゃ、また明日会いま

えーそれでは新しい人事の発表をー

Studio Kōsen

しょう *Well, let's meet again tomorrow.* This expression can be contracted into それじゃ、また明日 *Well, (see you) tomorrow,* and even more so to じゃね、また *Well, see you* (notice how even the それ is "cut"). There is also the concise but extremely common じゃね (literally "well" or "well then," but used with the meaning of "see you later").

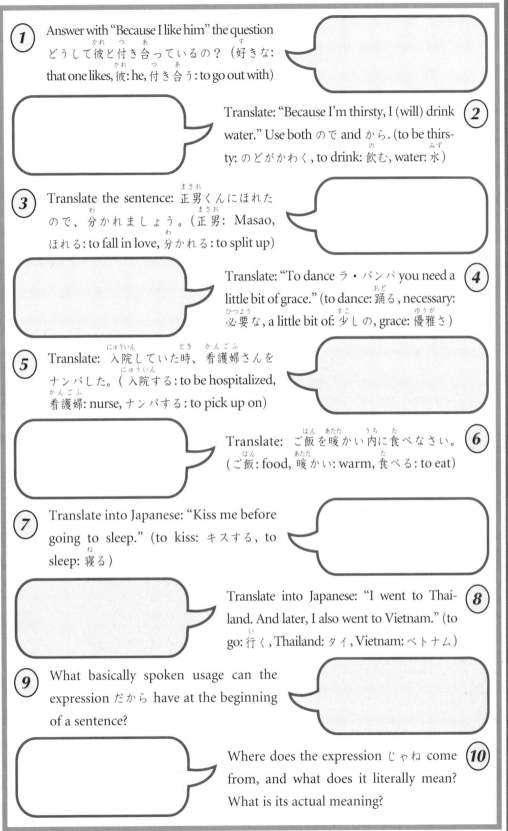

1. Answer with "Because I like him" the question どうして彼と付き合っているの？（好きな: that one likes, 彼: he, 付き合う: to go out with)

2. Translate: "Because I'm thirsty, I (will) drink water." Use both ので and から. (to be thirsty: のどがかわく, to drink: 飲む, water: 水)

3. Translate the sentence: 正男くんにほれたので、分かれましょう。（正男: Masao, ほれる: to fall in love, 分かれる: to split up)

4. Translate: "To dance ラ・バンバ you need a little bit of grace." (to dance: 踊る, necessary: 必要な, a little bit of: 少しの, grace: 優雅さ)

5. Translate: 入院していた時、看護婦さんをナンパした。（入院する: to be hospitalized, 看護婦: nurse, ナンパする: to pick up on)

6. Translate: ご飯を暖かい内に食べなさい。（ご飯: food, 暖かい: warm, 食べる: to eat)

7. Translate into Japanese: "Kiss me before going to sleep." (to kiss: キスする, to sleep: 寝る)

8. Translate into Japanese: "I went to Thailand. And later, I also went to Vietnam." (to go: 行く, Thailand: タイ, Vietnam: ベトナム)

9. What basically spoken usage can the expression だから have at the beginning of a sentence?

10. Where does the expression じゃね come from, and what does it literally mean? What is its actual meaning?

The time has come for the third and final touch in our intensive series of lessons on compound sentences. This time, we will study essential adversative constructions so that your Japanese sounds as natural and fluent as possible.

But / however: けれども/けれど/けど/が

First of all, we will study the most typical adversatives: the constructions used to form sentences such as "x, but y" or "x, however y." The basic word is けれども *(but, however)*, although it is quite formal and is usually reduced to けれど (also formal, but less so). This can be reduced even more to the informal expression けど. On the other hand, we have が, with an equivalent meaning (we already studied its usage as "but" in L.37 (book 2); you should review it before going on). <u>Usage</u>: We add nothing after verbs and -*i* adjectives. Nouns and -*na* adjectives need the verb to be in its simple form, だ.

- ボブは先生だけれども、教えるのが嫌いです *Bob is a teacher, but he doesn't like teaching.*
- カメラを買いたいけれど、お金がない *I want to buy a camera, but I don't have money.*
- バイクを運転できるけど、バイクがない *I can drive motorcycles, but I don't have a motorcycle.*
- 彼は映画は好きだが、アニメは好きではない *He likes cinema, but not animation.*
- 昨日は病気だったけど、今日は大丈夫だ *Yesterday I was sick, but today I'm fine.*

Just like with が (L.37, book 2), sometimes the variations of けれども are used to link sentences and don't necessarily have the adversative meaning "but."

- 後で梅田へ行くけど、美穂も来る？ *Later, I'll go to Umeda, will you go too, Miho?*
- 相談したいんですが、時間がありますか？

I would like to consult with you about something, do you have time?

The same words are used in spoken language to soften sentences, especially when making requests or giving excuses: they are placed at the end, leaving the continuation in the air.

- 今ちょっと忙しいんですけれども... *Now I'm a little busy, but...*
- そのパソコンを見たいんだけど... *I would like to see that computer, but...*

Although / in spite of: のに

Be very careful with this construction, because it has nothing to do with its homophone −のに with the meaning of aim / intention−, which we studied in the previous lesson. The のに we are about to study is, like けれども and its "family," an adversative expression meaning "although" or "in spite of." The adversative expression のに has a quite distinct "subjective" and "emotional" component: we use it to indicate that something that was almost a fact finally has not been possible and it, therefore, provokes in the speaker a feeling of surprise, frustration, or even annoyance.

If you want to form normal adversative sentences, that is, without adding any subjective or emotional nuance, then you had better use けれども, けれど, けど, or が. <u>Usage</u>: Nothing is added after verbs or -i adjectives, while nouns and -na adjectives require the usage of な.

● ダイエットをしているのに、全然やせない

I'm on a diet and, in spite of that, I'm not losing any weight.

● 眠かったのに、徹夜をしました *Although I was sleepy, I worked all through the night.*
● 彼女が好きなのに、告白できない *Although I like her, I'm unable of declaring my love.*
● いい天気なのに、外に出られない *In spite of this nice weather, I can't go out.*

In a colloquial register, sentences cut by のに are common. These sentences express displeasure or frustration, and could be translated as "and to think that..."

● 彼はすごく金持ちなのに... *And to think that he's so rich...*

● なんでそれが欲しくないの？ただなのに... *Why don't you want that? But it's free...*

Although / in spite of: くせに

Here we have a very similar expression to the adversative のに we have just seen: くせに. While のに can be used both with formal and colloquial sentences, the usage of くせに is restricted to colloquial and even vulgar sentences. Its meaning, despite being "although" or "in spite of," just like のに, implies something which could be even defined as "pejorative," and seems to lay blame on the subject. <u>Usage</u>: Nothing is added after verbs or -i adjectives. With nouns, の is required, and with -na adjectives, we use な.

● 何も知らないくせに、何を言っているの？ *You don't know anything; what are you saying?*
● 医者のくせに、病気を治せない *Although he's a doctor, he's unable to cure sicknesses.*

Just like with のに, we will sometimes find くせに at the end of a cut sentence.

● 何だ、その態度？がきのくせに... *What's with that attitude? You're nothing but a little brat...*

Interrogatives + 〜ても

何_{なに}を言_いっても	No matter what he says...
誰_{だれ}に言_いっても	No matter who he says it to...
どう言_いっても	No matter how he says it...
どんな説明_{せつめい}しても	No matter how he explains...
どこへ行_いっても	No matter where he goes...
いつ行_いっても	No matter when he goes...
いくら払_{はら}っても	No matter how much he pays...

言_いう: to say ｜ 説明_{せつめい}する: to explain
行_いく: to go ｜ 払_{はら}う: to pay

Even / even if: 〜ても

In L.32 (book 2) we saw the expression 〜ても いい, which, as you probably remember, was used to form sentences to ask for permission. We are now to study a related expression, since the basic structure is exactly the same: 〜ても.

The expression 〜ても means "even" or "even if," and is used only to give an adversative meaning to sentences expressing hypothesis or conjectures – unlike のに, which is used with sentences whose certainty is ensured. Usage: Verbs, nouns, and adjectives of both kinds must be conjugated in the *-te* form (L.35, book 2), to which も is added.

● 雨_{あめ}が降_ふっても、試合_{しあい}を行_{おこな}います *Even if it rains, the match will be held.*
● 免許_{めんきょ}がなくても、このバイクを運転_{うんてん}できる *Even without a license, you can drive this motorcycle.*
● パソコンを買_かっても仕事_{しごと}ができない *Even if I buy a computer, I can't work.*
● 難_{むずか}しくても、試験_{しけん}に合格_{ごうかく}したい *No matter how difficult it is, I want to pass the exam.*
● この問題_{もんだい}、アホでも解_とける *Even a fool can solve this problem.*

On the other hand, if we add an interrogative pronoun or adverb (L.34) to a verb + ても, we obtain sentences such as: "no matter what I do..." or "no matter what it is..." (see table).

● いつ行_いっても、あの店_{みせ}は閉_しまっている *No matter when I go, that shop is closed.*
● 何_{なに}を言_いっても、君_{きみ}を許_{ゆる}すつもりはない *No matter what you say, I won't forgive you.*

Strong recommendation: 〜方_{ほう}がいい

Let's now leave aside adversative expressions, and go on to take a look at other types of constructions. The first one, 〜方_{ほう}がいい, is used to make recommendations or suggestions of a strong kind, which are not quite orders, but almost. Usage: This expression is only used with verbs, which must be conjugated in the past tense – except with negative expressions, when verbs are conjugated in the negative present tense.

● 彼女_{かのじょ}に花_{はな}をあげた方_{ほう}がいいと思_{おも}うよ *I think you should give her some flowers.*
● 彼_{かれ}を殺_{ころ}すのをあきらめた方_{ほう}がいいよ *If I were you, I'd forget about killing him.*
● その水_{みず}を飲_のまない方_{ほう}がいいよ *I recommend that you not drink that water.*
● 腐_{くさ}っているから、みかんを食_たべない方_{ほう}がいいよ *Don't eat the mandarins, because they are rotten.*

More usages of the -ō conjugation

Let's now see two expressions using the -ō conjugation, which we studied in L.34 (book 2), and which on its own meant "let's…"

All you need to do is add ～とする or ～と思う to a verb in the -ō form to create two new expressions with different meanings, which can be very useful.

We will start with the construction -ō form+とする. It means "to try to" or, more literally, "to be in the process of doing something."

● マンガを描こうとしているけど、難しいね *I'm trying to draw a comic book, but it's difficult.*
● バカなのに大学に入ろうとしている *Even though i'm stupid, I'm trying to enter university.*
● 私は銀行強盗をしようとしていた *I was trying to rob a bank.*
● バスに乗ろうとした時、死んだ *When he was going to get on the bus, he died.*

As to the expression -ō form + と思う, it is used to indicate something like "I think I'm going to…," that is, it is nothing but the simple combination of the -ō form ("let's…," L.34, book 2) plus と思う ("I think that…" L.41, book 2).

● 彼女に告白しようと思っています *I'm thinking of declaring my love to her.*
● 失敗したから、自殺しようと思う *Because I've failed, I think I'm going to commit suicide.*
● 勉強をやめようと思っている *I'm thinking about abandoning my studies.*
● 鈴木さんは家を買おうと思っている *Mr. Suzuki is thinking of buying a house.*

Compound sentences (3): general summary table		
～けれども ～けれど ～けど ～が	"But," "However," "Nevertheless" (～けれども: formal, ～けれど: neutral, ～けど: informal, ～が: neutral / formal)	彼は歯科医ですけれども、歯を抜けません He is a dentist, but he can't pull out a tooth. (formal) 彼は歯科医だけど、歯を抜けない He is a dentist, but he can't pull out a tooth. (informal) 彼は歯科医だが、歯を抜けません He is a dentist, however he can't pull out a tooth. (neutral / formal)
～のに	"Although," "In spite of"	彼は歯科医なのに、歯を抜けない In spite of the fact that he is a dentist, he can't pull out a tooth.
～くせに	"Although," "In spite of" (informal / pejorative)	彼は歯科医のくせに、歯を抜けない Although he is a dentist, he can't even pull out a tooth! (pejorative)
～ても	"Even if," "Although" (In hypothetical sentences)	彼は歯科医でも、歯も抜けない Even if he is a dentist, he can't pull out a tooth.
～方がいい	"You had better…" "You should…" (Strong recommendation or suggestion)	歯が痛いだろう？歯科医に行った方がいいよ Your tooth is painful, isn't it? You should go to the dentist.
～おうとする	"To try to," "To be in the process of doing something"	歯科医が歯を抜こうとしていた The dentist was trying to pull out a tooth.
～おうと思う	"I think I'm going to…"	歯が痛いから、歯科医に行こうと思っている Since my tooth is hurting, I think I'm going to go to the dentist.
かれ: he | しかい: dentist | は: tooth | ぬく: to pull out | いたい: painful | いく: to go		

Conjunctions

We will finish this third lesson in our series devoted to the formation of compound sentences by studying a few essential conjunctions. On this page you also have a summary table with all the conjunctions we have seen thus far.

1) But / However / Nevertheless: だけれども / だけれど / だけど / でも / しかし

● 社長はとても優しいです。だけれど、その息子は鬼みたいに厳しいです

The director is very kind. However, his son is so demanding, he's like an ogre.

● 巻き寿司は大好きだ。でも、きゅうりの巻き寿司は大嫌いだ！

I love makizushi. *But I hate cucumber* makizushi!

● SPITZの新しいCDを買いに行った。しかし、もう売れ切れだった

I went to buy Spitz's new CD. However, it had already sold out.

2) In spite of that / However: それなのに / なのに

● 加藤さんはとても金持ちです。それなのに、非常にけちです

Mr. Katō is very rich. In spite of that, he is extremely stingy.

● 僕はかっこいい。なのに、女が寄ってこない *I'm handsome. However, the girls don't come near me.*

			Summary table: conjunctions (L. 45, 47 and 49)
L.46	例えば	For example	花が好きです。例えば、桜や椿が大好きです I like flowers. For example, I like *sakura* and camellias very much.
L.46	ところで	By the way	いい天気だね。ところで、桜はもう咲いた？ Isn't the weather fine? By the way, have the *sakura* bloomed yet?
L.46	それに	Besides	椿は満開です。それに、桜もきれいです The camellias are in full bloom. And besides, the *sakura* are pretty too.
L.48	そして	And later / And then	昼ご飯を食べた。そして、桜を見に行った I ate lunch. And then, I went to see the *sakura*.
L.48	それで	Then / Therefore	今日、昼ご飯を食べなかった。それで、今とてもお腹がすいている I haven't had lunch today. Therefore, I'm very hungry now.
L.48	それでは	Well then / Then	おはようございます！それでは、桜を見に行こう！ Good morning! Well then, let's go and see the *sakura*!
L.48	それから	After that	今日は桜を見に行きます。それから、昼ご飯を食べるつもりです Today, I'm going to see the *sakura*. After that, I intend to have lunch.
L.48	だから	Therefore	桜が咲いた。だから、見に行きました。 The *sakura* have bloomed. Therefore, I went to see them.
L.49	だけれども だけれど だけど でも しかし	But However Nevertheless	椿はもう咲いています。だけれども、桜はまだ咲いていません The camellias have already bloomed. However, the sakura haven't bloomed yet. もう昼ご飯を食べた。でも、まだお腹がすいている I have already had lunch. But I'm still hungry. 今日はいい天気です。しかし、明日は雨が降るそうです Today the weather is fine. But, apparently, it is going to rain tomorrow.
L.49	それなのに なのに	In spite of that However	桜が咲いている。なのに、見に行けない The *sakura* have bloomed. In spite of that, I can't go to see them..

はな: flower | (だい)すきな: that one likes (a lot) | さくら: cherry blossom *(sakura)* | つばき: camellia | いい: fine
いま: now | てんき: weather | さく: to bloom | まんかい: full bloom | きれいな: pretty | ひるごはん: lunch
たべる: to eat | みにいく: to go to see | きょう: today | おなかがすく: to be hungry | あした: tomorrow | あめがふる: to rain

漫画例 Manga-examples

We are sure you have noticed how the rhythm and the difficulty have increased in the last lessons: we have been studying more and more complicated aspects of the language, so that our Japanese improves at a very fast pace. Don't give up now, you are doing very well!

a) *kedo* at the end of a sentence and *no ni* (although)

George: これ、おいくらですか？
this, how much be Q?
How much is this?

Man: それなら安くしとくけど...
that (cond.) cheap put but...
I can make that cheap for you...

Man: あんた外国人なのに、ミョウなもんに興味あるんだね。
you foreigner although, strange thing IOP interest there are be EP
Despite being a foreigner, you are interested in very strange things, aren't you?

We get to see two expressions in this example. To start with, take a look at the clerk's first sentence, それなら安くしとくけど... and the けど closing it. The meaning of this けど is not exactly a "but" (as usually is the case in the word's most orthodox usage), but it is used to leave the sentence unfinished, thus softening the statement. Here, it implies something like "but... why the hell would you wana buy something like that?!" Regarding the のに in あんた外国人なのに, notice how, as it goes placed after a noun (外国人, *foreigner*), it needs the help of な. Here, the speaker expresses some surprise, therefore, it is not unusual that he uses のに, as you will remember that this construction has a relevant ingredient of subjectivity. Here, のに can be translated as "despite."

Notes: The prefix お before the word いくら (*how much*) is honorific and implies respect (L.52). The ～とく in 安くしとく is a spoken contraction of ～ておく (L.35). The adverb 妙に (here written in katakana) is difficult to translate: it has the connotations of "strange," "unexpected." もん is the colloquial contraction of the word 物 (*thing*).

b) *Shikashi* and *no ni* at the end of a sentence

Satoru: しかし...どうしてこんなに水_{みず}がにごっているのだろう...?

however... why like this water *SP* muddy *POP* be...?

However... I wonder why the water is so muddy?

大雨_{おおあめ}も降_ふっちゃいないのに...

heavy rain neither fall although...

But it hasn't rained that heavily...

Here we also have two expressions to comment. The first one is しかし meaning *but, however, nevertheless...* It is certainly a very useful word, although in colloquial register でも *(but)* is used more often.

The second expression is のに, closing the panel and leaving the sentence's conclusion in the air. Its meaning is adversative (it could be translated as "although") but in this con-

Gabriel Luque

text we can interpret it as *To think it hasn't rained...* or *But it hasn't rained...*

Note: 降_ふっちゃいない is the contraction of 降_ふってはいない *(it hasn't rained)*. Notice the emphatic particle も in this construction: go back to L.37 (book 2) to review its usage.

c) A pejorative expression: *kuse ni*

Kisaki: 何_{なに}もできないくせに...妙_{みょう}に人_{ひと}の心_{こころ}を動_{うご}かしやがる...

nothing can in spite of... strange person *POP* heart *DOP* move *(vulg)*

Despite his incompetence... he can oddly move people...

Javier Bolado

We have learnt how the expression くせに means "although," "in spite of," but with a pejorative nuance. With this same pejorative intention, we have translated the 何_{なに}もできないくせに part, literally *In spite of not being able to do anything,* for *Despite his incompetence,* because the word

"incompentence" can give the connotation of "superiority" or "disdain" in くせに.

Note: The construction ～やがる shows violence, extreme roughness, threat... We will study it in L.53. As you have probably noticed, using くせに and やがる in the same sentence gives it a layer of "threat" or "disdain" almost impossible to convey in a translation.

d) Even: -te mo

> **Tetsuya:** そのために死んでも後悔はしないぞ！
> *that for die regret TOP do EP! PTM hacer !*
> **Even if I die for that, I won't regret it!**

Bárbara Raya

It is now time to review the usage of the construction -*te* form + も (or 〜ても, as we have seen in the theory pages) which, you will remember, has the meaning of "even" or "although," and is used in sentences expressing hypothesis. In this sentence, the speaker expresses the hypothesis 死んでも *(even if I die)*, and then the result if that supposition finally became true: 後悔はしない *(I won't regret it)*.

Notes: Notice the usage of ために *(for)*, which in this case comes with the *kosoado* その *(that)*, forming そのために *(for that)*, as we saw in L.48. Notice, too, the emphatic usage of the particle は in 後悔はしない *(I won't regret it)* (L.37, book 2).

e) No matter how...

> **Seiji:** いくら電話しても出ないので心配になって、来てみたんだ
> *how much telephone do go out since worry become come try be*
> **Since no matter how much I called, no one answered, I got worried and came.**

We have also studied in the theory pages that if we combine an interrogative plus a verb and the 〜ても construction, we obtain sentences such as: "no matter what I do…" Here we have one of them: いくら電話しても *(no matter how much I call...)*. Usually, いくら has the meaning of "how much" when talking about quantity of money, but here it is used in a more general meaning of "how much / many." Another option would be

Studio Kōsen

何回 *(how many times)*: 何回電話しても *(no matter how many times I call...)*.

Notes: Take the opportunity to review ので *(since, because, L.48)*, and notice, as well, the 〜てみる construction (giving the nuance of "try to do something," L.35) of きてみた. Last of all, the んだ closing the sentence is the typical tag used to give "security" or to "soften" the sentence, and which we studied in the manga-example d) in L.40 (book 2).

f) Strong suggestion: *hō ga ii*

Chie: あたしやっぱり死んだほうがいいんかなぁ
I after all die better if Q? EP
After all, it is better if I die, isn't?

Studio Kōsen

And now we focus on 〜方がいい: it indicates "suggestion" or "advise," and it is rather strong; it is not quite an order, but it comes very close.

Usually, 〜方がいい is used to advise other people. However, we see here a slightly different usage: the speaker is consulting about something that she thinks might be necessary to do with herself: あたしは死んだ ほうがいいのか? (*should I die?*). Notice how the proposed translation above is more "poetic." Remember that the verb before 〜方がいい must be conjugated in the past-affirmative (死んだ方がいい, *you should die*) or present-negative (死なない方がいい, *you shouldn't die*).

Note: やっぱり has no direct translation: it's something like "after all" or "I knew that."

g) To be in the process of: *-ō to suru*

Noriko: ああわたしは...わたしはまたいつかのように逃げようとしている...
aah I TOP... I TOP again someday like in the process of...
Aah, I... I'm trying to escape, like some other time...

Gabriel Luque

The example closing this intense lesson – and the series of three lessons which has shown us countless constructions to form much more complex sentences than the ones we were used to–, will help illustrate the usage of the 〜おうとする construction (*to try to, to be in the process of doing something*).

In our sentence, Noriko says 逃げようとして いる, that is, *I'm in the process of escaping* or *I'm trying to escape*. In order to master this construction, you should thoroughly review the -ō form (L.34, book 2).

Note: Notice the いつかのように part. いつか means *some time,* and we studied it in L.41 (book 2). のように is a comparative (*like*) we briefly saw in L.43 (book 2), and which we will study in depth in L.54. いつかのように means *like (I did) some other time.*

① Translate into formal Japanese: "I'm hungry, but I don't have any money." (to be hungry: お腹がすいている, money: お金)

② What differences of formality are there between the expressions: けれども, が, けど and けれど?

③ What is けど used for in the sentence すみません、これが欲しいんだけど…? (すみません: excuse me, 欲しい: to want)

④ Translate: 魚は好きなのに、どうして寿司は嫌いなの？ (魚: fish, 好きな: that one likes, 寿司: sushi, 嫌いな: that one dislikes)

⑤ Translate this sentence 彼女は大人のくせにそんな服を着ている。(彼女: she, 大人: adult, 服: clothes, 着る: to wear)

⑥ Translate: "Even if I go to Japan, I won't learn Japanese." (to go: 行く, Japan: 日本, to learn: 習う, Japanese: 日本語)

⑦ Translate: "No matter how much I study, I don't learn anything." (to study: 勉強する, to learn: 習う, nothing: 何も)

⑧ Translate: "I think you should / had better kiss the teacher." (to kill: キスする, teacher: 先生)

⑨ Translate: 山本さんは論文を書こうとしている。(山本: Yamamoto, 論文: thesis, 書く: to write)

⑩ Translate into colloquial Japanese: "There's a party today. But you should not go." (today: 今日, party: パーティー, to go: 行く)

第 50 課：関係節

Lesson 50: Relative clauses

In this lesson we will learn how to give more depth to our sentences by means of relative clauses, used as subordinate sentences to provide additional information about a noun. We will also enter the world of expressions with よう.

Relative sentences

Let's first define a relative clause: they are subordinate sentences acting as the complement of a noun; in other words, they give extra information about a noun. Relative clauses (underlined) would be: "The **house** <u>which is near the school</u> is blue," "That **man** <u>who is walking in the town</u> is my uncle," or "The **dog** <u>whose fur is black</u> is big." The relative clauses we have underlined give extra information about the nouns (in bold type) "house," "man," and "dog," respectively.

Notice how in English we use relative pronouns such as "which" or "whose" to introduce these kinds of clauses. Fortunately, in Japanese, we don't need any such particular pronoun, although we must bear in mind that the order followed by these kinds of sentences is, more often than not, the total reverse of the English order: the noun comes last.

● <u>あの学校に近い</u>家は青いです *The **house** <u>that is near the school</u> is blue.*

● <u>街を歩いている</u>あの男は叔父です *That **man** <u>who is walking around the town</u> is my uncle.*

● <u>あの黒い毛</u>の犬は大きいです *The **dog** <u>with black fur</u> / <u>whose fur is black</u> is big.*

How to form relative clauses

Forming relative clauses is not difficult, but you must bear in mind the following rules:

⇒ The noun about which information is offered must go <u>after</u> the relative clause.

⇒ If the relative clause ends in a verb or an -*i* adjective, these must be conjugated in the simple form. With -*na* adjectives, we require な, and with nouns, we must add の. However, in the past tense or in the negative, they both need the verb to be conjugated in the simple form.

⇒ The subject in a relative clause can never be marked with the topic particle は: using the subject particle が is compulsory. As we saw in L.37 (book 2), in subordinate sentences we must use が, unless we are looking to add emphasis. See this example:

Ex: 猫が食べた魚は高かった *The **fish** that the cat ate was expensive.* (With は after 猫 we would explicitly express that it was the cat and no one else who ate the fish.)

⇒ Sometimes, when there is nothing between the subject and the verb of the relative clause, the が (indicating subject) can be replaced by の without distinction.

Ej: 車が/の通った道路は狭い *The **road** where the car passed was narrow.*

"Internal" relative clauses

Let's now go over a more complex aspect of this subject, and distinguish two kinds of relative clauses: "internal" and "external."

"Internal" relative clauses are those where the noun (about which information is provided) is part of the original sentence from which the relative clause is derived. Refer to the table and you'll get a clearer idea: 少年, 倉庫, 友達 and 本 are part of a basic hypothetical phrase, and they can all be "embellished" by the other words in order to "stand out." Let's

Relative clauses
BASIC SENTENCE: 少年は倉庫で友達に本を見せた The boy showed a book to his friend in the warehouse
"Internal" relative clauses
倉庫で友達に本を見せた少年 The boy who showed a book to his friend in the warehouse.
少年が倉庫で本を見せた友達 The friend to whom the boy showed a book in the warehouse.
少年が倉庫で友達に見せた本 The book which the boy showed to his friend in the warehouse.
少年が友達に本を見せた倉庫 The warehouse where the boy showed a book to his friend.
"External" relative clauses
少年が倉庫で友達に本を見せた日 The day when the boy showed a book to his friend in the warehouse.
少年が倉庫で友達に本を見せたという理由 The reason why the boy showed a book to this friend in the warehouse.
少年が倉庫で友達に本を見せたということ The fact that the boy showed a book to his friend in the warehouse.
少年 しょうねん: boy | 倉庫 そうこ: warehouse | 友達 ともだち: friend | 本 ほん: book | 見せる みせる: to show | 日 ひ: day | 理由 りゆう: reason

now see a few sentences of this kind so you can form a clear mental diagram:

● 日本語を習っているあの女性は親切だ *That **woman** who is learning Japanese is kind.*

● 昨日聞いたCDが大好きだ *I like very much the **CD** that I heard yesterday.*

● 彼が使ったタオルは洗濯機に入れた *I put the **towel** that he used in the washing machine.*

● 日本語が上手だった人は少なかった *There were few **people** who were good at Japanese.*

● 汚れた服の女はどこに行った？ *Where has the **woman** whose clothes were dirty gone?*

● センスがよくない人が集まる場所に行かなければならない

*I must go to **a place** where people who don't have style meet.* (two relative clauses)

"External" relative clauses

On the other hand, there are also relative clauses where the noun (about which information is provided) is not a part of the basic hypothetical phrase (see table in the previous page). Some of these nouns cannot be directly linked to the sentence; to do so, they require という (or って in its colloquial form).

Never take という: nouns expressing feelings (音 *sound*, 匂い *smell*, 痛み *pain*...) or those that can be perceived through the senses (写真 *photo*, 音楽 *music*...).
- 腐った魚の匂いがひどいです *The **smell** <u>of rotten fish</u> is disgusting.*
- ビートの強い音楽が好きだ *I like **music** <u>with a strong beat</u>.*

Always take という: abstract concepts expressing thoughts or assertions (うわさ *rumor*, こと *fact / thing*, 意見 *opinion*, 理由 *reason*, 考え *thought*...).
- 政府が悪いという意見はありますか？ *Is your **opinion** <u>that the government is bad</u>?*
- 彼らがラス・ベガスで結婚したいってうわさは本当かな？

  *Is the **rumor** <u>that they want to get married in Las Vegas</u> true?*

In other cases, it doesn't matter whether we use という or not:
- マンガを翻訳する(って)仕事は楽しい *The **job** <u>of translating manga</u> is fun.*
- 男が死んだ(という)事件があった *There was an **incident** <u>in which a man died</u>.*

The many usages of よう

Let's now briefly forget about relative clauses and go on to study another subject. In Japanese there are several expressions and grammatical constructions, which use よう. Bringing them all together in one same lesson and having a look at them all at once might be interesting, since studying them gradually and separately could be confusing.

We will review now the よう constructions we already saw in L.43 (book 2). To begin with, we have ようだ, used at the end of a sentence to indicate "apparently," when the speaker has direct information on something and his degree of certainty is high:
- 天気が崩れたようだね *Apparently, the weather has worsened.*
- 彼女の弟さんは背が高いようだ *Apparently, her younger brother is tall.*
- 先生は娘をしかったようです *Apparently, the teacher scolded my daughter.*

We also have the ような and ように variations, which act as simile (L.54):
- あの鬼のような先生が嫌いだ *I hate that teacher who is like an ogre.*
- 彼は政治家のようにうそをつくね *He lies (tells lies) like a politician.*

−52− 第50課 Lesson 50

In order to: ように

Let's now begin to study those "unseen" usages of よう, the first of which is the usage of ように after verbs (only), usually in the simple form, and indicates "in order to" or "so that." This usage is for expressing that a certain action be implemented to urge or cause someting to be done; thus, enabling us to obtain the desired outcome.

The structure of this kind of sentences is always "*[result]* ように *[action]*." That is, before ように we specify the result we want to obtain and, afterwards, we detail the action or actions that must be done to achieve it.

- 日本へ行けるように働いている *I'm working in order to go to Japan.*
- 猫が魚を食べないように隠そう *I shall hide the fish so that the cat doesn't eat it.*
- 合格できるように祈りたい *I want to pray so that I can pass.*
- 事故がないように気をつけてください *Be careful (in order) not to have an accident.*
- 父が怒らないように謝ろう *I shall apologize so that my father doesn't get angry.*

Soft command or request: ように + verb

Knowing how to use the expression ように, combined with a verb like 言う *(to say)*, 頼む *(to ask), or* 命令する *(to command),* is very convenient. It has the implication of "to do as..." and it that can also be used with other verbs to form sentences which are not necessarily imperative or for requests.

However, you can't give an order or make a request using this structure directly. "ように + verb" is normally used either to indicate what kind of order or request oneself or a third person has received, or to describe an order or request in an indirect way or which was previously performed (in the past). It might sound somewhat intricate, but take a look at the following example sentences and you will understand much more clearly what we mean.

Note: Since we are talking about orders, you can review L.30 (book 1), where the imperative is explained, as well as the usage of 〜てくれ, which we studied in L.45.

- 先生は私に本を読むように言った *The teacher told me to read a book.*
- 社長は山崎にやめるように言った *The president told Yamazaki to resign.*
- 彼女はあそこで待つように僕に頼んだ *She asked me to wait there.*
- 川井にオフィスへ来るように言ってください *Please, tell Kawai to come to the office.*
- 私は息子に勉強するように命令した *I ordered my son to study.*

To get to the point of: ようになる

Another expression with ように is ようになる, which is used to indicate changes that are usually gradual (despite some exceptions), and indicate the end of processes that are usually long. It is translated as "to get to the point of...", "to finally manage to..." or "to become able to..." This expression can only be used with verbs conjugated in the simple form.

- 彼は泳ぐようになった *He managed to (learn to) swim.*
- 日本語を話せるようになりたい *I want to become able to speak Japanese.*
- タバコを吸わないようになった *I managed to not smoke. (I managed to quit smoking.)*
- やっと統計が分かるようになった *I have finally managed to understand statistics.*

To try to do something: ようにする

The last よう expression we will see is ようにする, used to express an intention or decision. An exact translation of this expression is very difficult to suggest, but we could define ようにする more or less as "to decide to do something...," "to try to do something...," "to have the intention of using all the necessary means to do something...," etc.

- 毎朝、運動するようにしたい *I want to try to exercise every morning.*
- 彼はあまり食べないようにしている *He is trying not to eat much.*
- 明日、十時に来るようにしてください *Tomorrow, make sure you come at 10.*
- 政治家はうそをつかないようにしないといけない *Politicians must try not to lie.*

Usages of よう		
ようだ (L.43)	"Apparently..."	彼は城に行ったようだ Apparently, he went to the castle.
ような (L.43 / 54)	Simile	彼は城のような家に住んでいる He lives in a house that looks like a castle.
ように (1)	Adverbial form of よう	あの家は城のように広い That house is as spacious as a castle.
ように (2)	"In order to..." / "So that..."	城に行けるように地図を書こう I'll draw you a map so that you can go to the castle.
ように (3)	Order / Request	彼は地図を書くように言った He told / asked me to draw a map.
ようにする	"To get to the point of..."	彼は地図を書けるようになった He has got to the point of being able to draw a map.
ようになる	"To try / decide to do something"	毎日、城まで走って行くようにする I'm going to try run to the castle every day.
かれ: he | しろ: castle | いく: to go | いえ: house | すむ: to live | ひろい: spatious, wide | ちず: map かく: to write, to draw | いう: to say | まいにち: every day | はしる: to run

As usual, we will take the opportunity by means of manga panels to see in a working context the expressions we have just studied. On the one hand, we will review relative clauses and, on the other hand, we will try to give a clearer idea of the numerous usages of よう.

a) A simple relative clause

Narrator: めのおおきなひとは、おなかがすいてしにそうです
eye POP big person TOP, stomach SP empty die be
The man who had big eyes was starving to death.

Javier Bolado

We start with this excerpt from a story written in hiragana alone. The author copies the style of children's stories, which are usually written in hiragana because children can't read kanji yet. The sentence would actually be: 目の大きな人はお腹がすいて死にそうです.

The relative clause is 目の大きな (*with big eyes*), and it provides information about the noun 人 (*person*). Notice how, as we commented in the theory pages, sometimes the subject particle が is replaced with の. Therefore, 目が大きな人 (*the man with big eyes*) would also be valid.

An interesting thing about Japanese is that the concepts of restrictive and non-restrictive relative clauses don't exist. That is, the sentence 目の大きな人は親切だ can mean both *The man, who has big eyes, is kind* (non-restrictive) and *The man who has big eyes is kind* (restrictive). Consequently, we will only be able to tell this nuance through the context. In this case, the relative clause is restrictive.

Notes: Notice how the sentences お腹がすいている (*to be hungry*) and 死にそうです (*he looks like he is going to die*) are linked by the *-te* form (L.35 and 46). Notice, too, the usage of the suffix for conjecture 〜そうだ in 死にそうです.

b) An "internal" relative clause

> **Zange:** 彼は、ミュンヘン大学の図書館で私が銃で撃った男だ！！
> *he* TOP, *München university* POP *library* PP *I* SP *gun* IP *shoot man be*
> **He is the man I shot with a gun in the library of the University of Munich!!**

Here we have a sentence with a long relative clause: ミュンヘン大学の図書館で私が銃で撃った (*I shot with a gun in the library of the University of Munich*) is the relative clause identifying the noun 男 (*man*). It is an "internal" relative clause because the noun 男 is part of a basic hypothetical phrase: 私はミュンヘン大学の図書館で男を銃で撃った (*I shot a man with a gun in the library of the University of Munich*). In this example we

J.M. Ken Niimura

observe an important point you should bear in mind: the subject of the relative clause (in this case 私, *I*) can never take the topic particle は: it needs が.

c) An "external" relative clause

> **Sayama:** おまえがムコ候補に肩入れしてるって噂は聞いてるぜ
> *you* SP *son-in-law candidate support do say rumor* TOP *hear* EP
> **I have heard the rumor that you support him as a candidate for son-in-law.**

Studio Kōsen

Let's now see an instance of an "external" relative clause, named so because the noun about which the information is given is totally independent. In other words, it is not part of a basic hypothetical phrase. In this case, the noun is 噂 (*rumor*), and the relative clause is おまえがムコ候補に肩入れしている (*you support him as a candidate for son-in-law*).

We mentioned in the theory pages that some nouns require という when linked to a relative clause. To be precise, we use という when the noun expresses abstract concepts, like thoughts or assertions. 噂 is one of those very concepts, therefore we will use either という or the shortened colloquial form って, like in this example.

d) Two usages of *yō*

Doctor: 彼女、食欲もそこそこでてきたようだし、会話もできるようになった

she appetite too a little go out apparently besides, conversation too to get to

Apparently, she has recovered some of her appetite and, what's more, she is able to talk now.

Javier Bolado

We will now leave the relative clauses behind, and we will focus on the usages of the multipurpose よう. In this sentence we have two different usages. On the one hand, in 食欲もそこそこ出てきたようだ (*she has recovered some of her appetite*), we have the well-known expression ようだ, indicating "apparently," which we studied in depth in L.43. Next, in 会話もできるようになった, we see ようになる, which indicates a change that has gradually happened. The phrase would be literally translated as *She has become able to hold a conversation (after a certain adaptation period which has taken place gradually and which has already concluded).*

Note: Notice the usage of し, indicating "not only x, but also y" which we saw in L.46.

e) In order to: *yō ni*

Boss: お客様に良いことがたくさんありますようにここで見守ってね！

Mr. client IOP good thing SP many there is so that here PP pay attention EP!

Stay here and pay attention in order to make sure the clients have everything they need!

In this panel we can see a usage of ように expressing an aim and the action that must be performed to achieve it. It could be translated as "so that" or "in order to."
In this case, the aim is お客様に良いことがたくさんあります (*that there are many good things for the clients*) and the action to be performed in order to achieve it is ここで見守って (*stay here and pay attention*). ように is placed in the middle – after the sentence indicating the "aim"– to link both sentences and give the meaning of "in order to."

Gabriel Luque

Note: Before ように the verb comes usually in the simple form, but since the register in this case is quite formal,
she has chosen to leave the verb あります (*to be, there is / are*) in the *-masu* form.

f) Request: *yō* + verb

Man: お母さん、銀行の支店長に融資を待つように言ったそうだね

mom, bank POP *branch director* IOP *funds* DOP *wait* (requ) *say looks like be* EP

Mom, you've told the bank manager to wait for the funds, haven't you?

Let's now see another usage of よう, used for soft orders or requests: it is the construction formed by ように + verb for request or order.

In our sentence, we must take a look at 待つように言った (*you told him to wait*). Although 言う (*to say*) is used, the sentence is obviously a request. Other possible sentences could have been: 待つように頼んだ (*you asked him to wait*) or 待つように命令した (*you ordered him to wait*), etc.

Bárbara Raya

Notes: Notice the expression of the conjecture 〜そうだ − be careful, this expression is different to the one we have seen in the manga-example a) − used to give information which has been obtained from another source (L.43, book 2). Thus, 待つように言ったそうだ literally means *I've heard / been told that you have told him to wait.*

g) To try to do something: *yō ni suru*

Naoya: これから、彼女と話すようにしたいなぁ...

this from, her CP *talk try to want* EP...

From now on, I want to try to talk to her...

Studio Kōsen

We will conclude this lesson with another of the many usages of よう: the ようにする construction. Although rather difficult to define, it indicates a nuance similar to "to try to" or "to decide to do something." In the text in this panel we find the sentence 彼女と話すようにしたい, which has the connotation of either *I want to try to talk with her* or *I want to have the intention of doing all I possibly can to talk with her.* That is, using ようにする is more or less the equivalent to a declaration of intentions of what one wants to do or is presently attempting to do.

Note: これから (literally, "from this") means "from now on," "after this."

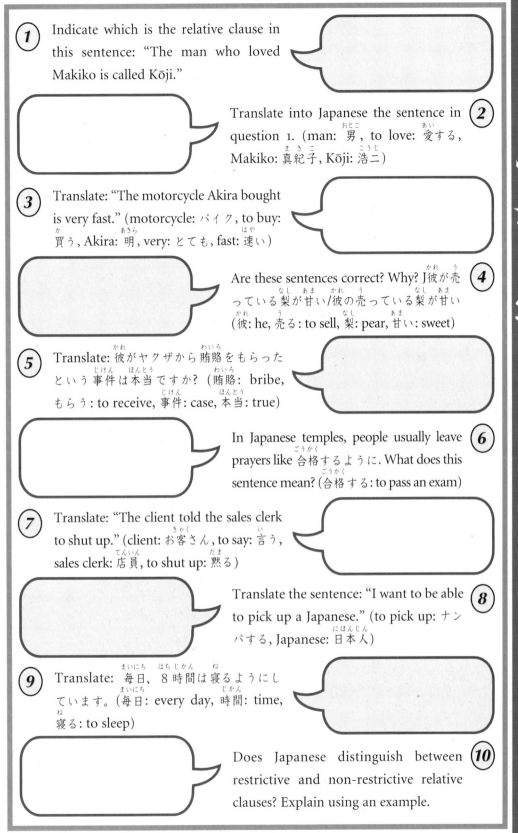

1 Indicate which is the relative clause in this sentence: "The man who loved Makiko is called Kōji."

2 Translate into Japanese the sentence in question 1. (man: 男, to love: 愛する, Makiko: 真紀子, Kōji: 浩二)

3 Translate: "The motorcycle Akira bought is very fast." (motorcycle: バイク, to buy: 買う, Akira: 明, very: とても, fast: 速い)

4 Are these sentences correct? Why? 彼が売っている梨が甘い/彼の売っている梨が甘い (彼: he, 売る: to sell, 梨: pear, 甘い: sweet)

5 Translate: 彼がヤクザから賄賂をもらったという事件は本当ですか? (賄賂: bribe, もらう: to receive, 事件: case, 本当: true)

6 In Japanese temples, people usually leave prayers like 合格するように. What does this sentence mean? (合格する: to pass an exam)

7 Translate: "The client told the sales clerk to shut up." (client: お客さん, to say: 言う, sales clerk: 店員, to shut up: 黙る)

8 Translate the sentence: "I want to be able to pick up a Japanese." (to pick up: ナンパする, Japanese: 日本人)

9 Translate: 毎日、8時間は寝るようにしています。(毎日: every day, 時間: time, 寝る: to sleep)

10 Does Japanese distinguish between restrictive and non-restrictive relative clauses? Explain using an example.

第51課：困ったことと事故

Lesson 51: Unexpected events and accidents

In any stay in a foreign country unexpected events —such as theft, loss, accidents, sickness— can arise. In this lesson we will learn how to face these kinds of situations in Japanese, and we will learn a lot of new vocabulary, as well.

The role of the police

Japan is a country with an extremely high level of safety in cities; so much so that pickpockets hardly exist, and the possibilities of being robbed or hurt are slim. Therefore, the role of the Japanese police is not quite "keeping the peace," but rather acting like "social workers," who watch traffic, take care of lost children or objects, show the way to those who get lost, etc.

Another curiosity in Japan are the town police boxes or 交番, mini-police stations with only two or three policemen who see to the safety in the neighborhood. If you ever get lost, go to the closest 交番: there they will kindly and diligently help you find your way.

Emergencies	
accident	事故
ambulance	救急車
bag	バッグ
emergency	緊急
injured person	けが人
injury	けが
pickpocket	スリ
police	警察官
to rob	盗む
thief	泥棒
wallet	財布
witness	目撃者

● すみませんが、道に迷ってしまいました *Excuse me, I'm lost.* (L.35/37)

● ここは何という町ですか？ *What is this city called?* (L.41)

● この住所はここから近いですか？ *Is this address near here?* (L.41)

● 電車の駅へ行く道を教えてください *Please, tell me the way to the railway station.*

● 東京タワーに行きたいんですが... *I'd like to go to Tokyo Tower...* (L.37/40)

● 地図を書いてくれますか？ *Could you draw a map for me?* (L.32/45)

● 私の地図でここはどこですか？ *According to my map, where are we now?*

● 代々木公園まで歩いて行けますか？ *Can I walk to Yoyogi park?*

Theft

As we have just mentioned, to be the victim of theft in Japan is extremely rare. Nevertheless, let's see a few sentences to practice vocabulary and grammar.

● 一番近い交番はどこですか？ *Where is the closest kōban?*

● 誰かが私の財布を盗んだ *Someone has stolen my wallet.* (L.41)

● 泥棒が私のバッグをひったくって逃げた *The thief snatched my handbag and ran off.*

● リュックには財布とクレジットカードが入っています

My wallet and my credit cards are in my (stolen) backpack.

● 盗難証明書を作ってください *Fill in the theft report, please.*

Loss

Something that is more likely to happen in Japan, like anywhere else, is losing an object. Generally, the Japanese are very considerate when they find a lost object, and they usually take it to the closest 交番. If the lost object is a wallet with money that is returned intact, it is customary to give 10% of the recovered money as a token of gratitude to the person who has found it and given it to the authorities.

● ここに財布がありませんでしたか？ *Wasn't there a wallet here?*

● 忘れ物係はどこですか？ *Where is the lost and found office?*

● 地下鉄にデジカメを忘れてしまいました *I forgot my digital camera in the subway.*

● どんなカメラですか？ *What kind of camera is it?*

● 銀色で、メーカーはカシオです *It's silver and its make is Casio.* (L.35 / 46)

● 見つかった場合、連絡してください *If you find it, let me know, please.* (L.46)

● パスポートをなくしました。再発行していただきたいのですが…

I have lost my passport. I would like you to reissue it... (L.35 / 31 / 45)

What's wrong with me, doctor?

During our stay in Japan, it could also happen that, at some time or other, we become sick. Now, we will focus on visits to the doctor and hospitals.

● 気分が悪いですが *I don't feel good...* (L.37)

● 医者(救急車)を呼んでください *Call a doctor (an ambulance), please.*

● 病院に連れていってください *Take me to a hospital, please.* (L.35)

● 診療の予約をとってくれますか？ *Can you make an appointment for a consultation, please?* (L.45)

In the hospital

We recommend that you review now the vocabulary of the parts of the body in L.26 (book 1). Also, on the next page we have given a large vocabulary table. However, you don't need to memorize it all; just learn the words you think are most important.

● どんな症状ですか *What are the symptoms? | How do you feel? | What symptoms do you have?*

● お腹が痛いです *I have a stomachache.* (L.26)

● 風邪を引いたようです *I think I've caught a cold.* (L.43)

● 熱があります *I have a fever.*

● せきが止まりません *I can't stop coughing. (lit. The cough doesn't stop)*

● 転んで腕を痛めました *I've fallen and hurt my arm.*

● 手をやけどしました *I've burnt my hand.*

● 足首をねんざしました *I've sprained my ankle.*

● ペニシリンのアレルギーがあります *I'm allergic to penicillin.*

● 毎日この薬を飲んでいます *I take (lit. drink) this medicine every day.*

● 生理中です *I have my period.*

● どのくらいで治りますか？ *How long will I take to recover?*

● 旅行は続けられますか？ *Can I continue my trip?* (L.32)

● 処方せんを書いてもらえますか？ *Could you please write a prescription for me?* (L.45)

Talking with the doctor

Let's see some typical doctor phrases so that we can understand what they are telling us:

● いつからその症状がありますか？ *How long have you had those symptoms?* (L.41)

● どこが痛いですか？ *Where does it hurt you?*

● 横になってください *Lie down, please.*

● シャツを脱いでください *Take your shirt off, please.*

● 深呼吸をしてください *Breathe deeply.*

● 血液(尿)検査が必要です *You need to have a blood (urine) test.* (L.37)

● アレルギーはありますか？ *Do you have any allergies?*

● 血圧(体温)を計りましょう *I'm going to take your blood pressure (your temperature).* (L.34)

● 大したことはありません *It's nothing serious.*

● この処方せんをもって薬局に行って、薬を買って飲んでください

Take this prescription, go to the pharmacy, buy the medicine and take it. (L.35/46)

Accidents

We will conclude the theory section with some useful phrases in case of an automobile accident; which we hope you will never have to use.

- こうつうじこ
交通事故があって、けがをしています *There has been a traffic accident, and I'm hurt.*
- ともだち くるま
友達が車にはねられました *My friend has been run over by a car.*
- きゅうきゅうしゃ く でんわ
救急車が来るように電話してください *Call for an ambulance to come, please.* (L.50)
- けいさつ よ
警察も呼んでください *Call the police as well.* (L.37)
- みぎうで お
右腕を折ったみたいです *I think I've broken my right arm.* (L.43)
- しゅっけつ はげ と
出血が激しくて止められない *I am bleeding heavily and I can't stop it.*
- じこしょうめいしょ か
事故証明書を書いてください *Fill in the accident report, please.*

Medical vocabulary					
Basic vocabulary (きほん基本)		diarrhea	げり下痢	joint	かんせつ関節
doctor	いしゃ医者	food poisoning	しょくちゅうどく食中毒	kidney	じんぞう腎臓
hospital	びょういん病院	fracture	こっせつ骨折	liver	かんぞう肝臓
hospitalization	にゅういん入院	gastric ulcer	いかいよう胃潰瘍	lung	はい肺
insurance	ほけん保険	gastritis	いえん胃炎	muscle	きんにく筋肉
leaving the hospital	たいいん退院	inflammation of the ear	ちゅうじえん中耳炎	skin	ひふ皮膚
medicine	くすり薬	influenza	インフルエンザ	urine	にょう尿
pain	いた痛み	hepatitis	かんえん肝炎	**Doctors (いしゃ医者)**	
patient	かんじゃ患者	high blood pressure	こうけつあつ高血圧	dentist	しかい歯科医
pharmacy	やっきょく薬局｜くすりや薬屋	indigestion	しょうかふりょう消化不良	gynecologist	ふじんかい婦人科医
surgery	しゅじゅつ手術	low blood pressure	ていけつあつ低血圧	internist	ないかい内科医
symptom	しょうじょう症状	pneumonia	はいえん肺炎	ophthalmologist	がんかい眼科医
Sicknesses (びょうき病気)		rheumatism	リューマチ	otolaryngologist	じびいんこうかい耳鼻咽喉科医
allergy	Allergie アレルギー	rhinitis	びえん鼻炎	pediatrician	しょうにか小児科
anemia	ひんけつ貧血	sprain	ねんざ	surgeon	げかい外科医
appendicitis	もうちょうえん盲腸炎	sunstroke	にっしゃびょう日射病	**Others (いろいろ)**	
asthma	ぜんそく	tetanus	はしょうふう破傷風	bandage	ほうたい包帯
bronchitis	きかんしえん気管支炎	**Parts of the body (ないぞう内臓)**		blood pressure	けつあつ血圧
bruise	だぼく打撲	bone	ほね骨	breathing	こきゅう呼吸
burn	やけど	blood	ち血｜けつえき血液	injection	ちゅうしゃ注射
cancer	ガン（癌）	blood vessel	けっかん血管	pulse	みゃくはく脈拍
cold	かぜ風邪	heart	しんぞう心臓	temperature	たいおん体温
diabetes	とうにょうびょう糖尿病	intestines	ちょう腸	X-ray	Roentgen レントゲン

文化編：住所の読み方
Cultural note: Understanding addresses

One of the most surprising things in 日本(にほん) is that the vast majority of streets don't have a name, and that houses don't have numbers. The question is obvious: how do the poor postmen find their way around? And, if we want to go to a specific address (住所(じゅうしょ)), how will we find it? To get your bearings in 日本(にほん), you will have to learn how to walk along their streets from scratch. We will illustrate the explanation with an example:

We have chosen the address of the famous Nintendō's head office, in Kyoto: 〒601-8501 京都府京都市南区上鳥羽鉾立町 １１丁目１番地任天堂株式会社 (きょうとふ きょうとし みなみく かみとば ほこだてちょう じゅういちちょうめいちばんち にんてんどうかぶしきがいしゃ). The first number (601-8501) is the zip code (the sign 〒 means "zip code"). Then, we have the prefecture 京都府(きょうとふ) (府(ふ): prefecture, only when used with Kyoto and Osaka, with other prefectures we

If you get lost, go to the *kōban*! (Photo: M. Bernabé)

use 県(けん) − except for Tokyo, which is 都(と), and Hokkaidō, which is 道(どう) −), the city 京都市(きょうとし) (市(し): city), the district 南区(みなみく) (区(く): district), the town 上鳥羽鉾立町(かみとば ほこだてちょう) (町(ちょう): sector / town), the block within the town 11丁目(ちょうめ) (丁目(ちょうめ): block), and, finally, the plot number (番地(ばんち): plot). In the end, we have the name of the person or company, 任天堂(にんてんどう) 株式会社(かぶしき がいしゃ) (株式会社(かぶしき がいしゃ): public corporation). Notice how everything is the other way round compared to Western addresses: in Japan, they start from the prefecture and work their way down until they reach the plot of land. Following Western criteria, we would have something like Nintendō, 1-11 Kami-toba Hokodate-chō, Minami-ku, Kyōto-shi, Kyōto-fu 601-8501. That is, we would have to reverse the order of the elements, because we start from the plot and we finish with the prefecture or state. Consequently, to look for an address, we must have a good map, and look for the city first, then the district, then the town / sector, etc. It is no wonder the Japanese draw maps (usually from the nearest train or subway station) when they want to indicate the location of a place. However, there's a trick to everything: if you ever get lost or can't reach your destination, you can always go to the closest 交番(こうばん) so that the 警察官(けいさつかん) on duty can guide you. They are prepared for this, and will be glad to help you.

漫画例 Manga-examples

Although, ideally, you should never have to use the knowledge you have acquired from this lesson in real life, it will certainly be useful if you want to understand the jargon which appears in the thousands of comics and movies involving policemen or doctors. Let's see some examples.

a) Police jargon

Police.: えー本部本部 本町 3 丁目付近に不審人物発見 至急応援をー
err... headquarters headquarters this city 3 block vicinity PP *suspicious man discover immediately reinforcements* DOP...
Err... Headquarters, headquarters. I've discovered a suspicious man in the vicinity of the 3rd block in this sector. Send reinforcements immediately...

Javier Bolado

In this first example we find two different things. On the one hand, we have quite a lot of police jargon, essential if you want to enjoy police or *yakuza* movies and/or manga. The character is using very typical words of this jargon, such as 本部 *(headquarters)*, 不審 *(suspicious)*, 人物 *(person, man, woman)*, 至急

(immediately), *or* 応援 *(reinforcements)*. Typical words in police jargon which you won't usually find in dictionaries are デカ (colloquial word used when referring to a 刑事, *police officer, detective*), ガイシャ (contraction of 被害者, *victim*), ホシ (designating the *criminal* or 犯人), and チャカ (*gun*, also called 銃, 拳銃, ピストル or ハジキ).

On the other hand, we can review the subject of addresses studied in the **Cultural note.** Notice how the policeman indicates the place where he is at: 本町 3 丁目付近. You already know 町 means *city / town* and 丁目 means *block*. 本, in this case, means "this," "this here," as in the words 本日: *this day = today,* 本月: *this month,* 本校: *this school,* 本社: *this company,* etc. Thus, 本町 is *this city / town.* Whereas, 付近 means *vicinity.* Therefore, 本町 3 丁目付近 is *in the vicinity of the 3rd block of this city* (or *town* or *sector*).

b) Asking for directions

Man: すいません ちょっと道^{みち}をききたいのですが...
excuse me a little way DOP ask be but...
Excuse me, I would like to ask for directions...

すいません ちょっと道をききたいのですが…

Gabriel Luque

This time we see a man who wants to ask for directions and goes into a 交番^{こうばん} to do it. Notice how he expresses himself: he first breaks the ice with すいません (colloquial version of すみません, *excuse me*), and then he asks his question. At the end of the sentence he adds the のです tag (L.40), and a が (L.37), all in order to make the question less brusque. This is a very common way of expressing oneself in Japanese.

Observe now the ちょっと. It literally means "a little," like in ちょっと待^まって *(wait a little bit)*, but it really has countless usages: to call attention, ちょっとすみません *(excuse me a minute)*, to soften something difficult to say: ちょっと無理^{むり}ですね *(I'm afraid that's impossible)* or as an "aid" when asking something, like in this example: ちょっと道^{みち}をききたい *(I would like to ask for directions)*.

c) Calling the police

Man: お巡^{まわ}りさん 事故^{じこ}です！早^{はや}くきて！
police (suf.) accident be! quickly come!
Officer, there's been an accident! Quickly, come!

This is what we must say if we witness an accident and we want to call the police. By the way, the amount of names given to policemen is quite interesting. The generic name for the police force is 警察^{けいさつ}, from which the word 警察官^{けいさつかん} *(police officer)* is derived. Other names are 刑事^{けいじ} and 巡査^{じゅんさ}, or the colloquial 警官^{けいかん}, デカ or お巡^{まわ}りさん, like in this example. A crimi-

お巡りさん 事故です‼ 早くきて！

J.M. Ken Niimura

nal's most typical way of referring to the policemen is サツ (from 警察^{けいさつ}) or ポリ. **Note:** The telephone number for emergencies in Japan is １１０番^{ひゃくとうばん} (be careful with the irregular reading).

d) Phoning the hospital to report an emergency

Tel.: 事故（じこ）です！患者（かんじゃ）は胸（むね）を打（う）って呼吸（こきゅう）がうまくできないそうです！
accident be! patient TOP chest DOP hit breathe SP well can looks like be!
It's an accident! The patient has hit himself on the chest and can't breathe well!

Let's now enter the doctors' world. In this example, we can see how the doctor is being informed on the phone about a patient who has just been hospitalized. Since the sentence itself has no difficulty, we will focus on the grammar. We can see (in the 打（う）って... portion) two sentences linked with the *-te* form (L.37 / 46), and an adverb (L.22, book 1) formed from the *-i* adjective うまい. うまい is the colloquial version of いい *(well)*, therefore, うまくできない means *cannot do it well*. And, finally,

事故です！

患者は胸を打って呼吸がうまくできないそうです！

Studio Kōsen

notice the expression of the conjecture そうです (L.43, book 2), used to give information obtained from another source (similar to "I've been told that...").

e) A demanding patient

Miura: 痛（いた）み止（ど）め飲（の）んで2時間（にじかん）たったけど効（き）かないよ。ブスコパン頼（たの）むよ
painkiller drink 2 hours pass but take effect EP. Buscopan ask EP
Two hours have passed since I took the painkiller, but it doesn't take effect. Come on, give me some Buscopan.

痛み止め飲んで2時間たったけど効かないよ。ブスコパン頼むよ

Javier Bolado

Another medical example. This time we have a *patient* (患者（かんじゃ）) asking the nurse for some *medicine* (薬（くすり）). There are several points worth seeing. On the one hand, notice the word *painkiller* (痛（いた）み止（ど）め), literally something that "stops (止（と）める) the pain (痛（いた）み),"; and then we have the curious thing about the Japanese not "taking" medicine, but always "drinking" it (飲（の）む). By the way, the word 効（き）く means a medicine or something *takes effect*.

In the grammatical aspect, we have a sentence linked with the *-te* form (L.35 / 46) in the 飲（の）んで... portion, and an adversative construction with けど (L.49), indicating "but."
Note: ブスコパン (Buscopan) is the brand of a painkiller.

f) Names of sicknesses

> **Doctor:** 肺炎_{はいえん}じゃない... 食_{しょく}あたりじゃない... 扁桃腺炎_{へんとうせんえん}でもない...
> *pneumonia not be... food poisoning not be... tonsillitis neither be...*
> **It's not pneumonia... nor food poisoning... nor tonsillitis...**

Here we find some names of sicknesses (病気_{びょうき}), among which we find 食_{しょく}あたり (*food poisoning*), whose synonymous is 食中毒_{しょくちゅうどく}.

Notice the suffix 炎_{えん}, the equivalent to our suffix *-itis* (meaning "inflammation"). Thus, 肺炎_{はいえん} is *pneumonia* or "lung (肺_{はい}) inflammation (炎_{えん})," 扁桃腺炎_{へんとうせんえん} is *tonsillitis* or "tonsil (扁桃腺_{へんとうせん}) inflammation (炎_{えん})," and 胃炎_{いえん} is *gastritis* or "stomach (胃_い) inflammation (炎_{えん})," etc.

There are more suffixes, like 病_{びょう}, indicating "disease:" 心臓病_{しんぞうびょう} means *heart disease* (心臓_{しんぞう}), and アルツハイマー病_{びょう} is *Alzheimer's disease*.

Gabriel Luque

g) Tests and hospitalizations

> **Doctor:** これからいろいろ検査_{けんさ}を受_うけてもらいます
> *this from several tests DOP take (receive)*
> **From now on, we will have you take several tests.**
> くわしくは結果_{けっか}でわかりますから 明日_{あした}からさっそく入院_{にゅういん}しましょう
> *in detail TOP result IP understand because tomorrow from immediately hospitalize*
> **The results will give us more details, so tomorrow we shall hospitalize you.**

To conclude, here is a good example of medical jargon: notice how the doctor tells the patient she must be *hospitalized* (入院_{にゅういん}する) so that she can *take some tests* (検査_{けんさ}を受_うける), and that they will know more when they obtain the *results* (結果_{けっか}). In the grammatical level, we will highlight

Bárbara Raya

the 〜てもらう form (L.45), which adds the nuance that the listener will perform the action for the benefit of the speaker, and, besides, the *-ō* form (L.34) in 入院_{にゅういん}しましょう (*we shall hospitalize you*). Last of all, note the usages of から as the particle "from" (L.41) (これから and 明日_{あした}から), and as a connector indicating cause / reason (L.48) (わかりますから).

1 Translate into English the following words: 財布, 事故, 熱, 薬局, レントゲン, 心臓 and 痛み.

2 Translate into Japanese the following words: "doctor," "hospital," "injury," "ambulance," "cough," and "cold."

3 You go into a 交番 to inform them that you've lost a ring. What do you say? (to lose: 失くす, ring: 指輪)

4 Translate: "I've got a headache, a fever, and I can't stop coughing."

5 Translate into English: ただのインフルエンザかもしれないが、血液検査が必要です。(ただの: a simple)

6 Interpret this address: 〒101-8010 東京都 千代田区神田駿河台町 4丁目6番地日立 株式会社。(都: metropolitan area)

7 How many ways of calling a gun are there? And a policeman? List them.

8 Translate the sentence: ちょっと分からないので、説明してください。(分かる: to understand, 説明する: to explain)

9 Translate: "Because I have a headache, I take a medicine." (painful: 痛い, head: 頭, medicine: 薬)

10 What does the suffix 炎 mean? Write at least four words with 炎 that we have studied and give their meanings.

Lesson 52: Honorifics

Japanese, like any other language, has strategies to indicate respect and speak in a "polite" way: we are talking about the "formal language." In the Japanese case, however, this is specially complex because there are three modes of honorifics, its usage varying according to the occasion.

Honorifics or 敬語

The Japanese formal language is called 敬語, that is, "language (語) of respect (敬)." We will use 敬語 when speaking with or about people who are hierarchically superior to us (such as bosses, teachers, elders...) or with people we have just met, as well as in formal occasions like speeches, weddings, work meetings, dealing with clients, and so on.

Traditionally, in Japanese, there are three kinds of 敬語, that is: 尊敬語 (*language of respect*), 謙譲語 (*language of modesty*), and 丁寧語 (*polite speech*). Be careful, because each of them is used in different contexts, so it is very easy to mix them up. To end up using one in the wrong situation sounds awful!

Special verbs			
	Normal	Sonkeigo	Kenjōgo
to do	する	なさる	いたす
to be	いる	いらっしゃる	おる
to go / come	行く｜来る	いらっしゃる	参る｜伺う
to eat / drink	食べる｜飲む	召し上がる	いただく
to see	見る	ご覧になる	拝見する
to borrow	借りる	——	拝借する
to know	知っている	ご存知だ	存じている
to die	死ぬ	お亡くなりになる	——
to say	言う	おっしゃる	申す｜申し上げる
to give	くれる	くださる	——
to give (2)	あげる	——	さしあげる
to receive	もらう	——	いただく

The language of respect (尊敬語)

尊敬語 literally means "language (語) of respect (尊敬)." We use 尊敬語 when talking <u>with</u> or <u>about</u> another person, **raising his or her position** to express the utmost respect.

The subject of the action is always the other person, who normally is either someone the speaker considers superior or a stranger.

How do we use 尊敬語(そんけいご)?

In English, all we need to do is use relatively learned words and address people by their surname preceded by a title, such as Mr. or Miss, to speak with formality. One of the peculiarities of the Japanese formal language, however, is that it implies important grammatical and lexical changes regarding informal language. Bear in mind the following points:

(1) **Usage of the formal "versions" of certain verbs.** Take a look at the table on the previous page and you will see the 尊敬語(そんけいご) and 謙譲語(けんじょうご) versions of some verbs you probably already know. Let's see some examples in 尊敬語(そんけいご):

● 田中(たなか)さん、何(なに)をなさっていますか？ *What are you doing, Mr. Tanaka?*
● ご希望(きぼう)をおっしゃってください *Please, tell me what you wish.*
● 鈴木(すずき)さんはもうご存知(ぞんじ)です *Mr. Suzuki already knows it.*
● 先生(せんせい)は(私(わたし)に)ご本(ほん)をくださった *The teacher gave me a book.* (L.45)

(2) **Conjugation お + Root - になる.** Take any verbal root (L.31), and add お in the beginning and になる in the end. **Ex:** 書(か)く *(to write)* ⇒ -*masu* form: 書(か)きます ⇒ (without ます): 書(か)き ⇒ we add お and になる: お書(か)きになる. **Note:** This conjugation is not used with *suru* verbs (with those verbs we use なさる. Ex: 勉強(べんきょう)する ⇒ 勉強(べんきょう)なさる *to study*).

● 先生(せんせい)はお手紙(てがみ)をお書(か)きになった *The teacher wrote a letter.*
● すみません、お立(た)ちになってください *Excuse me, please stand up.*
● このご本(ほん)をお読(よ)みになっていないと思(おも)います *I think you haven't read this book.*

(3) **～られる Form.** There is a special conjugation you should learn from scratch (see table on the right). Verbs in group 1 replace the last -*ru* with -*rareru*, and verbs in group 2 replace the last -*u* with -*a* and add -*reru*. Thus, *kaku* ⇒ *kak-* ⇒ *kaka-* ⇒ *kakareru*. **Exceptions:** be careful with 買(か)う, which becomes *kawareru* and not *kaareru*, and with 待(ま)つ, which becomes *matareru* and not *matsareru*.

	Simple f.	Meaning	Rule	Sonkeigo
Group 1	教(おし)える	to teach	-~~る~~られる	教えられる
	起(お)きる	to wake up		起きられる
Group 2	貸(か)す	to lend	-~~す~~される	貸される
	待(ま)つ	to wait	-~~つ~~たれる	待たれる
	買(か)う	to buy	-~~う~~われる	買われる
	帰(かえ)る	to return	-~~る~~られる	帰られる
	書(か)く	to write	-~~く~~かれる	書かれる
	急(いそ)ぐ	to hurry	-~~ぐ~~がれる	急がれる
	遊(あそ)ぶ	to play	-~~ぶ~~ばれる	遊ばれる
	拒(こば)む	to refuse	-~~む~~まれる	拒まれる

● 清水さんは本を書かれたそうです *Apparently, Mr. Shimizu wrote a book.*

● (あなたは)仙台へ行かれましたか？ *Did you go to Sendai?*

● (あなたは)英語を教えられていますか？ *Do you teach English?*

● 木村さんは結婚されていますか？ *Mr. Kimura, are you married?*

You have probably realized that in the table there are no verbs ending in ぬ nor the irregulars する *(to do)* and 来る *(to come)*. There is only one verb of common use ending in ぬ, and that is 死ぬ *(to die)*, which already has its own 尊敬語 version: お亡くなりになる (see the first table). する and 来る, even though they have a *-rareru* version (される and 来られる), they also have 尊敬語 versions: なさる and いらっしゃる, respectively.

Important observation

We will sometimes find ourselves talking <u>about</u> somebody hierarchically superior <u>with</u> someone *equal* to us. In these cases, we use the different strategies we have seen to express respect towards the superior person but the verbal conjugation is usually left in the **simple form** to express familiarity with our interlocutor. Since this may seem somewhat intricate, let's take a look at an example:

● 先生はいらっしゃらないぞ *(Talking with a classmate) The teacher is not here.*

Since we are talking about someone we respect (先生, *teacher*) we use the verb いらっしゃる *(to be)*, but we leave it in the simple form because we are talking to an equal, a classmate. So that you can see this even better, we have also added the colloquial end-of-the-sentence particle ぞ. Let's see other examples:

● 社長はもうお帰りになったよ *The president has already gone.*

● 加藤さんは大学まで歩かれたよね *Mr. Katō walked to university, didn't he?*

The language of modesty (謙譲語)

Now we will go on to study the second kind of honorifics, the 謙譲語, literally "language (語) of modesty (謙譲)." We will use 謙譲語 when talking <u>with</u> another person who we consider superior, **lowering our position** in order to indirectly raise our interlocutor's position (hence the usage of the term 謙譲, *modesty*). The subject of the action is **always** "I" or someone in the *uchi* circle (L.45). We must never (absolutely never!) use this kind of honorifics when referring to actions performed by someone who is not "I" or doesn't belong to the *uchi* circle, because it would sound as if we were degrading the other person.

Using 謙譲語

Let's now see the various constructions and usages of 謙譲語:

① **Usage of the modest "versions" of certain verbs.** Just like with 尊敬語, there are "modest" versions of several of the most common verbs (see the first table in this lesson).

● 私はアルゼンチンから参りました *I come from Argentina | I'm from Argentina.*

● 妹はお医者さんと結婚いたしております *My younger sister is married to a doctor.*

● すみませんが、社長は出かけております *I'm sorry, but the president has gone out.*

Note: In the third example, the person performing the action is hierarchically superior, because he is the 社長 *(president of the company)*, but he still belongs to the speaker's *uchi* circle. Therefore, when talking with someone in the *soto* circle about anybody in our *uchi* circle we will use 謙譲語.

② **Conjugation** お + Root + する / いたす. Take any verbal root (L.31) and add お in the beginning and する or いたす in the end (with いたす it is even more formal). **Ex:** 書く *(to write)*⇒ -*masu* form: 書きます ⇒ root (without ます): 書き ⇒ we add お and する: お書きする. **Note:** With *suru* verbs, we only add ご (not お) in the beginning: ご運転する *(I drive)*, ご案内する *(I'll guide you)*.

● 先生のご本をお読みしたいです *Professor, I'd like to read your book.*

● ご相談いたしたいと思っております *I'd like to consult you.*

Observations

The same happens with 謙譲語 as with 尊敬語: when talking to somebody equal or inferior about an action we have performed in the interest of somebody superior, or in his or her presence, we will use 謙譲語 verbs and structures in their simple form.

● 私は先生に本をさしあげたよ *(To a classmate) I gave the teacher a book.*

● 社長の計画書を拝見したぞ *(To a colleague) I've seen the president's project.*

You have probably seen that sometimes the prefix お～ or ご～ is used before nouns or adjectives: this is a way of showing respect used in the three kinds of formal language. We will put お～ before words of Japanese origin –which are usually written with only one kanji–, such as お早い *(early)*, お車 *(car)*, お宅 *(your house)*, お手紙 *(letter)*, etc., and ご～ before words from Chinese origin –which are usually written with two or more kanji–, such as ご家族 *(your family)*, ご心配 *(worry)*, or ご相談 *(consultation)*. There are some exceptions, such as お食事 *(meal)*, お元気 *(healthy)*, お電話 *(telephone)*, etc.

Polite speech (丁寧語)

The third and last mode of honorifics is the 丁寧語, or "polite (丁寧) language (語)." This mode is, perhaps, the closest one in usage and concept to our English usage of "titles" (Mr., Mrs., etc.) and the corresponding polite language used with them. It is merely a politer way of speaking, involving no special hierarchies. Using 丁寧語 is quite simple, since it is based on always using the です and ～ます verbal forms, which we already studied in L.9 and 19 (book 1), respectively.

● 私は脳外科医です *I'm a neurosurgeon.*

● ここには亀がいます *There is a turtle here.*

● あの人は1億円も盗みました *That person stole up to one hundred million yen.*

If we want to be even politer, in the case of ある / いる, we can use ございます or, in the case of です, we can use でございます.

● 私は脳外科医でございます *I'm a neurosurgeon.*

● ここには有名な絵がございます *There is a very famous picture here.*

In 丁寧語, the prefixes お～ and ご～ are profusely used before nouns and adjectives, although it is women who, by far, tend to use them more often:

● このお花、お美しいですね *This flower is beautiful, isn't it?*

● お店でご飯を食べてきました *I have had lunch in the shop.*

Honorifics: summary			
そんけいご 尊敬語 *(language of respect)*	We raise somebody else's position.	1- Special verbs.	先生、何かおっしゃいましたか？ Did you say something, teacher?
		2- お＋Root＋になる	三浦さんは**お待ちになって**います Mr. Miura is waiting.
		3- ～られる	三浦さんは**待たれて**います Mr. Miura is waiting.
けんじょうご 謙譲語 *(language of modesty)*	Lowering our position, we raise someone else's.	1- Special verbs	その本を**拝見**しました I saw that book.
		2- お / ご＋Root＋する	あ、**お待ちして**おりました Oh, I was waiting for you.
ていねいご 丁寧語 *(polite speech)*	Formal language.	1- Usage of the -*masu* form	三浦さんは待っています Mr. Miura is waiting.
		2- Usage of でございます、よろしい, etc.	これは先生の本でございます This is the teacher's book.
		3- お～ / ご～ before nouns and adjectives	先生の**ご**意見は何ですか？ What is the teacher's opinion?

せんせい: teacher | なにか: something | おっしゃる: to say | まつ: to wait | ほん: book | はいけん: to see | いけん: opinion | なに: what?

漫画例 Manga-examples

Now you have realized how complex and difficult it is to master the usage of Japanese honorifics. For the moment, try to concentrate only on **understanding** what you are being told in formal Japanese; later on, when your Japanese has notably improved, you can try using it yourself.

a) *Sonkeigo*

> **Man:** ...お客様。なにをなさっていらっしゃるのですか...?
> *...client (noun suf.) what DOP do be be Q?...?*
> **Madam, what are you doing?**

Studio Kōsen

Our first example gives us an instance of the usage of the language of respect or 尊敬語. The normal version of the sentence in this panel would be 何をしているのですか？ Notice how the verb なさる is used here, it being the "respectful" version of する *(to do)*. An important point is that even when forming the gerund (L.24, book 1), which is usually formed with the *-te* form and the verb

いる *(to be)*, the latter is sometimes replaced with its respectful version いらっしゃる. Thus, the している part *(to be doing)* finally becomes なさっていらっしゃる.

It is worth mentioning that the verbs いらっしゃる, なさる, おっしゃる and くださる are slightly irregular, because their *-masu* forms are, respectively, いらっしゃいます, なさいます, おっしゃいます and くださいます. That is, before the final ます we add an い, which, according to the rules, should not be there. Therefore, if we changed the sentence we are now examining into the *-masu* form, we would obtain 何をなさっていらっしゃいますか. Likewise, it is essential to know that there are "formal" versions of some words. The most typical examples are 方 (replacing 人, *person*), どなた (formal version of 誰, *who?*), or the adjective よろしい (instead of いい, *good, well*). Likewise, in formal language, we opt for the *kosoado* こちら, そちら and あちら instead of ここ, そこ and あそこ (L.34, book 2).

b) *Sonkeigo* in the simple form

Dr.: 間もなく堀部教授がいらっしゃる
soon Horibe professor SP come
Professor Horibe will come soon.
教授みずから執刀されるとの事だ
professor himself operate do SBP (nom) be
It will be the professor himself who will operate.

J.M. Ken Niimura

In this example we see two instances of the formal language of respect or 尊敬語. On the one hand, we have the special verb いらっしゃる, here replacing 来る *(to come)*. On the other hand, the speaker also uses the *-rareru* form of the *suru* verb 執刀する *(to operate)*, that is, 執刀される. In this last case, 執刀なさる could have been used as well (remember なさる is the respectful version of する), with hardly any nuance differences.

Notice how in the sentence, the speaker talks <u>about</u> 堀部教授 *(Professor Horibe)*, who is someone he respects, someone superior to himself: that's why he uses 尊敬語 when speaking. However, since he is talking <u>with</u> someone who is his equal or inferior, he deliberately leaves his verbs in the simple form to denote familiarity towards him / her.

c) *Sonkeigo* and *kenjōgo* in the same sentence

Yoshida: 何もおっしゃらなくても、すべて判っております。
nothing say (although), everything know be
Even if you say nothing, I know everything.

Javier Bolado

The languages of respect and modesty can be used at the same time, combining forms as we see here. On the one hand, Yoshida is talking with a stranger, so he chooses to use the verb of respect (尊敬語) おっしゃる *(to say)*, with which he raises his interlocutor's position. On the other hand, when speaking about himself, he uses the verb of modesty (謙譲語) おる *(to be)*, lowering his position to indirectly raise that of his interlocutor. Notice how in 謙譲語 the gerund 〜ている is changed into 〜ておる (〜ております in the *-masu* form). **Notes:** We studied the 〜ても form *(although)* in L.49. The verb わかる *(to understand)* is usually written 分かる, but, sometimes, for either style reasons or because of the author's preference, 判る is used.

-76- 第52課 Lesson 52

d) Honorific prefixes and *kenjōgo*

Kumi: あのー お客様、ご出発までの間お休み出来る
well... client (noun suf.), departure until (nom) recess rest can
If you please... Ladies and gentlemen, I'll get a room ready at once...
お部屋をご用意致しますので、どうぞ。
room DOP prepare do because, go ahead
... where you can rest until departure time. Come in, please.

Bárbara Raya

In all three modes of formal language the honorific prefixes お～ and ご～ are very frequent. In this example there are several: お客様 (*client*), ご出発 (*departure*), お休み (*rest*), お部屋 (*room*), and ご用意 (*preparation*). By the way, there are some very common words from which we normally do not separate this honorific prefix, even when talking in colloquial Japanese: お茶 (*tea*), お金 (*money*), ご飯 (*rice, meal*), お湯 (*hot water*), お菓子 (*cake, pastry*), お風呂 (*bath / bathtub*), etc.

Notes: Sometimes we will find the ご～ or お～ prefix written in kanji: 御～. Notice in this sentence how the client (客) is usually treated as お客様, with the suffix of highest respect ～様 (L.15), and that's because, as you know, the client is "god" in Japan.

e) The *uchi-soto* relationship in formal language

Chiaki: ただいま川井が参りますので...
now Kawai SP come because...
Kawai will come right away...

Javier Bolado

As we saw in L.45, the difference between those who form part of one's own circle (*uchi*) and those who don't (*soto*) is very important. Here, Chiaki says that "Kawai is coming" using the verb 参る (*to come*), which belongs to the language of modesty (謙譲語). Moreover, for extra "humbleness," she chooses not to use the honorific ～さん after Kawai's name, something surprising if we think that he is actually Chiaki's boss, whom we would expect her to treat him with respect. Chiaki considers Kawai as an *uchi* member before her interlocutor (a visitor from another company who clearly belongs to the *soto* circle), and that's why she uses 謙譲語.

f) A new form

Recepcionist: ただ今お調べ致しますので 少々 お待ち下さい。
now investigate do because a little wait please
I'll check it at once. Wait a minute, please.

There is a very common request form which, despite being quite formal, is not considered part of 敬語: it is お ＋ Root ＋ ください, equivalent to the request made with ～てください (L.24 and 35), but more formal. This construction is formed with the verbal root (L.31), in front of which you add お (or ご with *suru* verbs), and then you add ください behind. In this panel we see お待ちください (*wait, please*), which comes from the verb 待つ (*to wait*).

Other examples would be: お書きください (*write, please*), お座りください (*sit down, please*), or ご注意ください (*be careful, please*), which come from the verbs 書く (*to write*), 座る (*to sit*), and 注意する (*to be careful*), respectively. Learn this form well, because you will find it more than once. In the panel we also have お調べ致します (*I check*), an instance of the structure お ＋ Root ＋ いたす, which belongs to 謙譲語. The verb 調べる means *to investigate, to check*. Notice how いたす is sometimes written in kanji (致す), like in the example.

g) *Teineigo*

Aiko: はい。こちら伊丹空港の受付でございます。
yes. here Itami airport POP reception be
Yes? This is Itami airport reception office.

Gabriel Luque

Finally, we will see an instance of polite speech or 丁寧語: notice how Aiko uses the verb でございます instead of です (*to be*). The usage of ございます is one of the most common characteristics in 丁寧語.

For the moment, you don't need to master honorifics. If it is any consolation, many native Japanese, mainly the young, make mistakes when trying to use it. However, recognizing the different patterns of usage will be helpful, because they are widely used in daily life, mainly in sales clerk-client relationships.

① What are the three kinds of honorifics in Japanese, and when do we use each of them?

② Give the 尊敬語 version of the verbs 言う, 知っている, 飲む, あげる and 行く.

③ To what normal verbs do these 謙譲語 verbs correspond: 申す, いただく, いたす, 拝見する and 伺う?

④ Translate: 野村先生は記事をお書きになっている. (野村: Nomura, 先生: teacher, 記事: article, 書く: to write)

⑤ Conjugate in the ～られる form the verbs 歩く (to walk), 寝る (to sleep, g.1), 殺す (to kill), and 走る (to run, g.2).

⑥ Translate: 私はご本の内容を存じております。(私: I, 本: book, 内容: contents)

⑦ Is the following sentence correct: 私は映画をご覧になっております? Why? If it isn't, correct it. (私: I, 映画: movie)

⑧ Translate: そちらにおいしいお魚のお店がございます。(おいしい: tasty, 魚: fish, 店: shop)

⑨ In which case would this sentence be correct: 先生はご質問したいと申し上げました? (先生: teacher, 質問する: to ask) Translate it.

⑩ Translate: そちらのいすにお座りください。(いす: chair, 座る: to sit) To which of the three kinds of 敬語 does it correspond?

Lesson 53: Casual speech

After the intense lesson on formal language, there is nothing better than taking a look at the other side of the coin: the casual speech, that is to say, the spontaneous street language. If you wish to become able to understand comic books and movies in Japanese, this lesson will be essential.

Overview

Before starting with the contents, we want to make it clear that within the casual speech there are several "gradations" which can give very different connotations to our Japanese. To simplify matters, we have only distinguished two modes: <u>colloquial</u> and <u>vulgar</u> language. You can use colloquial language to speak informally with very close friends, but *avoid* using the vulgar language, which is only used profusely in movies and manga; in real life you will seldom or never hear it. In this lesson, we will use the mark (C) to indicate "colloquial language," and (V) for "vulgar language."

Generally, Japanese casual speech has several patterns: elision of grammatical particles, frequent usage of end-of-the-sentence particles, usage of the imperative, dislocation of sentences, contractions, shortenings, particular grammatical patterns, phonetic changes, and, finally, special vocabulary. Let's study them one by one.

Particles

One of the most obvious characteristics of spoken and spontaneous Japanese is the frequent elision of grammatical particles. You can easily verify this by looking at the many manga-examples in the previous lessons.

● メアリー、帽子 買ったわ *Mary bought a hat.* (female C)
● 映画館、行きたいんだよ *I want to go to the movies.* (C)

In the first sentence the topic particle は, which should follow メアリー, is omitted (L.37), and the direct object particle を (L.40), after 帽子 is omitted as well. In the second sentence, the direction particle に (or へ, L.38) after 映画館 has been left out.

On the other hand, the end-of-the-sentence particles are used all the time in spoken Japanese. Review L.17 (book 1) very well, because it will be essential to understand casual Japanese. Take a look at the sentences we have just seen: in the first one, we have the female particle for emphatic statement わ; and in the second one, we have the statement particle よ. Likewise, the emphatic tag んだよ (L.40) to end a statement, as in the second sentence, is extremely common.

Imperative, swearwords, and dislocations

The Japanese vulgar language (and sometimes the colloquial) is characterized by being almost the only register where we use the direct imperative we studied in L.30 (plus the 〜てくれ form in L.45), and the various swearwords we saw back in L.23:

● 日本へ行けよ、バカ野郎！ *Go to Japan, you silly ass!* (V)
● 貸してくれよ、その辞書 *Come on, lend it to me, that dictionary.* (C/V)
● 行きたくないんだよ、クソ学校へ *I don't want to go the damn school.* (V)

Notice how we often find dislocated phrases, like the second and third ones, where the usual order of the elements has been changed to highlight a certain part of the sentence.

The most common contractions			
Normal ⇒ Colloquial	Type	Normal form	Colloquial version
-t/de iru ⇒ -t/deru (L.35)	(C)	食べている	食べてる
-t/den	(V)		食べてん(だ)
-t/de iku ⇒ -t/deku (L.35)	(C)	飲んでいく	飲んでく
-t/de oku ⇒ -t/doku (L.35)	(C)	食べておく	食べとく
-t/de ageru ⇒ -t/dageru (L.45)	(C)	食べてあげる	食べたげる
-t/da darō ⇒ -t/darō (L.43)	(C)	飲んだろう	飲んだろう
-te shimau ⇒ -chau (L.35)	(C)	食べてしまう	食べちゃう
-de shimau ⇒ -jau (L.35)	(C)	飲んでしまう	飲んじゃう
-te wa ⇒ -cha (L.32)	(C)	食べてはいけない	食べちゃいけない
-de wa ⇒ -ja (L.32)	(C)	飲んではいけない	飲んじゃいけない
-nai ⇒ -n (except: しない ⇒ せん)	(V)	食べない	食べん
-nakereba naranai ⇒ -nakya (L.32)	(C)	飲まなければならない	飲まなきゃ
-nakya nannai	(C)		飲まなきゃなんない
-reba ⇒ -rya (L.56)	(V)	食べれば	食べりゃ
-nakereba ⇒ -nakya (L.56)	(C)	食べなければ	食べなきゃ
to iu ⇒ tte	teyuu	ttsuu (L.41)	(V)	彼という	彼って	彼てゆう	彼っつう
-ai	-oi ⇒ -ee	(V)	高い	すごい	たけえ	すげえ
食べる: to eat	飲む: to drink	彼: he	高い: expensive, high	すごい: cool, amazing, fantastic			

Contractions

Now take a look at the table on the previous page: we have summarized there the most common contractions in the Japanese colloquial and vulgar registers. You might sometimes find a written contraction that is not there: when that happens, read the sentence aloud and try to imagine where it comes from; you'll probably be able to figure it out.

● ビール、買っといたぞ！ *I've bought beer (just in case)!* (C)
● 食べちゃっていいの、ケーキ？ *Can I eat it, the cake?* (C)
● 大阪って街、面白くてたまらん *The city of Osaka is great fun.* (V)
● 明日、すげえ雑誌を読んじゃおう *Tomorrow I'll read a fantastic magazine.* (C)
● 何遊んでんだ？ 働けって言ったろう？

What are you doing, playing? I've told you to work, haven't I? (V)

There are other "minor" contractions, such as 何か⇒なんか (*something*, L.41) | どこか ⇒どっか (*somewhere*, L.41) | これは/それは/あれは⇒こりゃ/そりゃ/ありゃ (*this, that, that over there*, L.34) | こちら/そちら/あちら⇒こっち/そっち/あっち (*this way, that way, that way over there*, L.34) | 仕方がない⇒しょうがない (*it's no use / it can't be helped*).

Shortenings

Another characteristic of casual speech is cutting or abbreviating certain constructions or words. The most typical are: もの⇒もん (*thing*, L.57) | ところ⇒とこ (*place*, L.58) | かもしれない⇒かも (*perhaps*, L.43) | のだ⇒んだ (*emphatic tag*, L.40), among others. Notice as well the elision of ら in the potential form of verbs in group 1: 食べられる⇒食べれる, which we already studied in L.32.

Patterns in the casual Japanese		
～てやがる	(V)	歩いてやがる He's walking
～たまるか	(V)	飲んでたまるか I won't drink it
ぶっ～	(V)	ぶっ殺す I'll kill you
すごく	(C)	すごく高い Really expensive
すごい	(C)	すごい高い Really expensive

歩あるく: to walk | 飲のむ: to drink | 殺ころす: to kill | 高たかい: expensive, high | すごい: cool, terrific

● どっかいいとこ行かなきゃよな

We must go somewhere good. (C)

● おっす！ピーマン食べれる？

Hey! Can you eat (do you like) green pepper? (C)

● 俺んちにはすごいもんがあるかも

In my house there might be something cool. (C)

Notice the おっす in the second sentence: it is the abbreviated version of おはようございます (*good morning*). The 俺んち in the third sentence is the simplification of 俺の家 (*my house*).

Colloquial vocabulary					
Nouns		奴（やつ）	guy / man	**Verbs**	
こいつ	this guy	野郎（やろう）	guy / moron	エッチする	to have sex
そいつ	that guy	**Adjectives**		なめる	to take so. for a fool
あいつ	that guy over there	エッチな	sexual	ナンパする	to pick up
ガキ	kid / brat	かっこいい	handsome / cool	びびる	to be scared stiff
きさま	you (threat)	かっこわるい	ridiculous	ふざける	to mess around
ちび	kid / midget	すごい	great / cool	むかつく	to get angry
チャリ	bicycle	せこい	stingy	**Expressions**	
つら	face / mug	ださい	tacky	こら！	hey! (threat)
てめえ	you (threat)	でかい	huge	ざまみろ	serves you right
変態（へんたい）	weird / pervert	ひどい	horrible	超（ちょう）〜	super (very)
マジ	truly	やばい	risky / dicey	めっちゃ〜	very

Grammatical patterns

Take a look at the table in the previous page. There are a few grammatical patterns only used in colloquial or vulgar language. For instance, 〜てやがる is a very rough and vulgar expression with a very strong nuance of contempt, 〜てたまるか is used to indicate in a rough way that "I'll be damned if..." or "I won't allow...," and ぶっ〜 adds brusqueness to words like 殴る *(to hit)* or 殺す *(to kill)*.

● てめえ、なめてやがんのかぁ！？ *You, do you take me for a fool?!* (very V)
● この試合、負けてたまるかよ！ *I'll be damned if I lose this match!* (V)
● 何を笑ってんだ？ぶっ殺すぞ！ *What are you laughing at? I'm gonna kill you!* (very V)

The adverb すごく comes from すごい, an adjective constantly used in colloquial register to indicate "fantastic, great, wonderful, cool," etc. すごく is an adverb with the meaning of "very," synonymous of とても (L.45). The really peculiar thing is that very often すごい is used in the same position and with the same meaning of "very" as すごく; despite this being a *grammatically incorrect* usage, it is very common.

● すごく/すごい甘いんだね、このりんご！ *It's real sweet, this apple, isn't it?* (C)

Another curiosity is that there are words whose main consonant is "doubled" in casual register: ばかり⇒ばっかり *(only, L.58)* | やはり⇒やっぱり *(I knew it)* | あまり⇒ あんまり *(not much, L.45)* | さき⇒さっき *(a while ago)* | まま⇒まんま *(as it is, L.47)*.

● 文句ばっかり言うなよ、お前！ *Don't make only complaints (don't complain so much), man!* (C)
● ごめんね、友達のまんまでいたいけど *I'm sorry, but I want to remain as friends.* (C)

In the table above you have a list of words almost exclusively used in colloquial contexts, which should be very helpful when reading manga or watching movies.

Questions in the negative

In English, like in the sentence *Won't you come?*, we sometimes make a request in the form of a question by using verbs in the negative. We are actually asking our interlocutor to come, in an indirect or "soft" way. The same happens in Japanese, but it is much more frequent and in all registers (formal, colloquial, vulgar...)

- こちらへ来ていただけませんか？ *Could you come here, please?*
- 私と一緒に博物館へ行かない？ *Won't you come with me to the museum?*
- 君、電話に出てくれない？ *You, how about answering the phone?*
- 遠いんじゃないの、それ？ *Isn't that very far?*

The first sentence belongs to the formal register, the second and the third ones are colloquial, and the fourth is colloquial, verging on the vulgar. Be very careful with these kinds of questions as, even though the verb is in the negative, they are actually requests.

We also find じゃない？ at the end of sentences, used when asserting something and trying to obtain our interlocutor's agreement (like the English tag questions). Be careful as well with the more colloquial version じゃん, used mainly in Tokyo and nearby.

- 彼女のかばん、高いんじゃない？ *Her bag is very expensive, don't you think?*
- あのマンガ、面白いじゃん？ *That manga is interesting, isn't it?*

Answering yes / no questions

Yes or no questions are those that can be answered with a yes or a no. For example: *Are you hungry?* or *Shall we go out for a walk?* From our point of view, Japanese is peculiar because it is "logical" in its answers. For example, if we are asked *Aren't you hungry?*, and we really are not hungry, in English we answer "No." In Japanese, we must answer "Yes," that is, "Yes, it's true that I'm not hungry." If we are hungry, in Japanese we would answer "No," that is, "No, it's not true that I'm not hungry:" in other words, we are denying a negative, which finally gives us an affirmative. It sounds complicated, but if you consider it carefully, you will realize it is more logical in Japanese than in English, although it may be difficult to get used to.

- お肉を食べたくないんですか？｜はい（食べたくない）

Don't you want to eat meat?｜Yes (I don't want to eat).

- 真理子が好きじゃないの？｜いいえ、違う（好きだ）

Don't you like Mariko?｜No, you're wrong (I like her).

漫画例　Manga-examples

After the theory, we will now see a few examples to clarify the usage of colloquial and vulgar language. A word of advice: take this lesson only as a simple guide of casual speech to understand comic books and movies. In real life, avoid using this kind of Japanese whenever you can.

a) Pure vulgar language

Gabriel Luque

Katsuichi: うるせえ！てめえらにゃ関係(かんけい)ねえ話(はなし)だ！引(ひ)っ込(こ)んでやがれ！
noisy! you IOP relation there isn't topic be! withdraw (vulgar)!
Shut up! This has nothing to do with you! Out!

The panel opening this section of manga-examples is a real instance of the most vulgar Japanese there is, full of contractions, rough words and even special grammatical constructions.

Notice first the words うるせえ and 関係(かんけい)ねえ, which are very vulgar transformations of the words うるさい (*noisy*) and 関係(かんけい)がない (*bearing no relation to*). In the beginning, contracting the last part of words ending in *-ai* and *-oi* into *-ee* was a characteristic of the vulgar dialect in Tokyo, but it has spread all over the Japanese geography and we will certainly see it extremely often in comic books and movies.

The word てめえら is the plural of てめえ, a very vulgar way of saying "you," with a very strong nuance of threat and insult. てめえ is a distortion of 手前(てまえ).

In this example we have a contraction we haven't studied: it is にゃ, its normal form being, as you have probably guessed, に and は together.

To conclude, notice the final 〜てやがれ, the imperative form of 〜てやがる. 〜てやがる is a very rough and rude form of the gerund 〜ている. You will find 〜てやがる in comic books and similar places, but never in real life.

Casual speech くだけた日本語－85－

b) Threat

ぶっ殺してやる

おどしじゃねーぞ

Javier Bolado

Kaneshiro: ぶっ殺<ruby>殺<rt>ころ</rt></ruby>してやる
(pref.) kill (give)
I'm gonna kill you.

おどしじゃねーぞ
threat not be EP
And I'm not bluffing.

Here is another instance of vulgar language. Notice first the end, じゃねえ, a vulgar contraction of じゃない, or the more orthodox form ではない (*it isn't*). では is usually contracted in all registers in Japanese into じゃ, and the ねえ in the end is a rough contraction of ない. In this example we also have an instance of the usage of the prefix ぶっ〜, which adds brusqueness to a word. By just adding ぶっ〜 to the verb 殺<ruby>殺<rt>ころ</rt></ruby>す *(to kill, to murder)*, the speaker is strengthening his sentence and adding, as well, the nuances of "threat" and "resolve."

Last of all, the 〜てやる form is very common in vulgar language to indicate disdain towards the interlocutor or to sound more "macho;" it hardly has anything to do with the meaning of "give or do a favor to someone inferior" of the 〜てやる we saw in L.45.

c) A belligerent girl

Tokiwa: ふざけんな デブ野郎<ruby>野郎<rt>やろう</rt></ruby>————っ
lark around (neg. imp.), fat guy
Stop fucking with me, fat-ass!!

ふざけんな デブ野郎〜〜〜っ

Studio Kōsen

Generally, a girl would never use this type of vulgar language, merely because this register is too rough and "macho" for a woman. However, in this example, we have quite an exception. The girl uses three very vulgar words: the verb ふざける *(to mess around, to bug)*, and the nouns 野郎<ruby>野郎<rt>やろう</rt></ruby> *(guy, man)*, and デブ *(fat guy)*. Except maybe for デブ, the other two are extremely vulgar.

Notice the ふざけんな. ふざけん is a vulgar contraction of ふざける (the る becomes ん when talking very fast), and the な, as we have seen before, is used to form the direct negative imperative. Therefore, ふざけんな means *Don't bug me*. As a curiosity, we will mention that in the most gangster-like register in Japanese some speakers roll their "r," that is, the Spanish way.

d) A very vulgar negative imperative

Kumasaka: いい気^きになってんじゃねえ！
good feeling become not be!
Don't get smart with me!

J.M. Ken Niimura

Here is another example of rough language. Colloquial language is much more obvious and easy to understand, therefore, it is worth looking at examples in the roughest and most distorted language, which, moreover, is the most common in manga.

Here we have a negative imperative of the kind exclusively used in vulgar register: "verb ＋ んじゃない." Take a look at the example: いい気^きになる is a set phrase with the meaning of *to get smart with, to be stuck up.* じゃねえ, as you know, is the distortion of じゃない. Therefore, いい気^きになってんじゃねえ, its non-distorted version being いい気^きになっているんじゃない, means more or less *don't get smart.* More examples of this kind of (very) vulgar negative imperative are: ケーキを食^たべるんじゃない！ *Don't eat the cake!,* こっちで遊^{あそ}ぶんじゃない！ *Don't play there!,* マンガを読^よむんじゃない！ *Don't read manga!*

e) Using the negative to ask

Studio Kōsen

Asakawa: この４人^{にん}見^みおぼえありません？
this 4 people see remember not there are?
Do these 4 people ring a bell?

We will use this example as a transition from the subject of casual speech to that of questions in the negative. Notice how, despite conjugating the verb in the *-masu* form (ありません), Asakawa omits all grammatical particles: it is a very obvious characteristic of spoken language. The sentence would be この４人^{にん}に見覚^{みおぼ}えがありませんか？ in its most orthodox form: the speaker has avoided the particles に, が, and か in her sentence, something we don't generally recommend.

On the other hand, notice how the question is in the negative: its literal translation would be *Don't these 4 people ring a bell?* In Japanese, the negative conjugation is used very often when asking things, since it works as a "softener" of a direct question.

f) A tag for agreement

> **Kawami:** だから...<ruby>自分<rt>じぶん</rt></ruby>を<ruby>責<rt>せ</rt></ruby>めないでよ...アンタのせいじゃないじゃない...？
> *so... yourself dop attack EP... you pop fault not be not be...?*
> **So... don't blame yourself... It wasn't your fault, right?**

Bárbara Raya

We mentioned in the theory section that the tag じゃ ない at the end of a sentence, together with an interrogative intonation, was the equivalent to our tag questions looking for the interlocutor's agreement.

The second but last example offers us a peculiar instance of this. The sentence we want our interlocutor to agree with is アンタのせいじゃない (*it's not your fault*). If we add the colloquial expression for statement じゃない, we obtain アンタのせいじゃないじゃ ない？, like in the example. This gives us two じゃない together, something that may sound really strange but which happens more ofthen than not in colloquial language. Therefore, the literal translation of this sentence is *It's not your fault, isn't it?* Giving this last じゃない an interrogative tone is very important, because, otherwise, the interlocutor would interpret it as a negative. The tag じゃない？ is extremely common in spoken Japanese.

g) Answer to a question in the negative

> **Man 1:** え？オレが<ruby>見<rt>み</rt></ruby>えない？　　**Man 2:** はい
> *hey? I SP not see?*　　　　　　　　　*yes*
> **Hey? Can't you see me?**　　　　　**No.**

We will conclude with an example of something which might confuse you. Take a look at the conversation in the panel: literally, it would be *You can't see me?*, and then the answer *Yes*.

In English, we would interpret that he can see him, but in Japanese we are saying that, "indeed, I <u>cannot</u> see you." That is, in Japanese we cor-

Gabriel Luque

roborate the speaker's words "you can't see me." In our final translation, however, we have followed the English convention, and have answered *No*. Don't feel discouraged if you are not grasping this inmediately, this is a "concept" that takes a while to master.

1 To what forms are these contractions equivalent: ～ちゃう, ～てゆう and ～なきゃ?

2 Give the casual or vulgar version of 買っ<ruby>か<rt></rt></ruby>ておく, 行<ruby>い<rt></rt></ruby>きたい and 遊<ruby>あそ<rt></rt></ruby>んではだめだ。 (買<ruby>か<rt></rt></ruby>う: to buy, 行<ruby>い<rt></rt></ruby>く: to go, 遊<ruby>あそ<rt></rt></ruby>ぶ: to play)

3 Translate: 買<ruby>か<rt></rt></ruby>ってくれよ、車<ruby>くるま<rt></rt></ruby>！ (買<ruby>か<rt></rt></ruby>う: to buy, 車<ruby>くるま<rt></rt></ruby>: car)

4 Translate: なんか言<ruby>い<rt></rt></ruby>えよ、これってつまらないんだよ (言<ruby>い<rt></rt></ruby>う: to say, これ: this, つまらない: boring)

5 What do we use the construction ～てやがる for? Form a sentence with it.

6 Is the following sentence grammatically correct: あの家<ruby>いえ<rt></rt></ruby>、すごいでかいね? Why? (あの: that over there, 家<ruby>いえ<rt></rt></ruby>: house)

7 Translate this sentence: あいつ、めっちゃむかつくんだ、すぐびびりやがって… (すぐ: at once)

8 Use the negative and the ～てくれる form (L.45) when translating this: "Can you give me a hand?" (to give a hand: 手<ruby>て<rt></rt></ruby>を貸<ruby>か<rt></rt></ruby>す)

9 Translate the sentence: 舞子<ruby>まいこ<rt></rt></ruby>ちゃん、やせたじゃん? (舞子<ruby>まいこ<rt></rt></ruby>: Maiko, やせる: to lose weight)

10 You <u>don't</u> have a stomachache and someone asks you お腹<ruby>なか<rt></rt></ruby>、痛<ruby>いた<rt></rt></ruby>くない? (お腹<ruby>なか<rt></rt></ruby>: stomach, 痛<ruby>いた<rt></rt></ruby>い: painful) What do you answer?

第54課：比較の表現

Lesson 54: Comparatives

After a brief interval of two lessons where we have seen the informal and formal registers in Japanese, we shall return to our grammar studies to see how to form comparative and superlative sentences. It is, undoubtedly, a very useful subject in any language.

As... as

If you go back in the course, and review L.43 and 50, you will see how we explained the expression ようだ with the meaning of "apparently...," and, in passing, we also mentioned how a small variation of this expression could be used to form sentences of the comparative kind: "A is as... as B." The basic structure of this kind of sentences is "AはBのように..."

Usage: After verbs and -*i* adjectives, we add nothing. -*na* adjectives keep the な, and we must add の between nouns and ように. **Be careful:** ように is an adverbial form that always modifies verbs and adjectives, but never nouns.

- 彼はきつねのようにずるいです *He is as sly as a fox.*
- この家は宮殿のように広い *This house is as roomy as a palace.*
- 今は夏のように暑いです *It is now as hot as in summer.*
- 美穂は宇多田ヒカルのように歌えるよ *Miho can sing (as well as) like Hikaru Utada.*

To establish a comparison between nouns, we use the adjectival form ような.

- 彼は宮殿のような家に住んでいる *He lives in a house that is like a palace.*
- 舞子の彼氏はゴリラのような男だ *Maiko's boyfriend is a man like a gorilla.*

Finally, we can also make metaphors and similes with ようだ:

- 舞子の彼氏はゴリラのようだ *Maiko's boyfriend is (looks like) a gorilla.*

Remember, like we saw in L.43, みたいに and みたいな are the colloquial versions of ように and ような, respectively. Usage: We don't need to add or eliminate anything.

- 彼はきつねみたいにずるいです *He is as sly as a fox.*
- 彼は宮殿みたいな家に住んでいる *He lives in a house that is like a palace.*
- 舞子の彼氏はゴリラみたいだ *Maiko's boyfriend is (looks like) a gorilla.*

More... than

Let's now see how to form comparatives of the kind "A is more... than B." The basic structure to form this kind of sentence is "AはBより ...." <u>Usage</u>: We don't add anything after a verb in simple form, -*i* adjective, or noun. -*na* adjectives take な. **Be careful:** "AはBよりも...," with identical meaning and usage, is another valid form, as well as the dislocated forms "BよりAは..." or "BよりもAは..."

● 日本語は英語より難しいだろう *Japanese is probably more difficult than English.*
● 美穂は宇多田ヒカルよりうまく歌える *Miho can sing better than Hikaru Utada.*
● この仕事は地獄よりも大変だ *This job is tougher than hell.*
● アニメより、マンガは面白いと思う *I think that manga is interesting, more than anime.*
● 寿司よりも、スパゲッティを食べたいな *More than sushi, I want to eat spaghetti.*

An important point to stress is that "AはBより ..." is only used when we know what we are talking about, that is, the subject has already been raised in the conversation or all interlocutors know about it (L.39).

If the subject is not known, we must use the expression "AのほうがBより ..." The のほうが part is used to introduce a new subject, to give the interlocutor a hint about what we are talking about. The dislocated form "BよりAのほうが..." is also possible.

● ジョンのほうがマイクよりハンサムだ *John is more handsome than Mike.*
● 天ぷらのほうがカレーよりおいしい *Tempura is nicer than curry.*
● 九州より、四国のほうが静かだ *Shikoku is quiet, more than Kyūshū.*

Less... than

Curiously enough, in Japanese there is no way of saying "A is less... than B," maybe due to the Japanese aversion to stating things clearly. The closest expression is "AはBほど...(neg.)," which literally means "A is not as... as B." <u>Usage</u>: The position of "B" can only be taken by verbs in the simple form and nouns. The overall sentence must *compulsorily* be in the negative.

● 英語は日本語ほど難しくない *English is not as difficult as Japanese.*
● カレーは天ぷらほどおいしくない *Curry is not as nice as tempura.*
● マイクはジョンほどハンサムじゃない *Mike is not as handsome as John.*
● 歌うのは踊るほど疲れない *Singing is not as tiring as dancing.*
● 富士山はエベレストほど高くない *Mount Fuji is not as high as Mount Everest.*

Adverbs of gradation

Knowing some adverbs of gradation that can be combined with comparative sentences is very important. They are usually combined with sentences of the kind "more... than" and "not as... as," and they clarify them in different ways.

These adverbs immediately follow より and ほど, and can give different gradations to our comparative structures. Let's see them one by one:

1) やや: slightly
● 秀は知宏よりやや背が高い *Hide is slightly taller than Tomohiro.*

2) 少し/ちょっと: a little (ちょっと is more informal than 少し)
● 秀は知宏よりちょっと背が高い *Hide is a little taller than Tomohiro.*

3) かなり/ずいぶん: quite (ずいぶん is somewhat stronger than かなり)
● 秀は知宏よりかなり背が高い *Hide is quite taller than Tomohiro.*

4) ずっと: much more
● 秀は知宏よりずっと背が高い *Hide is much taller than Tomohiro.*

Besides everything we have just seen, we will mention that the adverb もっと *(more)* can form comparative sentences on its own, without the aid of より or ほど.

● この本はもっと高いよ *This book is more expensive.*
● 彼(のほう)がもっと頭がいいです *He is more intelligent.*

The same... as / As... as

The next structure we will study is "AはBと同じぐらい...," used to form sentences of the kind "A is more or less the same... as B," or "A is as... as B.". The word 同じ means *the same as*, and the adverb ぐらい (L.40, book 2), means *more or less* or *about*. Usage: We will only find nouns or noun phrases (L.40 / 57) in the position of "B." **Be careful:** Although grammatically correct, the structure "AはBと同じ...," that is, without ぐらい, is hardly ever used in real life, probably because, as you know, the Japanese don't usually say things in a frank manner.

● 秀は知宏と同じぐらい背が高い *Hide is more or less the same height as Tomohiro.*
● ジョンはマイクと同じぐらいハンサムだ *John is more or less as handsome as Mike.*
● 天ぷらはカレーと同じぐらいおいしい *Tempura is more or less as nice as curry.*
● 数学は化学と同じぐらい嫌いです *I hate math more or less the same as chemistry.*
● そのパソコンは車と同じぐらい高い *That computer is more or less as expensive as a car.*

Questions

Let's now see how to make comparative questions of the kind "between A and B, which is more...?" The basic structure in Japanese is "AとBではどちらが...?"

Be careful: in this kind of sentences we always use the interrogative pronoun どちら or its colloquial version どっち *(which?)*: never use 誰 *(who?)*, どれ *(which?)*, or 何 *(what?)*.

- 日本語と英語ではどちらが難しいか？ *Between Japanese and English, which is more difficult?*
- 日本語は英語と同じぐらい難しい *Japanese is more or less as difficult as English.*
- 秀と知宏ではどっちが背が高いの？ *Who is taller: Hide or Tomohiro?*
- 知宏は秀ほど背が高くない *Tomohiro is not as tall as Hide.*
- 天ぷらとカレーではどちらがおいしいの？ *Which is tastier: tempura or curry?*
- 天ぷらはカレーよりずっとおいしい *Tempura is much tastier than curry.*

Superlatives

There are two ways of forming superlative sentences (that is, of the kind "A is the most (adj.) in...") in Japanese. Both structures must always be used with an adjective, and never with a noun or an adverb.

The first is "Aは...(の中で/で)一番(adj.)." Between の中で and just で, there is a difference of usage: で is used when we are talking about places, and の中で is used when we are talking about groups of something. However, both are used without distinction in many occasions, so you don't need to worry about this for the moment.

- 富江はクラスの中で一番頭のいい人です *Tomie is the most intelligent in the class.*
- エベレストは世界で一番高い山です *Mount Everest is the highest mountain in the world.*
- 山中は一番アホな科学者だろう *Yamanaka is probably the silliest scientist.*
- 世界で一番安全な国は日本でしょう *Japan is possibly the safest country in the world.*

The second structure used to form superlative sentences is "Aは...(の中で/で)最も(adj.)." We use it just like its "sibling" 一番.

- 富江はクラスの中で最も頭のいい人です *Tomie is the most intelligent in the class.*
- エベレストは世界で最も高い山です *Mount Everest is the highest mountain in the world.*
- 山中は最もアホな科学者だろう *Yamanaka is probably the silliest scientist.*
- 世界で最も安全な国は日本でしょう *Japan is possibly the safest country in the world.*

Note: 一番 means *the first* or, sometimes, *the best* (as in the sentence 彼は一番だ, *He is the first / the best*), while 最も is an adverb meaning *the most (something)*.

Too (much)

We will end the theory section taking a look at a grammatical structure which doesn't have much to do with comparatives, but which could, somehow, be in the same category: "too much." Whereas in English we have the adverbs "too" and "too much" which modify adjectives and verbs, giving them the nuance of "in excess," as in the sentences *To be too sleepy* or *To work too much*; in Japanese we must form compound verbs and adjectives (L.44, book 2) with the auxiliary verb 〜すぎる (which comes from 過ぎる, *to exceed*).

Verbs: We add 〜すぎる to the root of any verb. Ex: 働く (*to work*) ⇒ Root: 働き ⇒ we add 〜すぎる: 働きすぎる (*to work too much*).

-i and *-na* **adjectives:** we replace い (in *-i* adjectives) or な (in *-na* adjectives) with 〜すぎる: 広い (*wide*) ⇒ 広すぎる (*too wide*) | 静かな (*quiet*) ⇒ 静かすぎる (*too quiet*).

● あの人はいつも話しすぎますね *That man always talks too much, doesn't he?*
● 昨日はお酒を飲みすぎた *Yesterday, I drank too much (alcohol).*
● このサンドイッチはまずすぎるな *This sandwich tastes so / really bad.*

Exceptions: いい (*good*) ⇒ よすぎる (*too good*) | Negative: 〜ない ⇒ 〜なさすぎる.
● 君は寝なさすぎるんじゃない？ *Don't you sleep too little?*

Comparative and superlative expressions		
AはBのように...	A is as... as B	百合は天使のようにきれいです Yuri is as beautiful as an angel.
AはBみたいに...	A is as... as B (colloquial)	百合は天使みたいにきれいだ Yuri is as beautiful as an angel.
AはBより...	A is more... than B	百合は久美よりきれいだ Yuri is more beautiful than Kumi.
AのほうがBより...	A (new topic) is more... than B	百合のほうが久美よりきれいだ Yuri is more beautiful than Kumi.
AはBほど...(neg)	A is not as... as B	久美は百合ほどきれいじゃない Kumi is not as beautiful as Yuri.
AはBと同じぐらい...	A is more or less the same... as B	百合は久美と同じぐらいきれいだ Yuri is more or less as beautiful as Kumi.
...の中で/で一番(Adj.)	the most (adj.) in...	百合は会社の中で一番きれいだ Yuri is the most beautiful in the company.
...の中で/で最も(Adj.)	the most (adj.) among...	百合は会社の中で最もきれいな女性だ Yuri is the most beautiful woman in the company.
〜すぎる	too much...	百合は背が低すぎる Yuri is too short.
てんし: angel	きれいな: beautiful	かいしゃ: company	じょせい: woman	せがひくい: short		

And now let's get on with the manga-examples, which, as usual, will help us see in greater depth some of the aspects we have just studied in the theory pages. We will also expand on the lesson with some new expressions or nuances that we have previously missed.

a) A comparative "more than"

Falken: この薬の方が麻薬より効くかもしれないよ
this medicine on its part SP drug more than effective perhaps
This pill might be more effective than a drug.

Bárbara Raya

This is an example of the "A is more... than B" kind, its basic structure being "Aは Bより ..." in Japanese. However, this structure is only valid if both speakers are familiar with the subject they are talking about.

If you want to introduce a new topic in a comparative sentence of the "more than" kind, then remember that you must use the "AのほうがB より ..." structure, just like in this example, この薬の方が麻薬より効く *This pill might be more effective than a drug.* **Note:** ほう is written in kanji (方) here, a perfectly valid option and very common in written Japanese.

Take a look now at this short conversation: この薬は効くね *This pill is effective, isn't it?* | そうだね、この薬は麻薬より効くかもしれない *That's right, this pill might be more effective than a drug.* In this case, we haven't used の方が because the "pill" (薬) has previously appeared in the conversation, and it has become the topic in it. You can review the concept of topic in L.37 (book 2).

Note: Notice the usage of かもしれない, which we studied in L.43 and which, as you will remember, means "perhaps" or "maybe." It is always placed at the end of the sentence.

b) Comparative "to be like"

> Haruki: まるで女王のように見える
> *completely queen like see*
> **She looks just like a queen.**

Studio Kōsen

This example will help us review the usage of comparatives of the "to be like" kind, which are formed with the adverbial form ように (before verbs and adjectives) and the adjectival form ような (before nouns). There are colloquial versions, which are, respectively, みたいに and みたいな.

In our sentence, Haruki states that 女王のように見える, literally, *She is seen like (as if she were) a queen*. Remember that between noun and ように or ような, we must add の. A more colloquial version of this sentence would be 女王みたいに見える (be careful, with みたいに and みたいな, we don't need の).

Notice, too, the word まるで, which means something like "completely," "utterly," or "just like," and is often used in these kinds of sentences to strengthen them rhetorically.

c) A special usage of *yori*

> Jun: それより後半も今までの調子でいこうぜ！勝てるぞ みんな！
> *this more than 2nd part too now until POP way ip let's EP! win EP everybody!*
> **Aside from that, in the second part we must play the way we've been playing until now! We can win, guys!**

Gabriel Luque

Just like we said in the manga-examples d) and f) in L.48, finding grammatical structures together with the *kosoado* pronouns (L.34) is quite common. The case of より is somewhat special, because it is usually seen only with それ *(that)* —it is hardly ever combined with other *kosoado* pronouns—, forming the expression それより, like in this example.

それより is used when changing subject suddenly in a conversation, as its literal translation suggests "more than that." This expression is very difficult to translate directly, although we could paraphrase it with expressions such as *aside from that* or even *I agree with what we've just said, but now we must talk about...*

d) A comparative "not as"

Bárbara Raya

Hiroshi: ウチの雪子ほどじゃないけどな
inside POP Yukiko so much as not be but EP
Although she's not as much as my Yukiko.

We have seen in the theory section that in Japanese there are no comparative expressions of the "less than" kind, and that we must use subtleties such as "not as much as." The basic structure of this kind of sentences is " AはB ほど...(neg.)." In our sentence, 雪子ほどじゃない *She is not as much as Yukiko*, there is no comparative element because it has previously appeared in the conversation. Probably, the original sentence of this poor man was something like 彼女はウチの雪子ほど太っていない, that is, *She is not as fat as my Yukiko...* That would justify Yukiko's rage we see behind him! Remember that the verb or adjective to be compared (太っている in this case) must be in the negative.

Note: Notice the usage of ウチ (in kanji 内), a very multipurpose word that can be used when referring to oneself (particularly in the case of women), to one's family, or to close friends: it is the same concept of *uchi* that we analyzed in L.45 (book 2).

e) The superlative *ichiban*

Yūji: それが一番大事なコトだよ、きっと
that SP the most important thing be EP, sure
That's the most important thing, surely.

Javier Bolado

We will now review the superlatives, expressions of the "the most..." kind. There are two ways of forming superlative sentences: using 一番, like in this panel, and with 最も. The basic structure is "Aは...(の中で/で)一番(adj.)."
In our sentence, それが一番大事なこと *That is the most important thing*, the area the speaker is referring to is not mentioned, and the subject is replaced with the pronoun それ *(that)*. Now imagine the sentence was 合格するのは人生で一番大事なこと *Passing the exam is the most important thing in life,* that is, with a word naming a specific area – 人生で *(in life)*–, and the pronoun それ being replaced with 合格する *(to pass an exam)*.

Note: Notice how the adverb きっと *(surely, undoubtedly)* is dislocated to the end of the sentence. This is a very common characteristic of the colloquial language (L.53).

f) Superlative words

> **Shigeko:** 鈴木さんなんか大ッキライ！ 最低オトコです！！
> *Suzuki (noun suf.) (emph) hate! the lowest man be!!*
> **I hate you, Suzuki! You scum bag!**

Studio Kōsen

Besides the superlatives 一番 and 最も, there are compound words with superlative meaning, formed by the kanji 最 plus another kanji. Notice how 最も and 最 have the same kanji, but their reading is diffe-rent. Other superlative words of this kind are 最良 *(the best),* 最悪 *(the worst),* 最新 *(the newest),* 最高 *(the best / the tallest),* 最愛 *(the most loved),* 最強 *(the strongest),* 最終 *(the last / the final),* 最適 *(the most appropriate / the ideal),* and many more. Also worth mentioning are 最初 *(the beginning),* 最後 *(the end),* and the adverb 最近 *(lately, recently).*

In this example we have the word 最低, which literally means *the lowest,* but which is quite often used as some kind of insult hurled mainly by women, with the meaning of "you are scum," "you are pathetic," or even "you are despicable."

g) Too much

Gabriel Luque

> **Title:** 第４章　知りすぎた男
> *number 4 chapter know too much man*
> **Chapter 4: The man who knew too much**

The panel closing the manga-examples offers an ins-tance on how to form sentences with the meaning of "too much." If we have the verb 知る *(to know)* and we want to say "to know too much," we must add the au-xiliary verb ～すぎる to its root, thus obtaining the verb 知りすぎる *(to know too much).* Compound verbs with ～すぎる can be conjugated just like any other verb: 知りすぎない (negative), 知りすぎなかった (past negative), 知りすぎて (-te form), etc. Here, for example, we have the past form 知りすぎた, working as a relative clause of the noun 男 *(man).* Therefore, 知りすぎた男 means *The man who knew too much.* Review L.50 to brush up on the subject of relative clauses.

1 What differences of register and usage are there between the expressions ように and みたいに?

2 Translate: "This house is as big as a cathedral." (house: 家（いえ）, big: 大（おお）きい, cathedral: 大聖堂（だいせいどう）)

3 Translate: "This house is bigger than a cathedral." (house: 家（いえ）, big: 大（おお）きい, cathedral: 大聖堂（だいせいどう）)

4 Translate: "This house is not as big as a cathedral." (house: 家（いえ）, big: 大（おお）きい, cathedral: 大聖堂（だいせいどう）)

5 Translate: "This house is more or less as big as a cathedral." (house: 家（いえ）, big: 大（おお）きい, cathedral: 大聖堂（だいせいどう）)

6 Translate: "This house is much smaller than a cathedral." (house: 家（いえ）, big: 大（おお）きい, cathedral: 大聖堂（だいせいどう）)

7 Translate: "Between this house and a cathedral, which is bigger?" (house: 家（いえ）, big: 大（おお）きい, cathedral: 大聖堂（だいせいどう）)

8 Translate: "This cathedral is the biggest in the world." (big: 大（おお）きい, cathedral: 大聖堂（だいせいどう）, world: 世界（せかい）)

9 Translate: "This house is too big." (house: 家（いえ）, big: 大（おお）きい)

10 What do the following words mean: 最悪（さいあく）, 最初（さいしょ）, 最良（さいりょう）, and 最低（さいてい）? What do you think the words 最大（さいだい） and 最小（さいしょう） could mean?

第54課　練習　Exercises

第(55)課：観光で

Lesson 55: Sightseeing

This is the last strictly conversational lesson in the book: in it, we will study some typical sentences that can be useful when sightseeing in Japan. This lesson will act as a general review of all the conversational lessons we have studied until now.

Asking for directions

In L.51 we studied a few phrases enabling us to ask for directions in case we get lost and have to go to a police 交番 for help. We will now take the chance to expand on this subject, so we can find our way by asking people on the street. First, study the vocabulary table below thoroughly; then, you can start analyzing the example sentences.

● すみませんが、横浜ランドマークタワーへ行く道を教えていただけませんか？

Excuse me, could you tell me how to go to the Yokohama Landmark Tower? (L.45 / 54)

● 次の角を右へ曲がってください。そしてまっすぐ行ってください

Turn right on the next corner. Then, go straight on. (L.48)

● すみませんが、浅草寺は近いですか？ *Excuse me, is the Sensōji temple close by?*

● 歩くには遠すぎるので、地下鉄に乗った方がいいですよ

Since it is too far to walk to, I recommend you to take the subway. (L.48 / 49/ 54)

● この近くにバス停はありますか？ *Is there a bus stop near here?*

● はい、あの映画館の隣にあります *Yes, it is next to that cinema.*

● 奈良の見所は何ですか？ *What place is worth seeing in Nara?*

Giving and receiving directions			
behind	～の裏側に	that way	あそこに
to go straight on	まっすぐ行く	to the left	左側に
in front of...	～の前に	to the right	右側に
next to...	～の隣に	to turn left	左へ/に曲がる
on the corner of...	～の角に	to turn right	右へ/に曲がる
on the opposite side of...	～の向かいに	to walk 3 more blocks	3ブロック行く

- 東大寺には大仏があるし、それに春日神社と奈良公園も面白いですよ。

  There is the great image of Buddha in Tōdaiji temple and, then, Kasuga shrine and Nara Park are also interesting. (L.35 / 48)
- 市内地図をいただけますか？ *Could you give me a map of the city?* (L.45)
- この辺には商店街がありますか？ *Is there a shopping district around this area?*
- 二番目の信号を左に曲がってください *Turn left at the second traffic light.*
- こちらの方向でいいですね *This is the right way, isn't it?*
- 東寺は京都駅の裏側にありますよ *The Tōji temple is behind Kyoto Station.*

Taking photos

Another thing we will sometimes feel like is either having our photo taken or taking photos of people. You should always ask for permission before doing so.

- すみません、写真を撮っていただけますか？ *Excuse me, could you take a photo (of me)?* (L.45)
- シャッターを押すだけでいいです *You only need to press the shutter.*
- もう一枚お願いします *One more, please.* (L.40)
- (あなたの)写真を撮ってもいいですか？ *Could I take a photo of you?* (L.32)
- あなたと一緒に写真を撮りたいんですけど *I would like to have my photo taken with you.*
- ここで写真を撮ってもいいですか？ *Can I take photos here?* (L.32)
- このフィルムを現像したいんですが... *I'd like to have this film developed...* (L.31 / 40)

  Extra vocabulary. Developing photos: 焼き増しする *(to make additional prints)* | 引き伸ばす *(to enlarge)* | 光沢 *(glossy)* | つや消し *(with a matt finish)* | スライド *(slide)*. Digital cameras: (デジタルカメラ⇒デジカメ): バッテリー *(battery)* | メモリーカード *(memory card)*. Video cameras: テープ *(tape)* | ズーム *(zoom)* | 録画する *(to record)*

In the museum

If you are interested in art or general culture, you will probably want to go to a museum to feed your mind with new knowledge. The following sentences will help you when touring Japanese museums. Remember these sentences are just examples: we recommend that you thoroughly study the words we have provided in the vocabulary tables, and then try forming your own sentences using the grammatical patterns we have studied throughout the *Japanese in MangaLand* series. がんばってね!

● 東京国立博物館の開館時間を教えていただけませんか？

Could you tell me at what time does the Tokyo National Museum open? (L.45 / 54)

● 東京国立博物館は９時から１７時まで開いております

The Tokyo National Museum opens from 9 AM to 5 PM. (L.41 / 52)

● しかし、休館日は月曜日ですので、お気をつけください

However, please be aware that they are closed on Mondays. (L.48 / 52)

● 入場料はいくらですか？ *How much is it to get in?*

● 学生割引はありますか？ *Is there a student discount?*

● 大人２枚と子ども１枚ください *Two adult (tickets) and one child, please.*

● 館内ツアーはありますか？ *Is there a guided tour through the museum?*

● 江戸時代の浮世絵はどこにあるんですか？ *Where are the ukiyo-e of the Edo period?*

● 絵葉書を買えますか？ *Can I buy postcards?* (L.32)

● トイレを使ってもいいでしょうか？ *Can I use the toilet?* (L.32)

Sightseeing vocabulary					
In the city (市内で)		theater	劇場	**In the museum (博物館で)**	
aquarium	水族館	traffic lights	信号	adult	大人
art museum	美術館	zoo	動物園	child	出口
botanical garden	植物園	**In the countryside (田舎で)**		entrance	入口
Buddhist temple	お寺	bay	湾	exhibition	展示
castle	城	cape	岬	exit	子ども
city hall	市役所	coast	海岸	guided tour	館内ツアー
corner	角	harbor	港	painting	絵画
direction	方向	hill	丘	price of admission	入場料
garden	庭園｜庭	island	島	sculpture	彫刻
market	市場	lake	湖	**Photography (写真)**	
movie theater	映画館	mountain	山	battery	電池
museum	博物館	peninsula	半島	b/w film	白黒フィルム
monument	記念碑	river	川	color film	カラーフィルム
park	公園	sea	海	to develop	現像する
Shinto shrine	神社	valley	谷	flash	フラッシュ
shopping dist.	商店街	volcano	火山	lens	レンズ
statue	像	waterfall	滝	photo	写真
street	通り	wood	森	tripod	三脚

Making a telephone call

We will finish the lesson with a few phrases that will help us to use the Japanese telephone and mail services. By the way, a very convenient word to know is もしもし, which would be the equivalent to our "Hello?" when answering the phone.

● 千円のテレホンカードをください *A 1000 yen telephone card, please.*

● この公衆電話から国際電話はかけられますか？

Can I make international calls from this public telephone? (L.32)

● もしもし？浅原昭子さんをお願いします *Hello? Can I speak with Shōko Asahara, please?*

● オーストラリアへ電話をかけたいんですが *I want to call Australia.*

● カナダにコレクト·コールで電話したいです *I want to make a collect call to Canada.*

Note: You can't make international calls from all public telephones in Japan: look for the gray ones or those marked 国際電話. When making international calls, there are several dialing codes, depending on the telephone company, but one that usually works is 001010.

Mailing things

And last of all, some useful phrases for the post office:

● 切手は どこで 買えますか？

Where can I buy stamps? (L.32)

● アメリカまで手紙を出したいが、いくらですか？

I want to send some letters to the US. How much is it?

● １３０円です

It is 130 yen.

● じゃ、１１０円の切手を ５枚ください

Then, give me five 110-yen stamps, please.

● 航空便でお願いします

By air mail, please.

● 船便でチリに着くまで何日ぐらいかかりますか？

How many days will it take to Chile if I send it by sea mail?

● 中身は本だけですが、何かの割り引きはありますか？

(The packet) only contains books, is there a discount?

Telephone	
country code	国番号
collect call	コレクトコール
intl. call	国際電話
local call	市内電話
cell phone	携帯電話
public phone	公衆電話
telephone book	電話帳
telephone card	テレホンカード

Post office	
address	住所
envelope	封筒
fragile (item)	割れ物
mailbox	ポスト
packet	子包み
postcard	絵葉書
post office	郵便局
registered mail	書留
special delivery	速達
stamp	切手
zip code	郵便番号

文化編：神社とお寺
Cultural note: *Jinja* and *o-tera*

The various Buddhist temples (お寺) and Shinto shrines (神社) dotting the most historical Japanese cities, such as 京都, 奈良 and 鎌倉, are fascinating and exotic to Western eyes, but... what are the differences between the places of worship of the two main religions in Japan, Buddhism (仏教) and Shinto (神道)?

There is a great difference in color: whereas the お寺 are not painted and keep the original color of the wood, the 神社 are often painted in bright red.

In the 神社 we will see 鳥居 gates, which separate the earthly from the spiritual world and which mark the entrance to the sacred land, often protected by a fierce 狛犬 watchdog on each side. You can go to the 神社 to pray for anything: success in your career or studies, finding a boyfriend or girlfriend, getting well again... In fact, the sale of お守り (amulets) and 絵馬 (votive tablets on which you write your wishes and then hang) are an essential source of income. Also remarkable are the おみくじ, little bits of paper that tell your fortune for a reasonable price.

To pray at a 神社 you must first purify yourself (washing mouth and hands), sound a bell to let the gods (神) know of our

A *torii* from Kasuga Jinja (Nara), guarded by a *komainu* (Photo: M. Bernabé)

presence, throw a coin into the offertory box (賽銭箱), bow twice, clap twice, bow again, and finally pray.

On the other hand, the お寺 are much more frugal in appearance. There we can find beautiful pagodas (塔) and huge bells (鐘), and people light aromatic incense (お香) to pray to the Buddha. There are many Buddhist images, and standing out among them are the different Buddhas (如来), the bodhisattva (菩薩), the 明王 (fierce beings who protect the teachings of the Buddhas), and the 仁王, two huge statues of angry warriors who guard the temple gates: one (阿) has his mouth open, and the other (吽), closed, as an allegory of the characters opening and closing the Sanskrit alphabet, "a" and "hum," and which, together, represent the beginning and end of all things...

We will say goodbye to conversational lessons with a few manga panels, of course, where some of the subjects we have seen in this lesson will be illustrated. We will also see quite a few new things, especially culture-wise, so be sure to read carefully.

a) Going to the post office

Kimie: 郵便局の人に「速達でお願いします」って言うのよ
post office POP person IOP "special delivery IP please" say EP EP
And you tell the man at the post office "by special delivery, please," OK?

Kazuhiro: そくたつでおねがいします　そくたつでおねがいします
special delivery IP please special delivery IP please
By special delivery, please. By special delivery, please.

Bárbara Raya

The panel opening the manga-examples section shows us a boy going to the post office (郵便局) on his mother's request, to hand in a letter (手紙) for special delivery (速達). Ordinary mail would be 普通, and registered mail, 書留. Besides helping us review vocabulary and learn the sentence 速達でお願いします (*by special delivery, please*), this panel will be useful to review some grammar seen in previous lessons. For instance, the で in 速達で corresponds to the use #4 of the particle で we studied in L.38 (book 2): it indicates Adverbial Complement of Manner ("how"). Likewise, take a look at the って placed just after the sentence in quotation marks (「」): it is the colloquial version of use #3 (quote) of the particle と we studied in L.41.
Note: Notice how the boy repeats the sentence twice, but that in his bubble no kanji are used. Sometimes, we will find words or sentences fully written in hiragana when children repeat them: this is a strategy to let the reader know that the child is only repeating sounds and doesn't really understand the meaning of what he's saying.

b) How to ask to have our photo taken

> **Couple:** すみません シャッター押^おしていただけます?
> *excuse me shutter press (do a favor)?*
> **Excuse me, could you take a photo of us?**

Here we find the most common sentence when asking someone to take a photo of us. Notice how questions with ～ていただきます (L.45) are very often inflected in the potential form (L.32), that is, ～ていただ<u>け</u>ます, literally, *could you do me the favor of...?* Peculiarities about photos in Japan: almost all Japanese have the odd habit of "posing" for photos making the V sign for victory (Vサイン^{ブイ}) with the index and middle fingers, a truly compulsive habit. By the way, the word they use to urge someone to

Gabriel Luque

smile when taking their photo is チーズ, *cheese*, just like us in English.

Note: The man's answer, somewhat unsociable, is へい, a distortion of はい *(yes)*, denoting certain indifference and even annoyance.

c) A telephone conversation

> **Yuki:** もしもし... あ ママ? うん... 今^{いま}友達^{ともだち}来^きてる そう...じゃーね
> *hello... oh, Mom? yes... now friend come that's right... bye-bye*
> **Hello? Oh, Mom? Yes... I have a friend over now. Yes... Bye-bye.**

Studio Kōsen

This is a telephone conversation between a mother and her daughter. As you can see, it is a short conversation: typical in Japan. We will highlight the もしもし, the Japanese equivalent to our *hello?* or *yes?*, which apparently comes from the verb 申^{もう}す (*to say*, L52), which belongs to the formal language of modesty. Seemingly, when the telephone was first introduced in Japan, people needed to make sure they were being heard "from the other side" and so they repeated the verb 申^{もう}す twice −obtaining something like *I say, I say*−. This expression has taken root and has become the actual もしもし used today. Notice, too, うん, a colloquial word used to say *yes*, and the じゃね in the end, used to say goodbye.

d) Zen Buddhism

Monk: ジムさん、ドーナツには穴がありますね
Jim (noun suf.), doughnuts PP TOP hole there is EP
Mr. Jim, doughnuts have holes, don't they?

Jim: はあ...公案ですか
ah... kōan be Q?
Ah, is this a *kōan*?

Javier Bolado

In this example we have a conversation where a bonze (お坊さん or 坊主) remarks to Jim that "doughnuts have holes," and he replies asking whether it is a 公案.

You probably know the word 禅, which designates a very widespread branch of Buddhism (仏教) in Japan. Among the 禅 practices we have 座禅, in which the student sits in meditation for hours (in an uncomfortable position) and contemplate riddles called 公案, which help the student reach enlightment (悟り). Probably, the most famous 公案 is the enigmatic 片手で叩く音とは何だ？ *What is the sound of one clapping hand?*

Note: In the next panel, the monk says that when you eat a doughnut, the hole disappears, and he wonders where that hole goes to. A very 禅 reflection, no doubt.

e) The fortune in the *omikuji*

Man: 今年のうんせいは...
this year POP fortune TOP...
Let's see my fortune for this year...

Box: おみくじ
fortunes
Fortunes

Paper: 大吉
great good luck
Great good luck

We see in this panel a man in a Shinto shrine (神社), who puts a coin in a box with a sign reading おみくじ, takes out a piece of paper reading 大吉, and rejoices at it. Why? The おみくじ tells you what your fortune will be for the year, and there are several kinds. From the best to the worst: 大吉 *(great good luck)*, 中吉 *(medium good luck)*, 小吉 *(little good luck)*, 末吉 *(so-so luck)*, 小凶 *(little bad luck)*, 中凶 *(medium bad luck)*, 大凶 *(great bad luck)*.

Gabriel Luque

Note: Other typical things we can see are a big rope of straw (しめなわ), the bits of paper in zigzag (四手), and the 破魔矢 arrows, which frighten evil spirits and devils away, and are sold during 初詣, the year's first visit to the temple.

f) Praying at a Shinto shrine

Michiko: 母^{かあ}さん、神様^{かみさま}に千円^{せんえん}もふるまって、なに祈願^{きがん}したの？

Mom, god (noun suf.) IOP 1000 yen very much donate, what prayer do EP?

Mom, you've just given 1000 yen to the gods, what have you prayed for?

In this example, which also takes us to a 神社^{じんじゃ}, we have a conversation between a mother and a daughter. The mother is praying before an offertory box (賽銭箱^{さいせんばこ}), which is where prayer money is thrown and where the praying ceremony we saw in the Cultural Note takes place.

The daughter asks why she has donated so much as 1,000 yen to the gods (神様^{かみさま}); because, usually, one throws in 10, or 50 or 100 yen coins, at the most. Larger offerings are only made when you are asking the 神^{かみ} for something especially important.

Note: Notice the use of the particle も, which in this case indicates the idea of "no less than" (L.37, book 2).

Javier Bolado

g) Festivals

Tomo: 「宵山^{よいやま}」とは、祇園祭^{ぎおんまつり}3日^{みっか}め、いちばんもりあがる日^ひ。

"Yoiyama" ref. TOP, Gion festival day 3 (ordinal), the most liven up day

The "Yoiyama" is on the third day of the Gion Festival, the liveliest day.

J.M. Ken Niimura

We could not conclude this lesson without mentioning the variety of bustling Japanese festivals (祭^{まつり}). In this example, we see an image of a 山鉾^{やまほこ} float, which corresponds to one of the most famous festivals in Japan: the 祇園祭^{ぎおんまつり}, celebrated between the 17th and the 24th of July, in the beautiful city of 京都^{きょうと}. They say this festival has a history of more than one thousand years! The three most famous festivals in Japan are the abovementioned 祇園祭^{ぎおんまつり}, the 天神祭^{てんじんまつり} (in the city of 大阪^{おおさか}, on the 25th of July), and the 神田祭^{かんだまつり} (in 東京^{とうきょう}, on the 15th of May), which are all worth seeing.

Notes: Notice the use of the superlative 一番^{いちばん} – in hiragana here –, which we saw in L.54, and the relative clause (L.50) 一番^{いちばん}もりあがる日^ひ, *the day it livens up most.*

1 Translate into English the following words: 動物園, 切手, 城, 展示, テレホンカード, 住所 and 美術館.

2 Translate into Japanese the following words: "flash," "garden," "direction," "cell phone," "street," and "traffic lights."

3 You are heading for the Atsuta Jingū (熱田神宮) in Nagoya (名古屋), but you don't know how to get there. Ask somebody.

4 Translate the answer to the previous question: この通りをまっすぐ行って、そして右へ曲がってください。交番の隣にあります。

5 Translate: "Walk two more blocks, and then turn right before the third traffic lights."

6 Ask someone if you can take their photo. If they agree, don't forget to ask them to smile for the photo!

7 You are going to the museum, and you need to buy tickets for an adult and three children. What do you say?

8 Translate: スペインまで手紙を出すのに110円の切手が必要です。(必要な: necessary)

9 What is the process to follow when praying at a 神社? What are 絵馬, and what are they for?

10 What are 禅, 公案, and the practice of 座禅, and what is their aim?

Lesson 56: The conditional form

We now begin one of the weightiest lessons of the whole *MangaLand* series: here, we will study the various expressions for the Japanese conditional form. There are four different constructions to express the conditional, and the differences of usage are often difficult to distinguish clearly.

The four expressions of the conditional form

We will start with the conditional form taking look in outline at the characteristics of the four expressions of the conditional (と, 〜ば, 〜たら and なら), studying their conjugation and how they generally work. Next, we will study their different usages and nuances, one by one.

と Our first "guest" will be と. The expression と is used to indicate natural relations derived from habit or logic (if / when x happens, then y usually happens). It is very often used in sentences expressing events derived from natural phenomena, habits, etc. After a clause with と, we never have sentences expressing will, wish, order, or request. This kind of sentence usually has the nuance of "whenever," more than the more familiar conditional "if."

Usage: と is placed directly after verbs and -*i* adjectives. -*na* adjectives and nouns require だ.

● １５日になると、給料が振り込まれる *When the 15th comes, my wage is transferred (to my account).*
● 毎日仕事が終わると、ビールを飲む *Every day, when I finish work, I have a beer.*

A different usage of と expresses a relation of "discovery:"

● あの橋を渡ると、学校があります *When you cross that bridge, there is a school.*

〜ば Our second construction of the conditional is 〜ば. This expression is used to form conditional sentences just as we know them (if x, then y). It is similar to と in some ways, but 〜ば has a much stronger nuance of hypothesis or supposition. Just like with と, after a clause with 〜ば we never have sentences expressing will, wish, order, or request.

<u>Usage</u>: Verbs have a special conjugation with 〜ば, so you will have to study the table below. *-i* adjectives replace the last 〜い with 〜ければ: 甘^{あま}い *(sweet)* ⇒ 甘^{あま}ければ *(if it is sweet)*. The negative is formed the same way: 甘^{あま}くない *(it is not sweet)* ⇒ 甘^{あま}くなければ *(if it is not sweet)*. After *-na* adjectives and nouns, we use ならば: きれいならば *(if she were pretty)*, 学生^{がくせい}ならば *(if he were a student)*. In the negative, we need the verb です in the negative (ではない/じゃない), and we will replace the last 〜い with 〜ければ: きれいではなければ *(if she weren't pretty)*, 学生^{がくせい}じゃなければ *(if he weren't a student)*.

● ワインを飲^のめば、気持^{きも}ちよくなります *If you drink some wine, you will feel well.*
● そのカメラは安^{やす}くなければ、買^かわないよ *If that camera is not cheap, I won't buy it.*
● 彼^{かれ}がもし親切^{しんせつ}ならば、助^{たす}けに来^くると思^{おも}う *If he were kind, I think he would come to help me.*

(〜たら) Now, let's go on to the next expression, 〜たら. It is a very versatile form, because it can be used in most conditional cases. If you always use 〜たら to form your conditional sentences, there is less of a possibility that you might make a mistake. Although there are always some exceptions, so you still need to be careful.

Unlike と and 〜ば, after 〜たら you can have sentences expressing will, wish, order, or request, consequently, its field widens considerably.

	Simple f.	Mening	Rule	Conditional	Rule	Negative	Negative cond.
Group 1 Invariable	教^{おし}える	to teach	-~~る~~れば	教えれば		教えない	教えなければ
	起^おきる	to wake up		起きれば		起きない	起きなければ
Group 2 Variable	貸^かす	to lend	-~~す~~せば	貸せば		貸さない	貸さなければ
	待^まつ	to wait	-~~つ~~てば	待てば		待たない	待たなければ
	買^かう	to buy	-~~う~~えば	買えば		買わない	買わなければ
	帰^{かえ}る	to return	-~~る~~れば	帰れば	Negative form -~~い~~ければ	帰らない	帰らなければ
	書^かく	to write	-~~く~~けば	書けば		書かない	書かなければ
	急^{いそ}ぐ	to hurry	-~~ぐ~~げば	急げば		急がない	急がなければ
	遊^{あそ}ぶ	to play	-~~ぶ~~べば	遊べば		遊ばない	遊ばなければ
	飲^のむ	to drink	-~~む~~めば	飲めば		飲まない	飲まなければ
	死^しぬ	to die	-~~ぬ~~ねば	死ねば		死なない	死ななければ
Group 3 Irregular	する	to do	*Irregular verbs: no rule*	すれば		しない	しなければ
	来^くる	to come		来^くれば		来^こない	来^こなければ

The conditional form 条件の表現 –111–

<u>Usage</u>: All you need to do is add ら after the <u>past</u> form of verbs (買ったら, *if I bought*), -*i* adjectives (甘かったら, *if it were sweet*), -*na* adjectives (きれいだったら, *if she were pretty*), and nouns (学生だったら, *if he were a student*).

● もし、ハワイに行ったら、お土産を買って来てね *If you go to Hawaii, buy me a souvenir, OK?*

● 行きたくなかったら、家に残ってもいい *If you don't want to go, you can stay home.*

● 彼が父親じゃなかったら、殴ったのに！ *If he wasn't my father, I would have hit him!*

Note: In the first sentence we use the word もし, which is an adverb with a meaning and usage very similar to our conditional "if." もし isn't strictly necessary when forming conditional sentences, but is used to emphasize the condition.

(なら) Last but not least, we will see the fourth form, なら, the most peculiar of the four. Its usage is more obvious in a conversation: we use it to reiterate what the interlocutor has said, and then add data. なら can be used in will, wish, order, and request sentences. **Note:** Its colloquial version is のだったら or んだったら.

<u>Usage</u>: We will sometimes find の before なら; it adds the nuance of "in the case of..." and is just an option. We place nothing between verbs, adjectives (-*i* and -*na*), nouns and なら. In the past form, nouns and -*na* adjectives need だった.

● A: 韓国に旅行したい | B: 韓国へ行く(の)ならビビンバを食べなきゃね

A: I'd like to travel to Korea | B: If you are going to Korea, then you must eat bibimbap.

● 外に出るんだったら、ごみを捨ててきてね

If you are going outside, then take out the garbage, OK?

To conclude this very intensive first section, we highly recommend that you study the table below and look carefully at the different nuances of the conditional expressions.

Conditional forms		
と	雨が降ると、カエルが鳴く If (when) it rains, frogs croak.	Since what is said in the first clause always comes true naturally then what is said in the second clause will come true, as well.
~ば	雨が降れば、水不足が解決する If it rained, the drought would be solved.	This is the "orthodox" conditional, close to the one in English. If the condition in the first clause (to rain) comes true, the following action comes true too.
~たら	雨が降ったら、試合は中止になる If it rains, the match will be cancelled.	Provisionally, the match will be held, but if in the future the condition in the first clause (to rain) came true, then, in that hypothetical future, the match would be cancelled.
なら	雨が降るなら、家にいよう If (what happens is that) it rains, I'll stay home.	The speaker indicates a condition that he himself imposes: the second clause can be an intention.

あめがふる: to rain | カエル: frog | なく: to croak, chirp, mew, etc. | みずぶそく: drought | かいけつする: to solve
しあい: match | ちゅうしする: to cancel | いえ: house | いる: to be

Nuances and usage

In the second section, we will see different nuances of the conditional forms:

① Hypothetical conditions ("if" / "in case"). <u>We may use</u>: と, ～ば, ～たら or なら.
- 試験に合格すれば、卒業できます *If I pass the exam, I would be able to graduate.*
- この音楽が好きだったら、CDをあげるよ *If you like this music, I'll give you a CD.*

In this kind of "pure" conditional sentence we can use ～たら most times without making a mistake. **Note:** ～ば is usually perceived as more formal than ～たら.

② The second action always and unavoidably follows the first one, as in the case of a naturally occuring event or the force of habit ("whenever" / "on... -ing"). <u>We use</u>: と.
- 夏になると、蛍が出てきます *Whenever summer comes, fireflies appear.*
- 国の経済が成長すると、豊かになる *Whenever the economy of a country develops, it becomes rich.*

③ An action immediately follows the first one, but not necessarily in a natural or predetermined way ("when" / "as soon as"). <u>We may use</u>: と or ～たら.
- 彼女に会うと、いつも緊張する *Whenever I come across her, I get nervous.*
- 先生が呼んだら、すぐ行ってください *As soon as the teacher calls you, go at once.*

④ Idiomatic usage introducing a conversation. It doesn't necessarily imply condition. <u>We use</u>: ～ば, ～たら.
- よかったら、今度家に来てください *If you'd like, please come to my house some time.*
- 考えてみれば、私たちは長い付き合いだね *Come to think of it, ours is a long relationship, isn't it?*

Notice how in this case only, ～ば can go before sentences expressing will, wish, order, or request. **Note:** the conjugation of the adjective いい (*good*) is irregular: it becomes よかったら (～たら form), and よければ (～ば form).

⑤ Something is either learned or discovered as a result of a certain action ("when" / "as a result of" / "after"). <u>We use</u>: と, ～たら.
- 納豆を買いに行くと、もうなかった *When I went to buy* nattō, *there was no more left.*
- 泳ぎに行ったら、プールには水がなかった *When I went swimming, there was no water in the pool.*

A less literal translation, and closer to the meaning they would have in English: *I went to buy* nattō, *but there was none left* and *I went swimming, but the pool was empty.*

⑥ To introduce a specific topic in the conversation ("regarding"). <u>We use</u>: なら.
- 赤松さんなら、家に帰りましたよ *Regarding Mr. Akamatsu, he has already come home.*
- 旅行なら、インドがいいな *Talking about trips, I'd like (to go to) India.*

Idiomatic usages and derivatives

We will now see a few usages which are not necessarily related to the conditional, but which derive from these forms we have just studied.

① 〜ばいい. "You need to" / "You should" / "Ideally... would." This expression is very often used to clarify doubts and ask about things we are not sure about. It is really useful and easy to use.

● この書類に記入すればいいんですね *I only need to fill in this document, right?*

● こんなこと、誰にきけばいいの？ *Who should I ask about this?*

② 〜たらどうですか？ Suggestion: "How about...?" / "Why don't...?"

● 疲れているなら、休んだらどうですか？ *If you are tired, why don't you take a rest?*

● 彼女を誘ってみたらどう？ *Why don't you try inviting her?*

③ At the end of a sentence, we use 〜ば or 〜たら to make soft proposals.

● 寝ないでよ！ちょっと勉強すれば？ *Don't sleep! How about studying just a little more?*

● 疲れている？休んだら？ *Are you tired? Why don't you take a rest?*

④ The expressions ったら and ってば（といえば）are used at the end of a sentence in colloquial spoken language to show annoyance.

● ぐずぐずしないでよ！勉強しなさいったら！ *Don't idle about! Get on with your study!*

● 君！こっちに来てってば *You! Come here, come on!*

Constructions #3 and #4 are very colloquial and only used in spoken language. Expression #4 is mainly used by women, when they repeat annoying orders to small children. **Be careful:** ったら is not conjugated: it goes directly at the end of a sentence.

⑤ 言えば: "This way" (explanation) / できれば: "If possible" (request).

● 簡単に言えば、彼はバカだ *In short / in a few words, he is stupid.*

● そう言えば、美紀が来ていないね *Now that you mention it, Miki hasn't come, has she?*

● できれば、あなたと結婚したいんです *If possible, I'd like to marry you.*

These last usages are basically idiomatic, and sometimes have little to do with the more orthodox conditionals. **Note:** できれば is a conditional and is extremely common.

To conclude, the conjunctions それなら and すると, placed at the beginning of sentences, have identical meaning to 〜ば and 〜たら (usage #1) and と (usage #5).

● 疲れている？それなら、休んでよ *Are you tired? If so, take a rest.*

● 彼に会った。すると、彼は太っていた *I came across him. Thus, (I saw) he had put on weight.*

漫画例　Manga-examples

You will have realized that the differences between the four conditional forms are very difficult to delimit clearly. For the moment, all you need to know is how to recognize them and how to form simple sentences with them. With time and practice, you will manage to use them properly.

a) The conditional *to*

Jun: これはウチとやる時にはボクがフルタイム出場しないと勝てそうにないな
this top "uchi" cp DO time TP TOP full time participate not do (cond) win not EP
**Seeing this, when we play against them, if I don't play full time,
I don't think we will be able to win.**

これはウチとやる時にはボクがフルタイム出場しないと勝てそうにないな

Gabriel Luque

We will start the examples taking a look at an instance of the usage of the conditional form と. The sentence in our panel is very long, so we will only select the extract we want to analyze, that is, ボクがフルタイム出場しないと勝てそうにない, with special attention, of course, to the と in the middle. This と corresponds to usage #1 in the "Nuances and usage" section on page 113. In other words, we use it to express a hypothetical condition.

Like in this example, we very often find と combined with a verb in the negative, with the "negative conditional" meaning of "if I don't do x, then Y." In this case, the translation of our sentence would be *If I don't play full time, I don't think we will be able to win.* Other examples: 食べないと大きくならないよ *If you don't eat, you won't grow.* | 行かないと死ぬ *If I don't go, I'll die.* We very often find と combined with だめだ or いけない, as in the sentences 食べないとだめだ or 行かないといけない This construction means exactly the same as ～なければならない and other expressions of the kind, which we studied in L.32 (book 2), that is "I must...," "I have to..." These sentences, then, would be *I must eat* and *I have to go*, respectively.

Note: 勝てそうにない *(it doesn't look like we can win)* is a kind of negation of the conjecture そうだ (2) (L.43), linked to 勝てる, the potential form (L.31) of the verb 勝つ *(to win.)*

The conditional form 条件の表現 −115−

b) The conditional -*ba*

Lee: そんなものがうまくいけばビルに飛行機は突っ込まないはずだ
that thing SP *well go (cond) building* PP *plane* TOP *crash look like*
If that worked out, nobody would think of crashing planes into buildings.

J.M. Ken Niimura

Here we have again an example of the most orthodox conditional, this time with the 〜ば construction: the うまくいけば part literally means *if it goes well*. 行けば is the conditional conjugation of the verb 行く *(to go)* (refer to the conjugation table in the beginning of this lesson). The rules for this conjugation are simple: basically, the last -*u* in the simple form of all verbs in all groups (including the irregular verbs, curiously enough) is replaced with an -*e* and, then, we add ば. Thus, *iku* ⇒ *ike* ⇒ *ikeba*. The only exception, as usual, are verbs ending in -*tsu*, which don't become -*tseba*, but change to -*teba*.

Notes: もの means "thing" (we will study it in depth in the next lesson). Notice the usage of the conjecture はずだ (L.43, book 2), which indicates a supposition that is almost a fact.

c) The conditional -*tara*

Taneda: パ...パ...パンチーをみせてくれたらな！！
pa... pa... panties DOP *show (favor) (cond)* EP!!
If... if... if you show me your panties, OK?!

In this humorous example we see how a dirty old man answers the girl when she asks him for a favor: パンティーを見せてくれたら *(if you show me your panties)*. A verb like やる *(to do)* or 助ける *(to help)* is supposed to go after くれたら, but it is omitted here. The part we want to high-

Studio Kōsen

light is, of course, the conditional 〜たら in 見せてくれたら *(if you show me)*: it is a conditional of the first kind (hypothetical), like those in manga-examples a) and b).

Note: The man says パンチー, but the correct spelling of "panties" is パンティー. Theoretically, old people can't pronounce the foreign and relatively "new" sound ティ *(ti)*, and so pronounce it チ *(chi)* instead: here, it reflects the humorous license of the author.

d) The conditional *nara*

> **Yūma:** 助けたほうがいいんなら助けよう！
> *save be recommended (cond) save!!*
> **If she had better be saved, then I'll save her!**

Javier Bolado

Here we have a slightly different usage of the conditional from those we have seen in the previous panels: the expression なら is used to reiterate a topic of conversation which appeared just before, and to then add more information (usage #6 on page 113). The sentence in the example is probably the answer to something like （彼女を）助けたほうがいいよ *She had better be saved.* What the speaker does is reiterate this piece of information, transform it into a conditional clause with the expression なら, and then add his own reply or opinion in the end. A more colloquial version of this sentence would be 助けたほうがいいんだったら助けよう.

Notes: Review here the usage of the strong recommendation 〜ほうがいい (L.49), and the *-ō* form (L.34), indicating a volitive action, in 助けよう (*I'm going to save her*).

e) An idiomatic usage: *yokattara*

> **Man:** もしよかったら、今度ママとパパと三人でお芝居を観に来てちょうだいよ
> *if well (cond), next time mom CP and dad CP the three theater DOP come to see please EP*
> **If you'd like, come to the theater next time with mom and dad, please.**

Bárbara Raya

We go back to the expression 〜たら, used this time as an example of usage #4, an idiomatic usage very often combined with the adjective いい (*good*) to indicate *If you'd like...* With this expression you can start sentences when you want to invite somebody or offer something. Bear in mind that the past conjugation of いい is irregular (よかった), and, therefore, its 〜たら conjugation is よかったら.

Notice, too, the usage of the adverb もし, translated as our conditional "if." In Japanese we don't need to place もし in each and every one of the conditional clauses, it is more often used when we want to emphasize the condition, or when we want to use it to help us introduce a conditional sentence.

Note: The 〜てちょうだい construction means the same as 〜てください (L.35).

f) Another conjunction

> **Shōji:** だとすれば左足が動かない原因は一つ
> *be CP do (cond) leg left SP move cause TOP one*
> **Then, there is one cause for the left leg not to move.**

だとすれば左足が動かない原因は一つ

J.M. Ken Niimura

There are several kinds of conjunctions −words placed at the beginning of a sentence, to connect its meaning to that of the previous sentence, or to follow a conversation in a coherent way− that are based on conditional expressions. Besides those we saw in the theory section (それなら and すると), we also have そうしたら, そうすれば, だとしたら, and, like in this example, だとすれば, among others.

Technically, だとすれば is not a conjunction, but the sum of だ (*to be*), the particle と (L.41) and すれば (the conditional ～ば of the verb する). Literally, it would be something like *if (that) is done,* in other words: "If that is the way it is," "in that case," "then..."

Note: In this example, we have a very clear instance of a relative clause: 左足が動かない 原因 (*cause for the left leg not to move*). Review L.50.

g) A "smart aleck" usage of the conditional *-ba*

> **Hina:** ふぇぇ～ん　　**Ken:** ふん 父ちゃんと母ちゃんにめんどう見てもらえば？
> *hueeennn* 　　　　　　*hum dad CP mom IOP problem look (receive)*
> **Waaah!** 　　　　　　**Humph! Then, let mom and dad take care of you...**

We will conclude this difficult lesson having a look at a funny usage of the conditional ～ば. You are probably curious to know whether there is a "smart aleck" answer of the kind *I'm hungry | Then eat,* or *I'm tired | Then sleep.* Well, there is, and it is very simple to obtain the "smart aleck" effect of "then x" using the conditional ～ば (usage #3 on page 114) and an interrogative intonation.

The translation of our "smart aleck" sentences would then be: お腹がすいている *I'm hungry* | 食べれば？ *Then eat,* or 眠いなぁ *I'm tired* | 寝れば？ *Then sleep.*

ふん 父ちゃんと母ちゃんにめんどう見てもらえば？

ふぇぇ～ん

Bárbara Raya

Notes: 面倒を見る (lit. *To look at a problem*) is a set phrase meaning "to take care of." 父ちゃん and 母ちゃん are childish distortions of お父さん (*father*) and お母さん (*mother*).

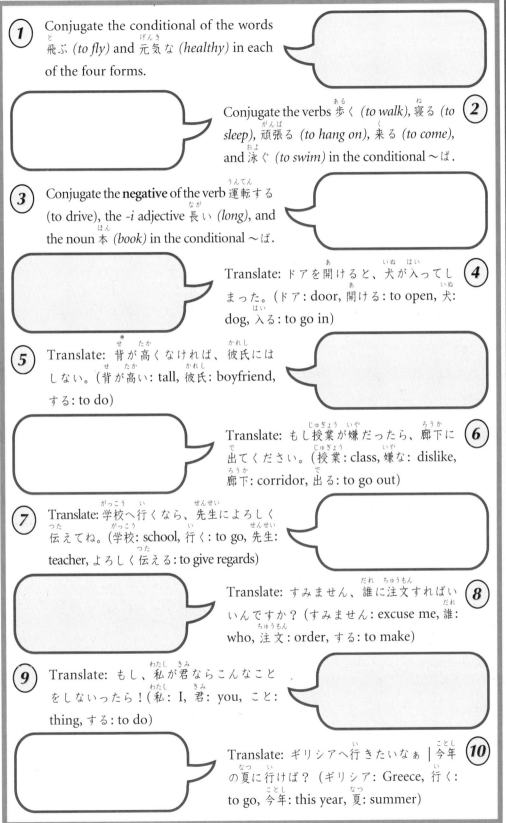

1. Conjugate the conditional of the words 飛ぶ (to fly) and 元気な (healthy) in each of the four forms.

2. Conjugate the verbs 歩く (to walk), 寝る (to sleep), 頑張る (to hang on), 来る (to come), and 泳ぐ (to swim) in the conditional 〜ば.

3. Conjugate the **negative** of the verb 運転する (to drive), the -i adjective 長い (long), and the noun 本 (book) in the conditional 〜ば.

4. Translate: ドアを開けると、犬が入ってしまった。(ドア: door, 開ける: to open, 犬: dog, 入る: to go in)

5. Translate: 背が高くなければ、彼氏にはしない。(背が高い: tall, 彼氏: boyfriend, する: to do)

6. Translate: もし授業が嫌だったら、廊下に出てください。(授業: class, 嫌な: dislike, 廊下: corridor, 出る: to go out)

7. Translate: 学校へ行くなら、先生によろしく伝えてね。(学校: school, 行く: to go, 先生: teacher, よろしく伝える: to give regards)

8. Translate: すみません、誰に注文すればいいんですか？(すみません: excuse me, 誰: who, 注文: order, する: to make)

9. Translate: もし、私が君ならこんなことをしないったら！(私: I, 君: you, こと: thing, する: to do)

10. Translate: ギリシアへ行きたいなぁ｜今年の夏に行けば？(ギリシア: Greece, 行く: to go, 今年: this year, 夏: summer)

Lesson 57: *Koto* and *mono*

In this lesson we will learn to distinguish between こと and もの, two different Japanese concepts which are both translated as "thing." We will study as well some very useful expressions where these two words take part as a grammatical element.

こと and もの

Before we start, let's make the differences between こと and もの very clear. Although both words are translated as "thing," their usage is very clearly distinguished.

こと (which you will sometimes find written in kanji: 事) designates a non-physical "thing," something that is intangible, such as thoughts, concepts, or words, for instance.

● 大事なことを君に言いたいんです *I would like to tell you an important thing.*
● とても悲しいことが起こりました *A very sad thing happened.*

こと is also used in "noun + のこと" constructions, which emphasize a noun and mark it more strongly than usual.

● 君のことが大好きだよ *I like you very much.*
● 大学のことを忘れてくれよ *Forget about university, come on.*

As for もの (which can also be written in kanji: 物), it designates a physical "thing:"

● そっちにある物を持ってきてくれない？ *Can you bring me that thing over there?*
● 今日、どんな物を買いたいの？ *What kind of thing do you want to buy today?*

Note: Don't mistake 物 *(tangible thing)* for 者 *(person, member of)*, a word with humble nuances which is only used to refer to oneself or someone in the *uchi* circle:

● はじめまして。星野という者です *Pleased to meet you. I'm (somebody called) Hoshino.*

こと as a nominalizer

In L.40 we talked about "nominalizing" sentences: it is the process of transforming a verb, an adjective, or a sentence into a noun phrase, so that it works exactly like any other noun. Well, then, in Japanese we have two nominalizers: の and こと. Go back to the epigraph "Indefinite pronoun and nominalizer" in L.40 (book 2) and review it to obtain more specific information about the nominalizer の. **Note:** Bear in mind noun phrases (underlined in the examples) with の and こと are subordinate sentences and, therefore, their subject will never be marked with the topic particle は —you must always use が (L.37, book 2).

● <u>彼が(notは)スキーをする</u>ことは皆が知っている *Everybody knows <u>he skis</u>*.

<u>Usage of the nominalizer の</u>: Nothing is placed after verb and -*i* adjective. After -*na* adjective and noun, we place either な or である in the present tense, and だった in the past tense. Let's see a few examples now to refresh your memory:

● <u>映画を見る</u>のは大好きです *I like <u>watching movies</u> very much*.
● <u>佐藤さんがゲイだった</u>のはよく知っている *I know very well that <u>Mr. Satō was gay</u>*.

こと is used just like の, in the same place and has the same characteristics of usage with verbs, adjectives and nouns, although there is one exception: after -*na* adjectives and nouns in the present tense, we can only have である, **never** な.

● <u>映画を見る</u>ことは頭にいいです *<u>Watching movies</u> is good for your mind*.
● <u>佐藤さんがゲイである</u>ことはよく知っている *I know very well <u>Mr. Satō is gay</u>*.

Differences between the nominalizers の and こと

Even though, as we have seen in the previous sentences, の and こと are used very often without distinction to nominalize a sentence. However, there are in fact some differences. In principle, we will use の when the noun phrase expresses something subjective, something the speaker feels "close" to, and こと when talking about something objective, or general, which doesn't imply any kind of emotion. Let's see an example:

● <u>寝る前に本を読む</u>こと/のは楽しいです *<u>Reading books before going to sleep</u> is fun*.

With こと, we are saying something objective; we simply state that the fact of reading books before going to bed is fun. Whereas, with の, we add an emotional component, indicating that the action is fun for us and it affects us specially.

There are some occasions when you can only use either の or こと:

<u>You can only use の</u>: When the verb in the main sentence is either a verb of perception —見る *(to see)*, 見える *(to be able to see)*, 聞く *(to hear)*, 聞こえる *(to able to hear)*, 感じる *(to feel)*, etc. —, or one of the following verbs: 待つ *(to wait)*, 手伝う *(to help)*, 邪魔する *(to bother)*, やめる *(to stop doing, to cease)* or 止める *(to stop)*.

- その時、<u>あの人が死ぬ</u>のを見た *At that time, I saw <u>that person's death</u>.*
- <u>大学の宿題が終わる</u>のを待ってね *Wait until <u>I finish my university homework</u>, OK?*
- <u>あの子どもをいじめる</u>のはやめてください *Please, stop <u>picking on that boy</u>.*

<u>You can only use</u> こと: When the verb in the main sentence either indicates "verbal communication" − 話す *(to speak)*, 命じる *(to command)*, 伝える *(to report)*, きく *(to ask)*, 約束する *(to promise)*, etc.− or when the last verb just after the nominalizer is です or だ *(to be)*. Take care not to mistake it with のです (L.40, book 2).

- <u>息子が病気だった</u>ことを彼に伝えてください *Tell him <u>my son was sick</u>.*
- 私の一番好きな運動は<u>走る</u>ことです *<u>Running</u> is the exercise I like most.*

Expressions with こと

こと and もの are used in several constructions in the Japanese language. In them, they lose their meaning as a tangible or intangible thing, and they strictly work as grammatical components. First of all, we will see some expressions with こと, of which we already know one: the potential ことができる (L.32, book 2).

- 私はバイクを運転することができる *I can drive motorcycles.*

The first of the new expressions with こと that we will study is 〜たことがある, used to indicate "I have the experience of having done x thing." It is a frequently used expression, so you should learn it well. <u>Usage</u>: Verbs and adjectives are always conjugated in the past. Nouns require だった.

〜たことがある can be conjugated in the negative (〜たことがない, not have the experience of...), past (〜たことがあった, had the experience of...), and past negative (〜たことがなかった, didn't have the experience of...).

- 彼はエベレストに登ったことがある *He (has the experience of) has climbed Mount Everest.*
- 僕はアメリカに行ったことがない *I have never been to the United States.*
- 私は十年前先生だったことがある *10 years ago, I (had the experience of) was a teacher.*
- 彼のギャグは面白かったことがなかった *His gags were never funny.*

An expression that is very easy to mistake for 〜たことがある is ことがある, which has the meaning of "now and then...," that is, it designates an action or state that seldom happens. <u>Usage</u>: It is conjugated differently from 〜たことがある, because verbs, adjectives, etc., preceding こと are in the **present infinitive**. *-na* adjectives require な and nouns require の or である.

● 弟は働くことがある *Sometimes, my younger brother works (he usually doesn't).*

● スイカはバカ高いことがある *Occasionally, watermelons are ridiculously expensive.*

Attention: In negative form, は, instead of が, is used with this expression: ～ことはない:

● 彼女が黙ることはない *There are no occasions when she keeps quiet. | She never keeps quiet.*

Decisions

Let's study some more expressions with こと: the next two we will now see are related to taking decisions, but have very different nuances.

We first have ことにする which indicates "a decision taken by oneself or someone in the *uchi* circle." Usage: This expression only comes after verbs, conjugated in the present infinitive or in the negative when the decision taken is negative.

● 日本語を学ぶことにします *(I decide that) I'm going to learn Japanese.*

● 先生と話さないことにしたそうだ *It looks like he has decided not to speak with the teacher.*

● 来年、大阪へ行くことにしました *I have decided that next year I'll go to Osaka.*

The second expression is ことになる, which indicates "a decision which affects oneself or someone in the *uchi* circle, but which has been made by someone or something external." It is often used for demands or commands. Usage: The same as ことにする.

● 私は英語を勉強することになっている *I must (I've been told to) study English.*

● パーティーはバーでしないことになった *It has been decided that the party won't be held at the bar.*

● 仕事をやめることになりそうだ *Apparently, I'll have to (they're demanding that I) quit my job.*

● 来年、大阪へ行くことになりました *It has been decided that next year I'll go to Osaka.*

The last sentence in each section is very clear: with ことにする it is obvious that the decision to go to Osaka is taken by the speaker himself, whereas with ことになる the speaker implies that the decision to go to Osaka has been made by someone else, they are telling him to do it (maybe someone from the company he works for).

Expressions with もの

After seeing some expressions with こと (more of them are studied in more advanced levels of Japanese), it is now time to study a few expressions with もの.

At an elementary level, you don't usually study any of the various expressions using もの, but we will study two very frequent ones in colloquial language, which you will come across very often in movies and comic books.

The first もの we will see is used to give the implication of an excuse when answering a question with *why?* The effect is almost the same as that of an answer introduced by "The thing is..." or "Because..." in English and it is mainly used by children and women in colloquial Japanese. <u>Usage</u>: もの is always placed at the end of a sentence. Verbs and -*i* adjectives go in the infinitive, while -*na* adjectives and nouns need だ. The construction んだもの is very common. **Note:** もの can be contracted into もん.

● 今行けないの。とても忙しいもの *I can't go now. The thing is I'm very busy.*

● 幼稚園、行きたくないもん！ *It's just that I don't want to go to kindergarten!*

● どうして食べないの？ *Why don't you eat it?* | だって、まずいんだもん *Because it's bad.*

The second expression is ものですか, which we will very often see as ものか or even もんか. This construction, which always goes at the end of a sentence, is quite rough and indicates a (very strong) refusal to do something. Note: although this expression ends with a か, it is not pronounced as a question. <u>Usage</u>: Verbs and -*i* adjectives go in the infinitive. -*na* adjectives and nouns need な and である, respectively.

● あの男と付き合うものですか！ *There's no way I'm going out with that man!*

● お前に１００万円を払うものか *I'm not paying you a million yen (not on your life).*

● あんたとは旅行に行くもんかよ！ *I'm not going on a trip with you (under no circumstances)!*

Expressions with *koto* and *mono*			
こと	こと（事）	Intangible thing (concept)	どんなことを言いたいの？ What kind of thing do you want to tell me?
	こと	Nominalizer: used to transform full clauses into nouns	運動をすることは体にいいです (The fact of) doing exercise is good for your health.
	〜たことがある	To have the experience of...	ハワイに行ったことがありますよ I have been (I have the experience of going) to Hawaii.
	ことがある	Sometimes... Now and then x happens...	彼は運動をすることがある He sometimes exercises (though he usually doesn't).
	ことにする	To decide something by oneself	ハワイへ行くことにしました I decided to go to Hawaii.
	ことになる	Something external to the speaker makes a decision which affects him	ハワイへ行くことになりました It has been decided that I will go to Hawaii.
もの	もの（物）	Tangible thing (object)	その物を持ってきてくれる？ Can you bring me that thing?
	もの（もん）	At the end of a sentence, childish or female expression implying "excuse"	今、行けないの。忙しいんだもん！ I can't go now. The thing is I'm busy!
	ものか（もんか）	At the end of a sentence, it emphasizes a categorical refusal	今、ハワイに行くものか！ There's no way I'm going to Hawaii!

言う: to say | 運動 うんどう: exercise | 体 からだ: body | いい: good | ハワイ: Hawaii | 行 いく: to go
かれ: he | 持 もってくる: to bring | 今 いま: now | いそがしい: busy

漫画例　Manga-examples

Let's go on now to illustrate with a few panels, as usual, what we have seen in the theory pages. The subject we are dealing with is the usage of こと and もの: both when they are used with their original meaning of "thing," and when they are part of set constructions.

a) *Mono:* tangible thing / excuse

Ryanki: だって 私はあなたのものだもの　〜でしょ？
the fact is I TOP *you* POP *thing (emph) (excuse) be?*
The fact is I'm yours (your thing)... am I not?

We start with a very peculiar example that will be great in order to see two very different usages of the word もの. Look at the あなたの<u>もの</u>¹だ<u>もの</u>² part: we have underlined and numbered both もの so that you can see them more clearly.

The first もの (物 in kanji) is a word designating our concept of "thing," but it refers to something palpable, physical. 私はあなたのものだ, then, means *I'm a thing of yours (I'm yours)*: notice how the girl speaks about herself as if she were an object. Here, he does so because she is speaking in terms of her "physical body."

We have just seen the second もの in the previous page: it is always placed at the end of a sentence and it indicates a sort of excuse or the intention of drawing attention. This expression is almost always used by children and women, although now young men are also using it more and more. Very often, we will see もの together with the emphatic のだ we studied in L.40: のだもの (like in the example). The の can be contracted into ん (んだもん). Likewise, this expression often comes with だって at the beginning of the sentence. だって is an expression that could be translated as "the fact is..."

Note: The last でしょ is a shortened and colloquial version of でしょう / だろう, the tag meaning "am I not?," "isn't it?," etc., which we studied in L.43.

b) The emphatic usage of *koto*

Kazuki: 母ちゃんは僕のこと愛してるって
Mommy TOP *I* POP *(thing) love do says*
Mommy says she loves me.

Man: そりゃよかったね
that thing good EP
Isn't that great?

Bárbara Raya

This time we will study a special usage of こと, which means "intangible thing." The construction "noun + のこと," we find in this panel, and which we studied in the first page of the theory section, is mainly used with personal pronouns: 私のこと *(I)*, 君のこと *(you)*, etc. It has no specific meaning, it just underlines the personal pronoun, so that it is stronger than on its own, 私 or 君. In the example, 僕のこと(を) 愛している *(she loves me)*, could perfectly well be 僕を愛している, but the first sentence has a stronger meaning.

Note: って is the contraction of という *(says that*, L.41), and そりゃ of それは *(that*, TOP, L53).

c) *Koto:* intangible thing / nominalizer

Mariko: かわったことといえば、俊さんが大学生になったことくらい...
change thing say (cond), Shun SP *university student become (nom) approx...*
Talking about changes, the only thing that has changed is that Shun has become a university student.

Javier Bolado

This panel offers us two very different こと: the first one, in かわったこと, indicates an "intangible thing," like a thought, a concept, words, etc. かわったこと literally means *thing that has changed* – notice how what has changed is not "something" physical but abstract: that's why we use こと instead of もの. The second こと is a nominalizer: it transforms the previous clause into a noun phrase that works as a noun. In this case, the girl's sentence, which is cut, would finish with です (大学生になったこと(です), *the fact of becoming a university student*).

Note: Look at the いえば, which is the idiomatic usage #5 of the conditional 〜ば that we studied in L.56. In the example, いえば is used to introduce an explanatory sentence.

d) To have the experience of...

> **Abeno:** あなたは人を傷つけた事がありますか？
> *you TOP person DOP wound put (have the experience of) Q?*
> **Have you ever hurt anybody?**

Gabriel Luque

In the next three examples, we will slightly change subjects, and we will go on to comment on some grammatical expressions that use こと. Remember that sometimes, like in this panel, こと is written in kanji: 事. The first one, as you can see in this manga-example, is 〜たことがある, which has the meaning of "having the experience of having done something." We must bear in mind that this expression is only used with relatively uncommon actions (things we don't do every day): for example, we can't say 呼吸をしたことがある *I have the experience of having breathed*. The ある in 〜たことがある can be conjugated: in this example we find it in the interrogative *-masu* form.

e) To decide something by oneself

> **Ishibashi:** 和解することにしたんです　小津先生と
> *reconcile with (decide) be that man CP*
> **I've decided to make up... with him (Professor Ozu).**

This is a good example of ことにする, which means "to decide that..." and is used when one makes a decision for oneself. In the example, it is the speaker himself who decides, on his own initiative, to make up with Professor Ozu; in theory, no one is forcing him to do it, he is doing it because he wants to. Notice how the sentence is dislocated (the correct order would be 小津先生と和解することにしたんです): this is a typical characteristic of the spoken language (L.53).

J.M. Ken Niimura

Note: Notice how the speaker says 小津先生. The correct reading of these characters would obviously be 小津先生 *(Professor Ozu)*. The provided reading, カレ, belongs to the well-known kanji 彼 *(he)*. This kind of strategy is used sometimes in written Japanese to indicate to the reader that the speaker says 彼 but he is really referring to 小津先生.

f) An outsider makes a decision

Hanako: 私 この 人 と 結婚 する ことになりました
I this person CP marry (it has been decided)
I'm going to marry this man.

Studio Kōsen

Here we have ことになる, which indicates "it has been decided that..." (the decision has been taken by someone else). This implies that somebody (or circumstances) determine something that affects the speaker −very often in a negative way−, for instance, in the sentence 僕はレポートを書くことになった *It has been decided that I will write a report*. This denotes the idea that we are not too happy about it, but that there is a certain obligation to do it. Our example here, 結婚することになりました, is somewhat special. Although it can be interpreted as *The circumstances have prompted the decision that we marry*, the truth is that, sometimes (not often) ことになる is used in a "humble" way to refer to one's own decision, the importance of which one minimizes.

g) Categorical refusal

Shigekatsu: ふん 腹に赤児をもつ女なんか斬れるか
humph belly PP baby DOP have woman (emph) cut (neg)
Humph! I could never kill a woman with a baby in her belly.

We will finish with a slightly complicated example: the expression ものか, as we studied in the theory section, implies "categorical refusal to do something." It can be contracted into もんか, and even into a simple か, like in the example. Mistaking it with the interrogative particle か (L.17) is very easy, and there is no way to distinguish them, except by deducing it from the context. Don't worry, this か

Gabriel Luque

with the meaning of categorical refusal of ものか is not used too profusely.

Notes: Look at the relative clause (L.50) 腹に赤児をもつ女 (*woman who has a baby in her belly / pregnant*). 赤児 is an archaic word that designates what we now call 赤ちゃん or 赤ん坊 (*baby*). 斬る means, like 切る, *to cut*, but the usage of the kanji 斬 implies *cutting with a sword* and, by extension, in the language of the ancient 侍, *to kill*.

1 Translate: "What sort of thing are you thinking about?" (what sort of: どんな, to think: 考える)

2 Translate: "Put this thing on the table, please." (to put: 置く, on: 上, table: テーブル)

3 What two "nominalizers" are there in Japanese?

4 Nominalize the clause 彼は行く and replace the ○ in: 私は○を命じた. (彼: he, 行く: to go, 私: I, 命じる: to command)

5 Translate: "I have never read (I don't have the experience of reading) Tezuka's manga." (to read: 読む, manga: マンガ, Tezuka: 手塚)

6 What is the difference between 美香は酒を飲んだことがない and 美香は酒を飲むことがない? (美香: Mika, 酒: sake, 飲む: to drink)

7 Translate: "It was decided that I will translate a novel." (I: 私, to translate: 翻訳する, novel: 小説)

8 What is the difference between 美香は酒を飲むことにした and 美香は酒を飲むことになった?

9 Translate: このバッグが欲しいんだもん！ (バッグ: handbag, 欲しい: to want). What is the nuance of this もん?

10 Translate: "There's no way I'm going to drink sake!" (sake: 酒, to drink: 飲む) Use all options (4 altogether).

第58課：いろいろな文型

Lesson 58: Grammar scramble

We are now approaching the end of the book, therefore, we will make use of this lesson to study a few grammatical constructions which we have ended gathering together in this hodgepodge called "Lesson 58." We will be seeing the usages of だけ, しか, ばかり, ところ, せい and おかげ.

The expression だけ

Let's start then with だけ, a word that means "only" and which is extremely simple to use. We will give some examples that will be better than an explanation:

● 昨日はコーラだけ(を)飲みました *Yesterday I only drank cola.*
● 関西といえば、大阪だけ(は)「都会」だと言えるだろう

Regarding (the region of) Kansai, only Osaka could be called a "big city."
● 僕にだけ教えてくださいよ *Say it only to me, please.*
● 毎日、図書館でだけ勉強している *Every day, I study only in the library.*

Usage: だけ is placed directly after verbs, -*i* adjectives, and nouns, whereas with -*na* adjectives it needs な. **Note:** Notice how だけ is usually placed in the same position as grammatical particles. While it can precede を and は / が, it may also optionally replace them, so that they disappear altogether. However, it may not replace other particles (に, で, の, へ, etc.), and they will remain in the sentence, preceding or following だけ.

できるだけ is a special clause which means "as much as one can / as much as possible:"
● できるだけ日本語で話してください *Speak in Japanese as much as possible.*

Let's now see the expression X だけで(は)なく、Y(も), which means something like "not only x, but also y." Usage: Just like だけ.

● 彼はハンサムなだけでなく、頭がいい *He is not only handsome, but also intelligent.*
● 楽しいだけでなく、役にも立つホームページを作りたい

I want to create a web page that is not only fun, but also useful.
● 能はおもしろいだけの芸能ではなく、歴史的でもある

Noh (theatre) is not only an interesting performing art, but it is also historical.

The expression しか

The second expression we will study, しか, also means "only" somehow, but with a different nuance to that of だけ. While だけ means "only" in a neutral way, しか has a more "negative" nuance, closer to "nothing but." <u>Usage</u>: しか is used only after nouns. The verb in the sentence must <u>compulsorily</u> be in the negative. Regarding particles, しか completely replaces が and を, and optionally に and へ. Particles で, の, と, から and まで remain in the sentence together with しか.

- こんなことは先生しか知らないと思う *I think the teacher alone knows this.*
- 龍彦はラーメンしか食べない *Tatsuhiko only eats / eats nothing but* rāmen *noodles.*
- 大学へはバスでしか行けないよ *You can only go to university by bus (and by no other means).*
- 昨日は吉田さんとしか会わなかった *Yesterday, I met nobody but Mr. Yoshida.*

The end-of-the-sentence expression しかない has to be mentioned apart as it has the meaning of "to have no choice but to." <u>Usage</u>: It always goes after a verb in the infinitive.

- これから勉強するしかないな *From now on, I have no choice but to study.*
- 岡山に行くしかないと思うよ *I think we have no choice but to go to Okayama.*

The expression ばかり

The next item in our group is ばかり, a multipurpose expression of which we will study five usages. Although its basic meaning is "only," just like だけ and しか, the expression ばかり has a nuance of "only that (but I consider it is a lot / too much)," that is, it contains a certain idea of "excess."

①The first usage is similar to that of だけ and しか: "only." <u>Usage</u>: just like だけ.

- 彼はビールばかり飲んでいる *He drinks nothing but / only drinks beer (and excessively, I think).*
- あの女は文句ばかり言う *That woman does nothing but complain (and she's annoying).*
- 図書館でばかり勉強している *I only study in the library (and I study there a lot).*

Notice how ばかり replaces particles は, が and を. へ and に are optionally replaceable, while the rest must go together with ばかり in the sentence.

②The second usage, Xばかりで(は)なく、Y(も), is almost the same as Xだけで(は)なく Y(も), which means "not only x, but also y," but it has the idea of "excess" of ばかり.

- 彼はハンサムなばかりでなく、頭がいい *He is not only handsome, he is also intelligent.*
- このロックバンドはいい音楽を作るばかりではなく、スタイルもすごい

  That rock band not only creates good music, it also has a great style.

③ When placing ばかり in the middle of a gerund ～ている (L.35), we obtain ～てば かりいる, which means "to do nothing but," but with a negative nuance.

● その時、母は泣いてばかりいたよ *That time, my mother did nothing but cry.*
● 彼女は食べてばかりいて働かない *She does nothing but eat and she doesn't work.*
● 美根子ちゃん、遊んでばかりいると試験に落ちるぞ

Mineko, if you do nothing but play (have fun), you will fail your exams.

④ The expression ～たばかりだ, that is, ばかり after a verb conjugated in the past, means "to have just finished doing something."

● 今、ご飯を食べたばかりだよ *I have just finished eating lunch now.*
● 授業が終わったばかりだよ *The class has just finished.*
● A: だいぶ待ちましたか？ | B: いや、さっき着いたばかりです

A: *Have you waited long?* | B: *No, I just arrived a moment ago.*

⑤ And finally, ばかり after a counter (L.25) means "more or less" or "about," quite like ぐらい/くらい (L.40), but more formal.

● バナナを１０本ばかりください *Give me about ten bananas, please.*
● 彼は車を３台ばかり持っているかもしれません。*He might have ten cars more or less.*

The expression ところ

We will now leave aside the expressions meaning "only," and go on to study ところ, which, just like ばかり, is a multipurpose expression.

① The basic meaning of the word ところ is "place," "spot" (kanji: 所).
● この所はとても涼しいですね *This place is very cool, isn't it?*

② But, grammatically, ところ has many usages, like the meaning of "state" or "moment" it adopts when it modifies a verb, an adjective or a noun. <u>Usage</u>: ところ goes directly after verbs and -*i* adjectives, whereas, with -*na* adjectives and nouns, it requires な and の, respectively.

● ２人でラブラブしていたら、一番盛り上がっている<u>ところ</u>に母が部屋に入ってきた

The two of us were making out when, at the most exciting <u>moment</u>, mom came into the room.
● お忙しい<u>ところ</u>お邪魔してしまって、本当にごめんなさい

Please, excuse me for bothering you, when you are so busy (in such a busy <u>state</u>).

You must now read through the following three expressions carefully, as each has a very different meaning depending on the conjugation of the verb preceding ところ.

③ "Infinitive + ところだ" means "to be just about to do something."

● 手紙を書くところだ *I'm just about to (start writing) write a letter.*
● この間、妻はすごく怒って離婚するところだったよ

The other day, my wife got really angry and we were about to divorce.

④ The construction 〜ているところだ means "to be in the process of doing something."

● 手紙を書いているところだ *I'm in the middle of writing / in the process of writing a letter.*
● 今、大学院の入学試験のために勉強しているところだよ

Now I'm studying for the entrance examination for graduate school.

⑤ The construction 〜たところだ means "to have just finished doing something" and its meaning is very similar to usage #4 of ばかり.

● 手紙を書いたところだ *I have just finished writing a letter.*
● それは広美さんに言ったところだよ *I have just told Hiromi.*
● 授業が終わったところだよ *The class has just finished.*

Be careful when using expressions like ばかり or ところ, because they can give the sentence many different meanings depending on the verb conjugation that goes with them.

The expressions せい and おかげ

Let's now see a couple of expressions that are very useful and easy to remember, although, for some reason, they are not usually studied in a basic course of Japanese. Nevertheless, since they are very frequent as well as easy to use, we will see them here.

The first of these expressions is せい or せいで (で is optional), and it means "because of," with negative nuances. Usage: せい is placed directly after verbs and -i adjectives. With -na adjectives, it needs な and, with nouns, の.

● 太郎のせいで試合に負けた *It is because of Tarō that we lost the match.*
● 友達が死んだのは彼のせいだよ *It was his fault that my friend died.*
● 昨夜、あまり眠れなかったせいで、今日は仕事に集中できない

Because I couldn't sleep much last night, today I can't concentrate on my work.

The second expression, as you have probably guessed, has exactly the opposite meaning: おかげ or おかげで, "thanks to." We use it just like せい.

● 太郎のおかげで試合に勝った *Thanks to Tarō we won the match.*
● 石原さんに数学を教えてもらったおかげで、高校を卒業できた

Thanks to Ishihara teaching me math, I could graduate from senior high school.

A couple of conjunctions

We will conclude this lesson with two conjunctions that (even though they have completely different meanings), due to their resemblance in form, are very easy to confuse.

The first expression, ところで, can be translated as "by the way" or "now then." We already studied it in L.46, so we recommend that you review that lesson.

● ところで、哲治は来てない？ *By the way, hasn't Tetsuharu arrived?*

The second expression is ところが, and means quite the same as けれども and its "family" (L.49), that is, "but," "however," "nevertheless," etc.

● お母さんは東京では元気だった。ところが、尾道に帰ると、とても病気になった

Mom felt well in Tokyo. However, on going back to Onomichi, she fell seriously ill.

			Grammar scramble	
だけ	だけ	Only	私の猫は魚だけ食べる My cat only eats fish.	
	だけでなく	Not only x, but also y... (similar to ばかりでなく)	私の猫は魚を食べるだけでなく、肉も食べる My cat not only eats fish, it also eats meat.	
しか	しか+neg.	Only / Nothing... but...	私の猫は魚しか食べない My cat eats nothing but / only eats fish.	
	Inf.+しかない	To have no choice but....	今は魚を食べるしかないね Now, we have no choice but to eat fish, don't we?	
ばかり	ばかり	Only (similar to だけ)	私の猫は魚ばかり食べる My cat only eats fish.	
	ばかりでなく	Not only x, but also y... (similar to だけでなく)	私の猫は魚を食べるばかりでなく、肉も食べる My cat not only eats fish, it also eats meat.	
	～てばかりいる	To do nothing but x	私の猫は魚を食べてばかりいる My cat does nothing but eat fish.	
	Past+ばかりだ	To have just finished doing x (similar to Past + ところだ)	今、食べたばかりです I have just finished eating now.	
	ばかり	More or less / about (similar to ぐらい, L.40)	私の猫は毎日、魚を五匹ばかり食べる My cat eats about five fish every day.	
ところ	ところ	Place	ここは食べるところです This is the place to eat.	
	Inf.+ところだ	To be just about to do x	今、食べるところです I'm just about to start eating now.	
	Ger.+ところだ	To be in the process of doing x	今、食べているところです I'm eating now.	
	Past+ところだ	To have just finished doing x (similar to Past + ばかりだ)	今、食べたところです I have just finished eating now.	
せい	せい（で）	Because of...	私の猫は食べすぎたせいで、太ってしまった Because my cat ate too much, it got fat.	
おかげ	おかげ（で）	Thanks to...	私の猫は魚を食べるおかげで、とても元気だ Thanks to the fact that my cat eats fish, he's very healthy.	
わたし: I | ねこ: cat | さかな: fish | たべる: to eat | にく: meat | いま: now | まいにち: every day ひき: counter for small animals | ふとる: to fatten | げんきな: healthy				

In the theory section we have seen a great number of new expressions, some of them very easy to confuse with one another. So there is nothing better than analyzing a few manga-examples to get a clearer idea of some of these constructions.

a) *Tokoro:* however / place

Jun'ichi: ところが そこから１０キロほど離れた所にあるこの家では...
however there from 10 km. approx. separate place PP be house PP TOP
However, in this house situated about 10km from there...

From the first manga-example we can get quite a lot of information, even though you can't tell at first glance. The most obvious point to highlight is, of course, ところが. a sentence connector we have just studied in the previous page, and which has the meaning of "however," that is, it indicates an adversative relation with the previous sentence or sentences.

Something less obvious, as it is concealed in its kanji form is 所, the word meaning "place" or "spot," whose synonym is 場所. In fact, 所 and 場所 can be used equally in any sentence without any change in

J.M. Ken Niimura

nuance – notice how 所 and the second kanji in 場所 are the same, and they are only pronounced in a different way because of the 音読み and 訓読み readings (L.3).

Finally, it is worth while mentioning that the ほど in the example means exactly the same as ぐらい / くらい (L.40) and ばかり (usage #5), that is: "more or less," "about:" this excerpt could also be １０キロぐらい or １０キロばかり *(more or less 10 km.).* Bear in mind that ほど is perceived as more formal than ぐらい but less so than ばかり.

Note: The translation of the sentence in the panel we have offered has been made so that it sounds "natural" to a certain point. Perhaps a more literal translation, more in keeping with what it really says, will help you understand the meaning better. Here you are: *However, in this house that is in a place about 10km apart from there...*

b) *Tokoro* as "state"

Mina: 機関車の答におかしいところはないわ　機能はすべて完全よ
locomotive POP *answer* PP *unusual place* TOP *there is* EP *function* TOP *all perfect* EP
There's nothing unusual in the locomotive's response. All its functions are perfect.

Gabriel Luque

We continue analyzing the usages of ところ: in this case we have an instance of usage #2, that is, the usage of ところ as a verb, adjective, or noun modifier, with the meaning of "state" or "moment." In the case of 機関車の答におかしい<u>ところ</u>はない, the expression ところ is modifying the *-i* adjective おかしい *(unusual, strange)*. A more literal translation of the sentence in the example would be *In the response of the locomotive there is nothing (no state / point) unusual.*

Note: In colloquial registers, the word 所 *(place)* and the expression ところ are usually contracted into とこ, so that this sentence would become 機関車の答におかしい<u>とこ</u>はない.

c) About to

Naoya: あやうく他人の恋路をジャマするところだった！
dangerously others POP *romance* DOP *intrusion* DO *(about to) be!*
I have been about to intrude in someone else's love life!

Here we have yet another usage of ところ. Be careful with this one, because it is the easiest to confuse, since, depending on the conjugation of the verb preceding ところ, the meaning of the sentence changes.

In the example we have ジャマするところだった. The verb する is in the infinitive, which indicates it is usage #4 ("to be about to do something"). Thus, ジャマするところだった means *I was about to intrude*. If we had found ジャマしているところだった, that is, with the verb in the gerund, the sentence would have acquired the meaning of *I was in the process of intruding* (usage #3). Last of all, if we had found ジ

Studio Kōsen

ャマしたところだった, then, its meaning would have been *I had just intruded* (usage #5).

Note: As we saw in example e) in L.57, sometimes, the author takes the license of "imposing" the reading of some kanji. Here, 他人 *(another person)* is read ヒト (person, 人).

d) To have no choice but...

> **Shin'ichi:** やっぱり医者に見てもらうしかないかなァ
> *after all doctor ID see receive (nothing but) EP*
> **After all, I will have no choice but to go and have a doctor see me.**

After all these expressions of ところ, we will go on to see a different one: this time we'll look at しか ("nothing but"). In this panel we have an example of one of the variations of しか: the end-of-the-sentence expression しかない. As we saw in

やっぱり医者に見てもらうしかないかなァ

Javier Bolado

the second page of the theory section, this expression means "to have no choice but" and its usage merely consists of placing it at the end of a sentence; simple and effective.

Notes: やっぱり is the colloquial version of やはり, an adverb without direct translation and with the nuance of "I knew it," "just as I thought," although it has very different usages and its meaning changes depending on the context.

Take the opportunity as well to review the usage of the expression ～てもらう ("to receive a favor," L..45, book 2).

e) A very emphasized "only"

> **Man:** 妻にはただ山歩きに行くとだけしか言っていない
> *my wife ID TOP only mountain walk go SBP only only say*
> **I've told my wife nothing but that I was going mountain-walking.**

妻にはただ山歩きに行くとだけしか言っていない

Bárbara Raya

The expressions だけ and しか have the meaning of "only," and despite both having slightly different nuance and usage, they can be used together to give a much stronger idea of the negative concept of "only," like here: 山歩きに行くとだけしか言っていない *I have told her nothing but that I was going mountain-walking*. The word order is always だけしか, and not the other way around, and the verb must be in the negative. The sentence could be expressed neutrally (with だけ only) －山歩きに行くとだけ言っている *I have only told her that I was going mountain-walking*－, or with a negative nuance (with しか only) －山歩きに行くとしか言っていない *I've told her nothing but that I was going mountain-walking.*

f) The usage of *bakari*

> **Rena:** だって、あなた いつも織田さんのことステキってばかり言ってる
> *the thing is, you always Oda (noun suf.) POP thing adorable SBP only say*
> **The thing is you do nothing but say that Mr. Oda is adorable.**

We will now look at ばかり, an expression with lots of meanings depending on the context, as you have seen in the theory section. In this particular panel we have an instance of usage #1, a very similar usage to those of だけ and しか (meaning "only"), but with a slight nuance of "excess." 織田さんのことステキってばかり言う has the meaning of *You do nothing but say that Mr. Oda is adorable (and you say it a lot)*.

Studio Kōsen

Notes: In the colloquial register, ばかり is usually pronounced ばっかり, and there are some who even use ばかし or ばっかし. Take the opportunity to review, in L.57, the expressions "noun + のこと" (織田さんのこと) and だって ("the thing is").

g) Thanks to...

> **Daneel:** 国じゅうのロボットたちがぼくに投票してくれたおかげだ
> *country all POP robots (plural) SP I IOP vote do (favor) thanks be*
> **This is thanks to all the robots in the country voting for me.**

J.M. Ken Niimura

Here we have an example of the expression おかげ ("thanks to"). The 投票してくれたおかげだ part is then, *Thanks to them voting for me*. The opposite is せい, which has the negative meaning of "because of" and lays blame on someone or something. If we change the sentence a little into 投票してくれたせいだ, this acquires the negative nuance of *Because of them voting for me (something bad happened)*. Both expressions are very useful and easy to use.

Notes: We add 〜中 (be careful, here it is read じゅう, and not ちゅう as usual) after some words indicating time or place to give them the meaning of "throughout:" 国中 (throughout the country), 家中 (throughout the house), 一年中 (all year through), 冬中 (all winter), etc. The suffix 〜達 indicates plural after some nouns: ロボット達 (the robots), 君達 (you, in the plural), 学生達 (the students), 美穂達 (Miho and company), etc.

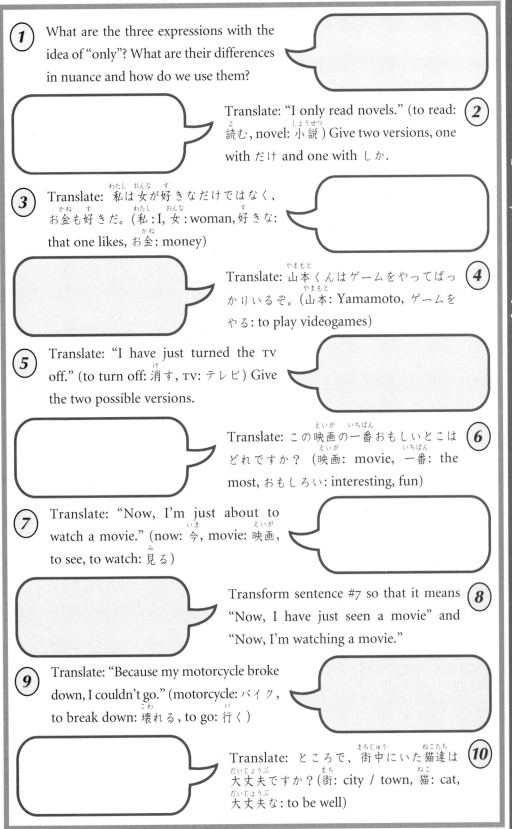

① What are the three expressions with the idea of "only"? What are their differences in nuance and how do we use them?

② Translate: "I only read novels." (to read: 読む, novel: 小説) Give two versions, one with だけ and one with しか.

③ Translate: 私は女が好きなだけではなく、お金も好きだ。(私: I, 女: woman, 好きな: that one likes, お金: money)

④ Translate: 山本くんはゲームをやってばっかりいるぞ。(山本: Yamamoto, ゲームをやる: to play videogames)

⑤ Translate: "I have just turned the TV off." (to turn off: 消す, TV: テレビ) Give the two possible versions.

⑥ Translate: この映画の一番おもしいとこはどれですか？(映画: movie, 一番: the most, おもしろい: interesting, fun)

⑦ Translate: "Now, I'm just about to watch a movie." (now: 今, movie: 映画, to see, to watch: 見る)

⑧ Transform sentence #7 so that it means "Now, I have just seen a movie" and "Now, I'm watching a movie."

⑨ Translate: "Because my motorcycle broke down, I couldn't go." (motorcycle: バイク, to break down: 壊れる, to go: 行く)

⑩ Translate: ところで、街中にいた猫達は大丈夫ですか？(街: city / town, 猫: cat, 大丈夫な: to be well)

第58課 練習 Exercises

Grammar scramble いろいろな文型 −139−

Lesson 59: Dialects and proverbs

The idea that Japanese is a uniform language and the same all over the country is wrong: there are hundreds of dialects, among which the Kansai dialect stands out the most. In this lesson we will see the characteristics of the best known dialects, as well as some proverbs.

Kansai ben

The region of 関西 ﹙かんさい﹚ —with the official name of 近畿 ﹙きんき﹚ — is, together with the region of 関東 ﹙かんとう﹚ (東京 ﹙とうきょう﹚, 横浜 ﹙よこはま﹚, 埼玉 ﹙さいたま﹚, 千葉 ﹙ちば﹚...), one of the driving forces behind the Japanese economy and society. The most important cities in 関西 ﹙かんさい﹚ are 大阪 ﹙おおさか﹚, 神戸 ﹙こうべ﹚ and 京都 ﹙きょうと﹚. A very distinct dialect called 関西弁 ﹙かんさいべん﹚ (弁 ﹙べん﹚: *dialect*) is spoken all over the region, with slight differences among cities. We will study some of 大阪弁 ﹙おおさかべん﹚ in this lesson.

● 儲 ﹙もう﹚ かりまっか？｜ぽちぽちでんなぁ *Are you making a profit?* | *Well, more or less.*

Most Japanese think that this is the "basic" sentence used in 関西 ﹙かんさい﹚ to greet people, together with its respective answer (大阪 ﹙おおさか﹚ = city of merchants). The truth is that it is not used at all nowadays, but you can use it when joking or impersonating.

Kansai dialect: vocabulary		
Kansai ben	**Standard**	**Meaning**
あほ	ばか	stupid
ええ	いい	good
おおきに	ありがとう	thank you
おもろい	おもしろい	funny
けったいな	変 ﹙へん﹚ な	odd, singular
しゃあない	しょうがない	can't be helped
しんどい	つかれる	tired
ちゃう	違 ﹙ちが﹚ う	you are wrong
なんぼ？	いくら？	how much?
べっぴん	美人 ﹙びじん﹚	beautiful woman
ほかす	捨 ﹙す﹚ てる	to throw
ほな	それじゃ	well, then...
ほんま	本当 ﹙ほんとう﹚	truth / really
まいど	こんにちは	hello / welcome
えらい	とても	very / much
ごっつい	すごく	very / much
めっちゃ	ちょう～	very / much

● 大阪弁 ﹙おおさかべん﹚ はよう分 ﹙わ﹚ からんわ！
（大阪弁 ﹙おおさかべん﹚ はよく分 ﹙わ﹚ からないぞ！）

I don't understand the Osaka dialect very well!

● 何 ﹙なん﹚ や、めっちゃ上手 ﹙じょうず﹚ やで、あんた！
（何 ﹙なん﹚ だ、とても上手 ﹙じょうず﹚ だよ、君 ﹙きみ﹚ ！）

What! You are great at it!

In the Osaka dialect we have intonation changes in sentences, some special vocabulary (take a look at the table on the left) and grammatical changes, like those specified on the table on the next page. Have fun studying some of them and surprise your friends!

The usage of や instead of the verb だ and the conjugation in the negative in ～へん or ～ん, instead of the standard ～ない, are the two most prominent features of this dialect. Besides, they use different end-of-the-sentence particles, like で instead of よ or ぞ and ねん instead of んだよ. わ has to be mentioned separately, since in standard Japanese this end-of-the-sentence particle is only used by women, whereas in 関西弁 (かんさいべん) it is also used by men with a similar meaning to the standard よ. The counterpart to the profusely used ね is な at the end of a sentence, with many different nuances, from invitation to surprise.

We will now see a sample conversation. Using the vocabulary and grammar tables we offer, try to "translate" it into standard Japanese. You will find the solution at the end of the book, together with the answers to the exercises of this L.59.

● 浩二(こうじ)はん、来(こ)られへんかった？ *Kōji couldn't come?*

● はい、ミナミの方(ほう)で仕事(しごと)があったさかい... *Yes (no), the thing is he had a job in Nanba...*

　Note: ミナミ, city / town of なんば | キタ, city / town of 梅田(うめだ). (Both in 大阪(おおさか).)

● 残念(ざんねん)やわ！ほな、ビール買(こ)うとこか？ *What a pity! Well, shall we buy some beer?*

● あかん、あかん！お酒(さけ)飲(の)めへんわ *No, no! I can't drink alcohol!*

● ほんまに？ なんでやねん？、けったいやなぁ！ *Really? Why is that? How strange!*

● コーラでええで。えらいうまいもん *I'm fine with cola. The fact is it's delicious!*

● しゃあないなぁ！ほな、おごるわ *Well, then! Come on, I'm buying.*

● おおきに！なんぼやろ、これ？ *Thanks a lot! How much will that be?*

Kansai dialect: grammatical aspects				
Standard	**Standard example**	***Kansai ben***	***Kansai ben* example**	**Translation**
だ (verb です)	行かないだろう？	や	行かへんやろう？	You're not going, are you?
～ない	大阪へ行かない	～へん ～ん	大阪へ行かへん 大阪へ行かん	I'm not going to Osaka.
んだよ	彼女はきれいんだよ	ねん	彼女はきれいやねん	She is beautiful (really).
よ/ぞ	彼女はきれいだぞ	で	彼女はきれいやで	She is beautiful (really).
~att~	車を買ったぞ!	~ō~	車を買(こ)うたで!	I bought a car!
いる	彼女、いる？	おる	彼女、おる？	Is she (here)?
～ていらっしゃる	どこへ行ってらっしゃる？	～はる	どこへ行ってはる？	Where are you going?
～てしまった	車を買ってしまった	～しもた	車を買(こ)うてしもた	I bought a car.
さん	香里さんはいない	はん	香里はんはおらん	Kaori is not (here).
から/ので	忙しいから、行かないよ	さかいに	忙しいさかいに、行かへんで	Since I'm busy, I'm not going.
だめ	これを使ってはだめだよ	あかん	これを使こうてはあかんやで	You can't use this.

いく(行): to go | かのじょ(彼女): she | きれいな: beautiful | くるま(車): car | かう(買): to buy | いそがしい(忙): busy | つかう(使): to use | かおり(香里): Kaori

Other dialects and languages

Although the 関西 (かんさい) is the most famous dialect in Japan, the truth is there are many more. Let's see a few characteristics of the best known ones.

We will use this sentence as a guide to move among them:

● 彼 (かれ) は毎日 (まいにち)、村 (むら) へ洗濯 (せんたく) に行 (い) っているよ *He goes into town every day to do the wash.*

Before we start, we will say that the samples and indications we give here are very general. There are many sub-dialects and variations within the regions themselves.

① 東北弁 (とうほくべん): Tōhoku covers the area from the north of Tokyo to the island of Hokkaidō (without including the latter). The most important cities are 仙台 (せんだい), 青森 (あおもり), 盛岡 (もりおか) and 秋田 (あきた). **Features:** The 東北弁 (とうほくべん) is the most different dialect from standard Japanese. It is characterized by the voicing of *t* and *k*, which become *d* and *g*, respectively, and by せ being pronounced as しぇ. Likewise, instead of the particles of direction へ and に (L.38) さ is used. The end-of-the-sentence particle べ is used with a similar usage to that of よ.

● 彼 (がれ) は毎日 (まいにち)、村 (むら) さ洗濯 (しぇんだく) に行 (い) ってるべ

② 愛知弁 (あいちべん): The area of Aichi is right in the middle of Japan and covers the whole region around the great industrial city of 名古屋 (なごや). **Features:** Usage of おる instead of いる (this is a characteristic which we find in all dialects to the west of Japan, from 名古屋 (なごや) to 九州 (きゅうしゅう)). All "ai," "ae" and "ei" sounds are pronounced "ya:" 帰 (かえ) る *(to return)* ⇒ 帰 (きゃえ) る. Usage of がなぁ at the end of the sentence.

● 彼 (きゃれ) は毎日 (みゃーにち)、村 (むら) へ洗濯 (せんたく) に行 (い) っておるがなぁ

③ 九州弁 (きゅうしゅうべん): The island of Kyūshū is to the far west of the main Japanese archipelago. The best known cities in Kyūshū are 福岡 (ふくおか), 長崎 (ながさき), 北九州 (きたきゅうしゅう) and 熊本 (くまもと). **Features:** Usage of おる instead of いる. Usage of な instead of the topic particle は, and of じゃ instead of だ *(to be)*. Usage of the desinence 〜ちょる instead of the gerund 〜てる.

● 彼 (かれ) な毎日 (まいにち)、村 (むら) へ洗濯 (せんたく) に行 (い) っちょるばい

④ 沖縄弁 (おきなわべん) or 沖縄語 (おきなわご): The specialists can't agree on whether what is spoken in the islands of Okinawa, to the south, almost in the tropic, is a separate language or a dialect. Some expressions: *mensooree* (hello) | *mata yassi* (goodbye) | *nifee deebiru* (thank you).

⑤ アイヌ語 (ご): The ancient settlers of Japan, the Ainu, have their own language. Nowadays, there are very few Ainu left and most of them live in Hokkaidō. Some expressions: *irankarapte* (hello) | *pirkano paye yan* (goodbye) | *iyayraykere* (thank you).

Proverbs

Like in any other language, in Japanese there are proverbs and sayings (ことわざ, or in kanji, 諺) that have been transmitted orally from one generation to another, since time immemorial. Many of them come from Ancient China or from the Buddhist scriptures.

In this page you have a small list with the ten sayings that, in our opinion, are most often used. The truth is that, nowadays, very few people use proverbs, but if they do, there is a high probability that you will find them in the table below. As you can see, we offer a literal translation and a more natural translation of each one of them. An example of usage:

● 娘さんも医者になりたいそうですね... *Apparently, your daughter wants to be a doctor too...*
● そうよ。カエルの子はカエルだもんね *That's right. "Like mother, like daughter."*

On the other hand, there are types of sayings that always consist of four characters (hence their name: 四字熟語, *words formed with four characters*), the majority of which were borrowed from China many centuries ago. Some have a literal meaning, such as 東西南北 (*east-west-south-north = in all directions*), but many are far from obvious. In the table you have the ten most frequent 四字熟語. An example of usage:

● 臼井さんはチョコレートが嫌いって！ *Mr. Usui says that he doesn't like chocolate!*
● ま、十人十色だよね *Well, "so many men, so many minds."*

ことわざ (諺) Proverbs		四字熟語 *Yoji-jukugo*	
猿も木から落ちる	Even monkeys fall from trees (Nobody is perfect)	一石二鳥	One stone, two birds (To kill two birds with one stone)
カエルの子はカエル	The frog's child is a frog (Like father, like son)	弱肉強食	Weak meat is food for the strong (The law of the jungle)
花より団子	Dumplings rather than blossoms (Bread is better than the songs of birds)	自業自得	One does, one earns (One reaps what one sows)
後の祭り	The festival after (The doctor after death)	自由自在	Freedom-freedom (With perfect freedom)
ウソも方便	A lie is also expedient (Pious fraud / White lie)	日常茶飯	Every day, tea and rice (An everyday affair)
郷に入っては郷に従え	When you enter a village, obey the village (When in Rome, do as the Romans do)	十人十色	Ten people, ten colors (So many men, so many minds)
出る釘は打たれる	The nail that sticks out gets hammered (A tall tree catches much wind)	一期一会	One's lifetime, one meeting (A chance in a lifetime)
仏の顔も三度まで	Buddha (gets mad if you touch) his face 3 times (There are limits to one's endurance)	花鳥風月	Flower, bird, wind, moon (The beauties of nature)
鬼のいぬ間に洗濯	To do the laundry while the ogre is out (When the cat's away, the mice will play)	順風満帆	Favorable wind, full sail (Smooth sailing)
能ある鷹は爪を隠す	The clever hawk hides its talons (He who knows most, speaks least)	天下無双	No twin under the heavens (Unique in the world)

文化編：武士の言葉
Cultural note: The language of the samurai

All languages in the world evolve and, of course, 日本語 (にほんご) is not an exception: in fact, the Japanese language has evolved at a frenzied pace, proof of which lies in literature. The language has changed so much since the 平安 (へいあん) period (794-1192), when the ひらがな and カタカナ syllabaries were invented, that there are many (and thick) 古語辞典 (こごじてん) *ancient language dictionaries.*

There are several curious things about ancient Japanese: for example, there were two kana which are not used nowadays: ゐ (hiragana) | ヰ (katakana), romanized *wi*, but pronounced "*i*," and ゑ (hiragana) | ヱ (katakana), romanized *we*, but pronounced "*e*." Other changes are that は was read "*wa*" (hence the present pronunciation of the topic particle は (wa)), ひ was read "*i*," and を was not only used as direct object particle, but also in words such as をとこ (男 (おとこ), *man*).

The castle of Matsumoto, great sample of samurai architecture (Photo: M. Bernabé)

The type of archaic Japanese you will mostly come across, especially when reading books / マンガ or watching movies / TV series set in the 江戸 (えど) period (1603-1867), will be the dialect used by the 武士 (ぶし), usually called 侍 (さむらい). Although the dialect of the ancient 武士 (ぶし) is not radically different from present-day Japanese, you will find some aspects that will surprise or perplex you, such as:

● Usage of first person pronouns *(I)* such as 拙者 (せっしゃ), 某 (それがし) or 我 (われ).
● Usage of the verbs なり and, especially, でござる instead of です.
● Extensive usage of the honorific suffixes 〜様 and 〜殿 (どの) (Ex: 徳川殿 (とくがわどの) Lord Tokugawa).
● Today's negative 〜ない was 〜ぬ (Ex: 行かない (い) *not to go* ⇒ 行かぬ (い)). Today's negative *-te* form 〜ないで used to link sentences was 〜ず (Ex: 行かないで (い) ⇒ 行かず (い)), etc.

An example: 拙者は忍びの者でござる (せっしゃ・しの・もの) *I am a fellow of stealth* (I'm a 忍者 (にんじゃ)).

Finally, some numbers were also written in a different way, like, for instance, to name the most relatively common, 壱 (いち) *(1)*, 弐 (に) *(2)*, 参 (さん) *(3)*, 伍 (ご) *(5)*, 拾 (じゅう) *(10)*. And they are still sometimes used... Take a look at the 10,000 yen note: it says 壱万円 (いちまんえん)!

漫画例 Manga-examples

We hope this curious lesson has helped you better understand the diversity of Japanese dialects and break the image you might have had of a "homogenous language." It is important to understand this, that way you can form a broader idea of what this language constitutes.

a) The Kansai dialect

Sakie: もー今からぜったい間食せえへんで！ぜったいやせたるんや
(excl.) now from swear snack do EP! swear lose weight be
Grrr! From now on, no more snacks! I'll positively lose weight!

Jirō: 何で関西弁になるの？
why Kansai dialect become Q?
Why are you speaking in the Kansai dialect?

J.M. Ken Niimura

We start with an example of someone talking in a dialect of Kansai: the Osaka dialect (大阪弁), to be precise. Take a look at the typical constructions of this dialect: the negative ～へん (せえへん ＝ しない), the emphatic particle で, or the や instead of だ. やせたる is a typical contraction in 大阪弁 of やせてやる (L.53). This sentence, "translated" into standard Japanese, would be 今からぜったい間食しないよ！ぜったいやせてやるんだ！ The 大阪弁 is usually used to characterize merchants, yakuza, and comedians. Why these characters? First of all, Osaka has been known for ages as a city of merchants, where earning money always comes first (hence the greeting 儲かりまっか？ studied in the first page of the theory section). Besides, the area of ミナミ is, so the cliché goes, swarming with yakuza and other organized criminals. Last of all, Osaka is the capital of 漫才, a kind of comedy performance very popular in Japan. All these clichés are exploited in novels, comic books, movies, and TV series. Therefore, curiously enough, you must master some of 大阪弁 to enjoy 100 % of all this!

b) Doing business in *Kansai ben*

> **Man:** あかん あかん シバではそんな高(たか)いもん必要(ひつよう)おまへんわ！
> *no no Shiba PP TOP as that expensive thing need there is EP!*
> **No way! No! In Shiba we don't need anything as expensive as that!**

あかん
あかん
シバでは
そんな
高いもん
必要
おまへん
わ！

Gabriel Luque

Another panel with an instance of Osaka dialect. Whereas in example a) the cliché of the comical aspect of this dialect was exploited, in this example it is the "commercial" or even "criminal" aspect which we can see. The man who is talking is the president of Shiba, a company with murky business with the local mafia. As you can see, the clichés of 大阪弁(おおさかべん) (business, mafia, and comedy) are truly exploited. However, if you go to Kansai you will realize people talk in 関西弁(かんさいべん) and, obviously, they are not all necessarily comedians, yakuza or merchants.

In this sentence you can see the word あかん (だめ in standard Japanese), the negative in 〜へん (おまへん is the equivalent to ない, the negative of ある), and the emphatic particle わ, which is used without distinction by men and women in Kansai.

c) The dialect of Kyoto

> **Ai:** 今(いま)私(わたし)が好(す)きなのは島(しま)さんしかいてしまへん これも真実(しんじつ)どす
> *now I SP like (nom) TOP Shima only there is this too truth be*
> **Now I like nobody but Mr. Shima. This is also true.**

We have said in the theory section that within a dialect there can be many variations and, therefore, it is difficult to define a "dialectal standard." For example, within 関西弁(かんさいべん) we have 大阪弁(おおさかべん), which we have studied quite in depth, 京都弁(きょうとべん),

今私が好き
なのは島さん
しかいてしまへん
これも真実どす

Studio Kōsen

神戸弁(こうべべん), etc. All these 関西弁(かんさいべん) sub-dialects are very similar, but they also have differences, quite marked sometimes. This example shows us a woman speaking in 京都弁(きょうとべん). As you can see, she uses the negative in 〜へん, a feature you find all over Kansai, although in Kyoto 〜ひん is sometimes used. Notice, too, the どす, the equivalent to the verb です. Generally, 京都弁(きょうとべん) is perceived as soft and melodic. The most typical phrase in this sub-dialect is おいでやす (*welcome*).

d) Does the Hokkaidō dialect exist?

> **Kimie:** 「シンちゃんのこっこがほしいべぇ...」
> *"Shin (noun suf.) POP egg SP want EP..."*
> **"I want a child by Shin..."**

Studio Kōsen

If in the Tōhoku region they speak a dialect so different from the standard language that the Japanese themselves have trouble understanding it, you will probably wonder what is spoken further north, on the island of 北海道. This is a very special case: the region was practically ignored until the beginning of the 明治 era (1868-1912), when the repopulation of the island started. Most settlers came from the 関東 area (Tokyo and its surroundings), and, so, the language spoken in Hokkaidō nowadays is very similar to standard Japanese. However, over the years, influences of the 東北弁 have permeated into 北海道弁, like the usage of the emphatic particle べ, or some words like こっこ (*egg / child*) or めんこい (*handsome / beautiful*).

e) A proverb

> **Shun:** それから『子供は親のこかんを見て育つ』ともいいますぞ
> *besides "child TOP father POP crotch DOP look grow up" SBP too say EP*
> **Besides, they say "children grow up seeing their parents' crotch."**

Bárbara Raya

> **Chieko:** 親の背中！
> *father POP back!*
> **Their parents' back!**

It is very easy to get mixed up with proverbs, as we can see in this funny example, where only one of the words in the proverb is changed. The saying goes 子供は親の背中を見て育つ, literally *Children grow up seeing their parents back*. It means that children are influenced by whatever their parents do or say and, even without being taught, they learn and copy their acts and words. The saying has negative nuances and is used to warn parents that what they are doing can be copied by their children, with negative consequences in their education. Here, the kid (deliberately?) changes the word 背中 (*back*) for 股間 (*crotch*)... No comment.

f) A *yoji-jukugo* proverb

Midori: あたし、若い女性ってほどでもありませんから　海千山千ですから

I, young woman say not so much be as sea-1000-mountain-1000 be because

I'm not what you would call a young woman. I'm a sly old fox.

Gabriel Luque

Here we have an example of the usage of 四字熟語, a kind of compact proverb with four kanji giving it a very specific and concentrated meaning.

In this manga-example we have 海千山千, literally *sea-thousand-mountain-thousand*. Apparently, this comes from a popular Chinese saying that goes "a snake who lives a thousand years in the sea and a thousand years in the mountain ends up becoming a dragon." 海千山千 is used, then, to designate someone with a lot of experience and wisdom, hardened in all aspects of life; in English we would say a "sly old dog" or a "sly old fox."

Note: Notice the usage of "ほど + neg.," the negative comparative we studied in L.54 with the meaning of "not as... as."

g) The language of the samurai

Maruo: 拙者は今も昔も変わらないでござるよ

I TOP now too before too change be EP

I haven't changed, I'm the same now as in the past.

We will conclude this lesson with an example of the language of the ancient samurai. Take a look at the panel and you will see how the speaker uses the first person pronoun 拙者 and the verb でござる (equiva-

Javier Bolado

lent to the modern です), two very typical and stereotyped characteristics of what was supposed to be the warriors' ancient dialect. The other social classes in the ancient feudal system of the 士農工商 (*warriors-farmers-artisans-tradesmen*, by order of importance) could not speak with these typical speech patterns of the samurai class, nor could they carry swords. We say that the usage of 拙者 and でござる is "stereotyped" because there is a tendency to characterize warriors with them in works of fiction. The samurai dialect was actually much more complex, but it is now simplified to make its comprehension easier.

1 What is 関西弁 and in which region is it used? What are the main sub-dialects in 関西弁?

2 What is the set answer to the greeting 儲かりまっか? What clichés are there about 大阪弁?

3 Translate into standard Japanese and into English: しんどい仕事はえらい嫌やなぁ。(仕事: work, 嫌: to dislike)

4 Translate into standard Japanese and English: キタは人がごっつい多いさかいに、歩けへんで。(人: people, 多い: many, 歩く: to walk)

5 Transform this sentence into 大阪弁: 光彦さんがまだいないので、行ってはだめだよ。(光彦: Teruhiko, まだ: still, 行く: to go)

6 To what dialect does this sentence belong? 開会式はまだ始まっておらんがなぁ。(開会式: opening ceremony, 始まる: to start)

7 What does the following proverb mean? 郷に入っては郷に従え

8 What is a 四字熟語? What does the expression 一石二鳥 mean?

9 Translate this into modern Japanese and English: 某は織田殿のところへ行かぬでござる。(織田: Oda, ところ: place, 行く: to go)

10 Does 北海道弁 exist? If so, could you name its main characteristics?

Lesson 60: The passive and causative forms

Welcome to the last lesson in the book! We are going to end the course taking a look at two of the most complicated constructions in Japanese: the frequently used passive and causative sentences.

The passive

We imagine you already know what the passive is, but in order to refresh your memory, we will mention it is a conjugation used to form sentences from the point of view of the recipient of the action. That is, the subject receives the action of the agent, taking no part in performing the action at all. In the sentence *Paul was fired by the president*, we are showing the action from the point of view of "Paul" (the subject), even though he doesn't take part directly in the "firing" process. The person performing the action of "firing" is "the president" (the agent). In Japanese, we have an almost identical kind of verbal conjugation: the form known as direct passive. The formation of passive sentences in Japanese depends on a special verb conjugation (see table) and on some changes in the grammatical particles.

Conjugations. <u>Group 1</u>: The last る is replaced by られる. 見る *(to see)* ⇒ 見られる *(to be seen)*. <u>Group 2</u>: The last *-u* is replaced by *-a*, and we add れる. 抱く *(to embrace)* ⇒ 抱かれる *(to be embraced)*. <u>Group 3</u>: Since they are irregular, you must learn them by heart.

When we study the passive form in English, we usually do the exercise of transforming a normal sentence into a passive one. **Example:** *The woman scolded Meg ⇒ Meg was scolded by the woman.* We will do the same in Japanese so that you can understand how it works:

● あの女性はメッグをしかった *That woman scolded Meg.*
● メッグはあの女性にしかられた *Meg was scolded by that woman.*

As you can see, the process is similar to English, in the way that both place the recipient of the action as the subject. Thus, Meg (the direct object marked with を in the normal sentence), becomes the topic of the passive sentence and is marked with は. The agent (performing the action) is almost always marked with the particle に.

- 警察は老人に棒で叩かれた *The policeman was hit with a stick by the old man.*
- 洋子ちゃんは彼氏にとても愛されている *Yōko is much loved by her boyfriend.*

Passive sentences without a specific agent (like in the sentence *This building was built fifty years ago*) also exist in Japanese:

- このビルは５０年前に造られました *This building was built fifty years ago.*
- この間、あの犯人は投獄された *The other day, that criminal was incarcerated.*

Finally, the construction によって is used instead of the particle に in passive sentences of a "historical" kind, sentences where the action of somebody important is described.

- 「源氏物語」は紫式部によって書かれた *"The Tale of Genji" was written by Murasaki Shikibu.*
- アメリカはコロンブスによって発見された *America was discovered by Columbus.*

"Victim" passive

In Japanese there is a very particular usage of the passive form: sometimes it describes an action that affects the subject and is performed by someone else. Almost always the effect is negative, that is why these kind of passive sentences are called "victim passive sentences." Take a look at the sentence in the following page.

	Simple f.	Mening	Passive	Causative	Causative-passive
Group 1 Invariable	教える	to teach	教えられる	教えさせる	教えさせられる
	起きる	to wake up	見られる	見させる	見させられる
Group 2 Variable	貸す	to lend	貸される	貸させる	貸させられる
	待つ	to wait	待たれる	待たせる	待たせられる
	買う	to buy	買われる	買わせる	買わせられる
	帰る	to return	帰られる	帰らせる	帰らせられる
	書く	to write	書かれる	書かせる	書かせられる
	急ぐ	to hurry	急がれる	急がせる	急がせられる
	遊ぶ	to play	遊ばれる	遊ばせる	遊ばせられる
	飲む	to drink	飲まれる	飲ませる	飲ませられる
	死ぬ	to die	死なれる	死なせる	死なせられる
Group 3 Irregular	する	to do	される	させる	させられる
	来る	to come	来られる	来させる	来させられる

The passive and causative forms 受身と使役 −151−

● 私は兄にコーラを飲まれた *(Lit: I had my cola drank by my elder brother).*

My elder brother drank (my) cola (and I didn't like that at all).

Here, the passive indicates that the fact that my brother drinks the cola (which is supposedly mine, or at least I consider it mine) affects me in a negative way.

In Japanese, there is a strong tendency to profusely use these kind of sentences, so it is essential that you learn to recognize and form them.

● （私は）隣の人にタバコを吸われたよ *The person next to me smoked (and I don't like it).*

● （私は）娘に秘密を知られた *My daughter found out about my secret (and I wasn't at all pleased).*

● ライバルチームにリーグを優勝された *The rival team won the league (and I don't like that).*

● 百合子は犬に死なれそうだよ *Yuriko's dog is about to die.*

Lastly, we'd like to point out that, in the case of the verbs in Group 1, the passive conjugation is identical to the potential (L.32) and to the conjugation in the formal language *sonkeigo* (L.52). Most times, we can infer from the context what kind of sentence it is, but very seldom it will be difficult. Have a look:

● 社長は窓を閉められた This sentence can be potential *(The president could close the window)*, respectful *(The president closed the window)*, or victim passive *(Someone closed the window (and the president didn't like that)).*

The causative

The causative is a feature which has no equivalent in English, and is used to indicate the action of "making" someone do something or "letting" someone do something.

Conjugations. <u>Group 1</u>: The last る is replaced by させる. 見る *(to see)* ⇒ 見させる *(to let / make see).* <u>Group 2</u>: The last *-u* is replaced by *-a*, and we add せる. 抱く *(to embrace)* ⇒ 抱かせる (to let / make embrace). <u>Group 3</u>: You must learn these verbs by heart.

When using the causative to indicate "permission," the particle に is usually used to mark the one receiving permission.

● お母さんは子どもにプールへ行かせた *The mother let the boy go to the pool.*

● 徹は犬に公園でいっぱい走らせた *Tōru let his dog run a lot in the park.*

On the other hand, if it is a sentence of "obligation," the particle を is usually used to mark the person being forced to perform the action.

● 先生は学生達を走らせた *The teacher made the students run.*

● 母は私をむりやりに勉強させた *My mother made me study.*

However, when the verb is transitive and the sentence has a direct object marked with を, we will use に for the person who is forced or allowed to do something: thus we avoid having two を in the sentence. In these cases, sentences are ambiguous and their meaning must be inferred from the context.

- ベロニカは弟にケーキを食べさせた *Veronica let my brother eat the cake.*
- 母は私にお風呂の掃除をさせた *My mother made me clean the bath.*
- 私は森さんにCDを聞かせた *I let / made Mr. Mori listen to the CD.*
- 社長は社員に酒を飲ませた *The president let / made his employees drink sake.*

As you can realize, whether it is an obligation or a permission sentence is quite clear in the first two sentences, whereas the two latter are ambiguous, and their meanings must be inferred from the context. **Note:** When an object or an inanimate being takes part in the sentence, を must always be used.

- 僕は車を愛媛まで走らせた *I made the car run up to Ehime / I drove the car up to Ehime.*
- 彼は飲み物を冷やさせた *He let (made) the drinks get cold / He chilled the drinks.*

The causative form has another curious usage, which consists of combining this form with 〜てください or 〜ていただく, to form sentences such as "let me do x" and "you let me do x," especially common in formal contexts.

- この映画を見させてくださいよ *Let me watch that movie, please.*
- この会社を辞めさせていただきたいです

Lit: *I want to be allowed to leave this company. | I want to leave this company.*

The causative-passive

And now we'll see an even more complex form called the causative-passive, which is used to indicate the idea of "being forced to do something (that one doesn't like)." That is, the causative is combined with the victim passive.

Conjugations. Using the causative form of a verb of any group, the last る is replaced by られる. 抱く *(to embrace)* ⇒ 抱かせる *(to let / make embrace)* ⇒ 抱かせられる *(to be made to embrace)*. Take a look at these sentences:

- 学生達は先生に走らせられた *The students were forced to run by the teacher.*
- 私は母にお風呂の掃除をさせられた *I was forced to clean the bath by my mother.*
- 僕は会社を辞めさせられた *I was forced to leave the company (I was fired).*
- 彼は彼女に告白させられそうだ *He seems to feel forced to declare his love to her.*

Important: Notice how these causative-passive sentences only have the connotation of "obligation," never that of "permission" which they had in plain causative sentences. Fortunately, these kind of sentences are not excessively frequent in everyday life, although you may come across them every now and then, so you must watch out.

Other constructions

We will make use of the last portion of this lesson to top off everything you've learned in the book with three new expressions that haven't appeared until now. They are について, ずつ and こそ.

について: This expression is the Japanese version of our "about" or "concerning." It is extremely easy to use and, needless to say, very useful in any context or situation. It is worth while remembering.

● 日本の歴史について話してください *Talk about Japanese history, please.*
● あの男について何かが分かりますか？ *Do you know anything about that man?*
● 禅について書くことが大好きです *I love writing about Zen Buddhism.*
● 彼について言えば、とても親切な人です *Concerning him, I'll say he is a very kind person.*

ずつ: This expression is used to indicate that something is distributed in an equal way (in English, it would be similar to "each" or "x by y"). ずつ can only go after counters (L.25) and some adverbs. Take a look at the examples and you will get a clearer idea:

● オレンジを２個ずつ食べてください *Eat two oranges each, please.*
● 各家にパソコンが１台ずつあればいいのに *It'd be nice if there was a computer in every house.*
● 漢字を毎日六つずつ覚えることにした *I decided to memorize six kanji a day.*
● 俳句が少しずつ上手になってきた *Little by little I have improved in (the composition of) haiku.*

こそ: This expression is quite common in written and spoken Japanese, and is used to emphasize the word preceding it. There is no exact translation in English, so take a look at the example sentences to understand how it works.

● 真理子はきれいだね｜違う、公江こそきれいだよ

Mariko is beautiful, isn't she?｜No, Kimie is the one who is beautiful.

● 今年こそ東大に入るぞ! *This year indeed I'll enter the University of Tokyo!*
● 今度こそダイエットしてやせるぞ！*I do swear next time, for sure, I'll go on a diet!*

● どうもありがとうございました｜いいえ、こちらこそ

Thank you very much.｜No, I'm the one (to thank you).

漫画例　Manga-examples

The passive, causative, and causative-passive conjugations are very easy to confuse due to their similarity, as you have probably realized. But don't worry, with practice, you will get used to them. Let's now see a few examples (the last in the book!) to clarify ideas.

a) Victim passive

> **Yama:** ちょうどトイレに行ったら自分の名前が歌われてビックリしましたよ
> *just toilet DP go (cond.) I POP name SP sing surprise do EP*
> **When I went to the toilet, I heard my name being sung and I was surprised.**

We start with an example of one of the so called victim passive sentences, a very particular usage of the Japanese passive that you will find quite often. The part we will take into consideration is 自分の名前が歌われる *(my name is being sung)*. 歌われる is the passive form of the verb 歌う, *to sing*. Remember the rule for the conjugation of verbs in group 2: The last *-u* is replaced with *-a*, and we add れる. With verbs ending in

Studio Kōsen

-u, the conjugation is somewhat special, because, for example, the passive form of 歌う is not 歌あれる, but 歌われる. The same happens with other verbs ending in *-u*, like 買う *(to buy)* ⇒ 買われる *(to be bought)*. The so called "victim" passive is used to indicate an action performed by someone else which affects (negatively most of the time, hence its name "victim") the subject in the sentence. 自分の名前が歌われる, then, would literally mean *my name is sung (and this affects me)*. In this specific case, we can't say the effect is a negative one, although the usage of ビックリする *(to be surprised)* right after, denotes that the fact of hearing his name "being sung" has affected the speaker.

Note: Notice the usage of the conditional 〜たら in トイレに行ったら *(when I went to the toilet...)*. It is usage #5 on L.56: to learn or discover something as a result of a certain action ("when," "as a result of," "after").

The passive and causative forms 受身と使役 −155−

b) The passive

> **Yoshiko:** ワタシはこんな男に殺されたりしないわ
> *I TOP this kind of man SBP kill or something do EP*
> **A man like him won't kill me.**

In this panel we have an instance of a "normal" passive sentence, where a subject (ワタシ, *I*) receives the action (殺す, *to kill*) from an agent (こんな男, *a man like this*) without taking part in it. The usage of grammatical particles is interesting to see: the passive subject is marked with the topic particle は or the subject particle が, while the agent is followed by に. The literal translation of this sentence would be *I won't be*

J.M. Ken Niimura

killed by a man like this, although we propose a more natural translation in English: *A man like him won't kill me.*

Note: Notice the usage of 〜たり, used to make non-exhaustive lists of actions (L.46). 殺されたりしない literally means *I won't be killed (or anything like that).*

c) The causative: obligation

> **Sally:** かっこよく爆発させようぜ
> *nice big explosion do EP*
> **Let's blow it to smithereens!**

Let's see an example of the causative (used to give the idea of "making" or "letting" do something). Here, the verb is 爆発する, a *suru* verb that means "to explode." Since する is an irregular verb, we must learn the conjugation by heart: The causative form of する is させる.

Thus, we have 爆発させる *(to make explode)*, here conjugated in the -ō form (爆発させよう, L.34), which gives the idea of "let's make it explode." Although the sentence doesn't show who or what is receiving the obligation, we will imagine it is a 戦車 *(tank)* that, being an inanimate object, must be marked with を, as we have seen in the theory pages. Therefore, we would have 戦車を爆発させよう *Let's make the tank explode.*

d) The causative: permission

> **Kishida:** もうこれ以上犠牲者は出させない！
> *any more this more victim TOP take out!*
> **I won't allow there to be any more victims!**

Javier Bolado

While in the previous panel we saw the causative of "obligation" (the tank is made to explode), we now have an instance of the causative of "permission." The verb here is 出す, a transitive verb (L.44) that means "to take out." The causative form is, then, 出させる (to let take out). 犠牲者を出す has the meaning of "causing victims," therefore 犠牲者を出させない would lite-rally be, *not to allow to cause victims.* In this case, there is no agent specified but, if there was one, it would be introduced with に, because there can't be two を in the sentence. An example: ジョンに犠牲者を出させない (*Not to allow John to cause victims*).

e) Causative + *morau*

> **Kumasaka:** 第一外科の熊坂俊介だ
> *num. 1 surgery POP Kumasaka Shunsuke be*
> **I'm Shunsuke Kumasaka, from the first section of surgery.**
> 君達2人の指導医をやらせてもらう事になっている
> *you 2 POP supervisor doctor DOP do receive (it has been decided)*
> **I have been appointed as the medical supervisor for both of you.**

We can find, especially in formal contexts, a com-bination of the causative with the 〜ていただく or 〜てもらう constructions (L.45). In this case, やらせてもらう comes from やる *(to do)*, which is con-jugated in the causative form (やらせる), which in its turn is conjugated in the *-te* form (やらせて) to be allowed to link to もらう. The literal transla-tion of やらせてもらう would be *To receive the favor of being allowed to do.* This form, like in the sentence 日光へ行かせていただきたいのです (*I*

Bárbara Raya

would like to be allowed to go to Nikkō | I want to go to Nikkō), is used to make sentences of request or action that sound humble and indirect at the same time.

f) The causative-passive

> **Jack:** やあ伊東先生 あなたは病院をやめさせられたんですってね
> *hey Itō-professor you TOP hospital DOP abandon be say EP*
> **Hi, Dr. Itō. I've been told that you have been forced to leave the hospital...**

Javier Bolado

One of the most difficult forms to conjugate without getting mixed up is the causative-passive. In the example we have やめさせられた, which comes from the verb 辞める *(to leave a job)*. To obtain a causative-passive form, we must first conjugate a verb in the causative and then in the passive. It sounds complex, but you'll understand better with an example: 辞める *(to leave a job)* ⇒ 辞めさせる (causative, *to force to leave*) ⇒ 辞めさせられる (causative-passive, *to be forced to leave*). For clarity, notice the difference between the following sentences: 信夫は千草にお酒を飲ませた *Nobuo made / let Chigusa drink sake* | 信夫は千草にお酒を飲まれた *Nobuo had his sake drunk by Chigusa = Chigusa drank Nobuo's sake (and Nobuo didn't like that)* | 信夫は千草にお酒を飲ませられた *Nobuo was forced by Chigusa to drink sake.*

g) The usage of *koso*

> **Emika:** 今こそあなたのラジコンがかつやくするときよ
> *now yes you POP radiocon SP activity do moment EP*
> **Now is indeed the moment to get your models to perform.**

And we finally arrive at the last example in the lesson and, by extension, in the course. Here we see an example of the usage of こそ, an adverb used to emphasize the word preceding it. In this case, 今こそ has the meaning of "now is indeed..." An example: Imagine you are on a diet, and you can't eat chocolate. You finally reach your ideal weight: this is the moment to say 今こそチョコレートが食べられるぞ! *Now, indeed, I can eat chocolate!*

Gabriel Luque

Notes: ラジコン is the contraction of ラジオコントロール, that is, "device controlled by radio," although the word in Japanese designates "radio-controlled toys." 活躍する is a difficult verb to translate: we could say it indicates "to be active," "to take active part in."

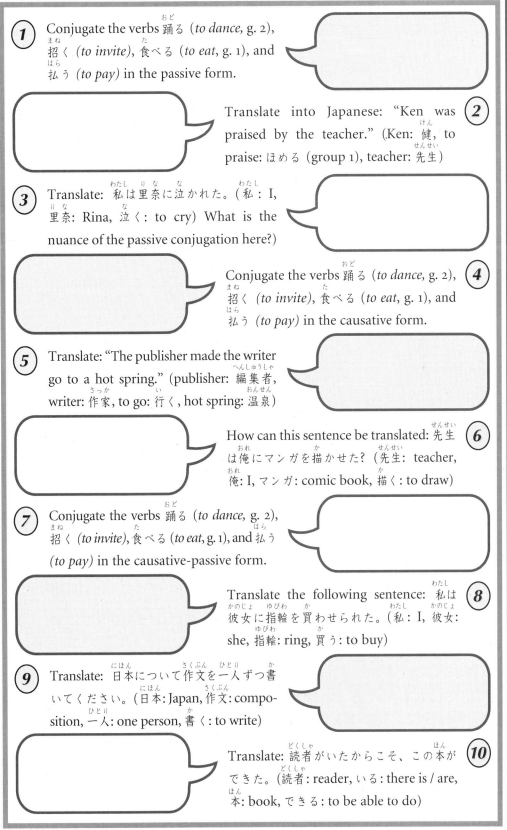

1. Conjugate the verbs 踊る (*to dance*, g. 2), 招く (*to invite*), 食べる (*to eat*, g. 1), and 払う (*to pay*) in the passive form.

2. Translate into Japanese: "Ken was praised by the teacher." (Ken: 健, to praise: ほめる (group 1), teacher: 先生)

3. Translate: 私は里奈に泣かれた。(私: I, 里奈: Rina, 泣く: to cry) What is the nuance of the passive conjugation here?)

4. Conjugate the verbs 踊る (*to dance*, g. 2), 招く (*to invite*), 食べる (*to eat*, g. 1), and 払う (*to pay*) in the causative form.

5. Translate: "The publisher made the writer go to a hot spring." (publisher: 編集者, writer: 作家, to go: 行く, hot spring: 温泉)

6. How can this sentence be translated: 先生は俺にマンガを描かせた? (先生: teacher, 俺: I, マンガ: comic book, 描く: to draw)

7. Conjugate the verbs 踊る (*to dance*, g. 2), 招く (*to invite*), 食べる (*to eat*, g. 1), and 払う (*to pay*) in the causative-passive form.

8. Translate the following sentence: 私は彼女に指輪を買わせられた。(私: I, 彼女: she, 指輪: ring, 買う: to buy)

9. Translate: 日本について作文を一人ずつ書いてください。(日本: Japan, 作文: composition, 一人: one person, 書く: to write)

10. Translate: 読者がいたからこそ、この本ができた。(読者: reader, いる: there is / are, 本: book, できる: to be able to do)

APPENDIXES

Answers to the exercises
Grammar index
Vocabulary index

第一 付録：解答

Appendix I: Answers to the exercises

In this first appendix you will find the answers to the exercises in each of the 15 lessons that constitute this book, arranged according to lesson and question number.

How to use this appendix

At the end of each lesson, small exercises have been provided with the aim of improving your overall comprehension of the subjects dealt within those lessons. The exercises also offer the tools you need to acquire practice in forming sentences in Japanese and they stimulate you to study the grammar points covered in the lessons in greater depth.

This book is designed for autodidactic study, which means you are meant to learn without the help of a teacher (although it is always much better if you do have one, of course). To make things as easy as possible, we enclose this appendix with the answers to the exercises.

In this appendix you will find suggestions for possible answers to the exercises that have been given, but we must mention that some exercises have more than one correct answer. Whenever possible, we have tried to provide all possible variations, although sometimes you might come upon with an option which is not listed in this appendix, though it may be perfectly valid. Therefore, we encourage you to use the suggested answers in this appendix as an approximate guide more than as a set of unbreakable rules etched in stone.

It goes without saying that the idea is to first do the exercises (looking up the theory explanations whenever you need to) and then to check this section to see whether your answers are right, or if, on the contrary, you have made some mistakes. Now remember to be fair to yourself by not checking this section before you have done the exercises, for, as we all know, when cheating, we only cheat ourselves.

Lesson 46

1- 浴衣を着て外に出ていきたい

2- 浴衣を着ないで外に出て行きたい | 浴衣を着ずに外に出ていきたい

3- この本は厚くなくて軽いです

4- In the first one (ビールを飲みながら踊ろう) the central action is dancing, that is, it would be translated as *Let's dance while we drink beer*, whereas in the second one (踊りながらビールを飲もう) the central action is drinking, that is *Let's drink beer while we dance.*

5- *I / he / she fell asleep with the air conditioning on.*

6- この夏は泳いだり、歩いたり、休んだりしました

7- この夏は泳いだし、歩いた

8- ところで、お茶でも飲みに行こうか？

9- 辛い⇒辛さ | 大切な⇒大切さ | 元気な⇒元気さ | 白い⇒白さ

10- 今はフラメンコを踊っている場合じゃない！

Lesson 47

1- 夕ご飯: dinner | 熱い: hot | ゆでる: to boil | 甘い: sweet | 焼く: to fry | 炒める: to stir-fry

2- Chocolate: チョコレート | water: 水 | cabbage: キャベツ | tomato: トマト | prawn / shrimp: えび | omelette: オムレツ

3- 焼きそば: *soba* noodles fried with a special sauce, vegetables and meat | おにぎり: stuffed rice balls (the stuffing can be tuna, salmon, *umeboshi, konbu*...) | 親子丼: bowl of rice with chiken and egg | 天ぷら: deep fried battered vegetables and fish.

4- You can use any of the following: あんこ, 大根, 大豆, だし, ごま, 白菜, かつおぶし, 昆布, みりん, 味噌, のり, 蓮根, しいたけ, 醤油, 竹の子, 梅干, わかめ or わさび. You will find their descriptions on the 5th page of L.47.

5- すみませんが、玉ねぎを2個と蓮根を一本ください

6- Any of the drinks specified in the sub table "Drinks" in page 25 plus 〜をお願いします or 〜をください (Ex: コーラをください / コーラをお願いします)

7- 天ぷら定食をお願いします

8- It is the way shop clerks greet customers when they come into the shop. It is used in restaurants, shops, and all sort of businesses. The customer doesn't need to answer anything when the shop clerk greets him or her with いらっしゃいませ.

9- 握り寿司 and 巻き寿司. They are called this way because, in the first kind, the fish is pressed directly on a small rice base (握る means "to clasp"), and in the second kind, the fish is in the center of a roll of rice wrapped in *nori* seaweed (巻く means "to roll").

10- The dish of Chinese origin called チャーハン (炒飯 in kanji), or "Three-variety fried rice" in English, costs 350 yen in the example.

Lesson 48

1- 彼が好きだから（付き合っている）

2- のどがかわいているので、水を飲みます｜のどがかわいているから、水を飲みます

3- *Because I have fallen in love with Masao, (we two) let's split (up).*

4- ラ・バンバを踊るため（に）、少しの優雅さが必要だ

5- *When I was hospitalized, I picked up the nurse(s) / hit on the nurse(s).*

6- *Eat your food while it's still warm.*

7- 寝る前にキスしてください

8- タイに行った。そして、ベトナムにも行った

9- Sometimes だから is used at the beginning of the sentence to show annoyance or insistence on a certain subject.

10- It comes from the expression それでは *(now / well then)*. It is actually used with the meaning of "see you later" when saying goodbye.

Lesson 49

1- お腹がすいているけれども、お金がありません
お腹がすいているけれど、お金がありません
お腹がすいているが、お金がありません

2- けれども is very formal. けれど and が are quite formal, but less than けれども. Finally, けど is the most informal version.

3- In this case, けど is used to soften the sentence, to leave the rest of the request in the air, thus allowing the interlocutor to realize what we really want, without having to tell him clearly.

4- *Although you like fish, why / how come you don't like sushi?*

5- *Although she is an adult, she wears those kinds of clothes.* The connotation is colloquial and disdainful, even pejorative.

6- 日本に行っても日本語を習わない

7- いくら勉強しても、何も習わない

8- 先生をキスした方がいいと思う

9- *Mr. Yamamoto is in the process of / is trying to write a thesis.*

10- 今日はパーティーがある。でも、行かない方がいい

Lesson 50

1- The relative clause is "who loved Makiko."

2- 真<ruby>紀<rt>き</rt></ruby>子を<ruby>愛<rt>あい</rt></ruby>した<ruby>男<rt>おとこ</rt></ruby>（の<ruby>名前<rt>なまえ</rt></ruby>）は<ruby>浩二<rt>こうじ</rt></ruby>です

2- 真紀子を愛した男（の名前）は浩二です

3- 明が買ったバイクはとても速い｜明の買ったバイクはとても速い

4- Both sentences are correct, because the が marking the subject of the relative clause can be replaced with の without changing its meaning in any way.

5- *Is the case of him receiving a bribe from the yakuza true?*

6- It means *So that (I can) pass the exam.*

7- お客さんは店員に黙るように言った

8- 日本人をナンパするようになりたい

9- *I try to sleep 8 hours every day.*

10- Japanese don't distinguish between restrictive and non-restrictive relative clauses. We must infer from the context what kind of sentence it is. For example, the sentence ガレージが/の広い家は大きいです can mean, depending on the context, *The house which has a large garage is big* (restrictive), and *The house, which has a large garage, is big* (non-restrictive).

Lesson 51

1- 財布: wallet｜事故: accident｜熱: fever｜薬局 or 薬屋: pharmacy / drugstore｜レントゲン: x-ray｜心臓: heart｜痛み: pain

2- Doctor: 医者｜hospital: 病院｜injury: けが｜ambulance: 救急車｜cough: せき｜cold: 風邪

3- すみませんが、指輪を失くしました

4- 頭が痛くて、熱があって、せきが止まりません

5- *It might just be the flu, but you need (to take) a blood test.*

6- 101-8010 Hitachi, Inc., 4-6 Kanda Suruga-chō, Chiyoda-ku, Tōkyō-to. (Block 4, plot 6, city of Kanda Suruga, Chiyoda district, Tokyo Metropolitan District)

7- Gun: 銃｜拳銃｜ピストル｜チャカ｜ハジキ
Police: 警察官｜警官｜刑事｜巡査｜お巡りさん｜デカ｜サツ｜ポリ

8- *I don't understand it very well, so can you explain it to me, please?*

9- 頭が痛いから/ので、薬を飲みます

10- 炎 is more or less the equivalent to our suffix *-itis*, that is, it indicates "inflammation." In this lesson we have seen the following words with 炎: 盲腸炎 *(appendicitis)*｜気管支炎 *(bronchitis)*｜胃炎 *(gastritis)*｜肝炎 *(hepatitis)*｜肺炎 *(pneumonia)*｜中耳炎 *(inflammation of the ear)*｜鼻炎 *(rhinitis)*｜and 扁桃腺炎 *(tonsillitis)*.

Lesson 52

1- There are three basic kinds of honorifics:

a) *Sonkeigo* or "language of respect:" It is used when talking with or about someone else, raising his or her position to express respect. The subject is the other person (someone superior to the speaker or a stranger).

b) *Kenjōgo* or "language of modesty:" It is used when talking with someone else who is either superior or a stranger. The subject is always "I" or someone in the *uchi* circle. The position of the speaker is lowered in order to indirectly raise the interlocutor's position.

c) *Teineigo* or "polite speech:" Polite way of talking.

2- 言う：おっしゃる｜知っている：ご存知だ｜飲む：召し上がる｜あげる：it doesn't exist｜行く：いらっしゃる

3- 申す：言う｜いただく：もらう｜いたす：する｜拝見する：見る｜伺う：行く or 来る

4- *Professor Nomura is writing an article.*

5- 歩かれる｜寝られる｜殺される｜走られる

6- *I know the contents of that book.*

7- It is not correct because the verb ご覧になる belongs to the *sonkeigo* and is only used when the subject of the sentence is someone towards whom the speaker expresses respect. The correct sentence would use the verb from *kenjōgo* with the meaning of "to see," 拝見する, so that the sentence would be 私は映画を拝見します, or 私は映画を拝見いたします, which is even more formal.

8- *There is a shop with tasty fish there.*

9- It would be correct if the teacher (先生) was someone in the *uchi* circle of the speaker. For example, if the teacher was the speaker's course tutor or something similar. The translation of the sentence is: *My teacher said he wants to ask you a question.*

10- *Sit on that chair, please.* Even though the construction "お + Root +ください" is a formal construction, it doesn't belong to any of the three kinds of formal languages, but to the everyday register.

Lesson 53

1- ～ちゃう：～てしまう｜～てゆう：と言う｜～なきゃ：Depending on the context, it can be the equivalent to the construction for "must" なければならない or to the negative conditional なければ.

2- 買っておく：買っとく｜行きたい：行きてえ｜遊んではだめだ：遊んじゃだめだ

3- *Buy me a car, come on!*

4- *Say something, 'cause this is boring.*

5- It is used to express the gerund in an extremely vulgar and rough way. 何を勉強してやがるんだ？ *(What the hell / fuck are you studying?)*

6- *That house (over there) is very big.* It is not grammatically correct, because the *-i* adjective すごい should become an adverb, replacing the last 〜い with 〜く, that is: あの家、すごくでかいね. However, using すごい instead of the correct すごく is very common in modern spoken Japanese, and, therefore, to a certain point, it could be considered "correct" usage wise.

7- *That guy makes me very angry, he gets scared stiff right away...*

8- 手を貸してくれない？ / 手を貸してくれませんか？

9- *Maiko, you've lost weight, haven't you?* or *Maiko has lost weight, hasn't she?*

10- はい（痛くない） *Yes (it is not painful).*

Lesson 54

1- みたいに is a more colloquial expression, it is used in conversations or writings between friends or acquaintances. ように is more formal, it is used in writings and conversations that require a certain distance from the interlocutor.

The only difference in usage is that, with ように, *-na* adjectives keep the な, and that after nouns we must place の, whereas with みたいに we don't need to use anything.

Example: *To fly like a bird* 鳥のように飛ぶ｜鳥みたいに飛ぶ.

2- この家は大聖堂のように大きい｜この家は大聖堂みたいに大きい

3- この家は大聖堂より大きい

4- この家は大聖堂ほど大きくない

5- この家は大聖堂と同じぐらい大きい

6- この家は大聖堂よりずっと小さい

7- この家と大聖堂ではどちらが大きいか？

8- この大聖堂は世界で一番大きい｜この大聖堂は世界で最も大きい

9- この家は大きすぎる

10- 最悪: the worst｜最初: the beginning｜最良: the best｜最低: the lowest / contemptible, pathetic｜最大: the biggest (most: 最, big: 大)｜最小: the smallest (most: 最, small: 小).

Lesson 55

1- 動物園: zoo｜切手: stamp｜城: castle｜展示: exhibition｜テレホンカード: telephone card｜住所: mail address｜美術館: art museum

2- Flash: フラッシュ｜garden: 庭 or 庭園｜direction: 方向｜cell phone: 携帯電話｜street: 通り｜traffic lights: 信号

3- すみませんが、名古屋(なごや)の熱田(あつた)神宮(じんぐう)へ行(い)く道(みち)を教(おし)えていただけませんか？

4- *Follow this street straight on and, then, turn right. It is next to the police box.*

5- ２ブロック行(い)って、そして3番目(さんばんめ)の信号(しんごう)を右(みぎ)に曲(ま)がってください

6- すみませんが、あなたの写真(しゃしん)をとってもいいですか？　チーズ！

7- 大人(おとな)１枚(いちまい)と子(こ)ども３枚(さんまい)ください

8- *To send a letter to Spain you need a 110-yen stamp.*

9- *The process to follow to pray at a* 神社(じんじゃ): 1: Purify yourself, washing mouth and hands | 2: Sound a bell to let the gods know of your presence | 3: Throw a coin or a bank note into the 賽銭箱(さいせんばこ) offertory box | 4: Bow twice | 5: Clap twice | 6: Bow once | 7: Pray.

Ema (絵馬(えま)): they are wooden votive tablets you can buy at Shinto shrines. They have a decorative drawing on one side. On the other side you can write a wish, and then you must hang the tablet with a string on a special place so that the wish comes true.

10- *Zen* (禅(ぜん)): it is a very widespread sect of Buddhism in Japan. | *Kōan* (公案(こうあん)): a sort of Zen riddle with an apparently cryptic meaning | *Zazen* (座禅(ざぜん)): the act of sitting for hours on one's knees, in an uncomfortable position, while meditating. | The practice of Zen Buddhism is some sort of way to reach the ultimate aim: enlightment or 悟(さと)り.

Lesson 56

1- 飛(と)ぶ：飛(と)ぶと，飛(と)べば，飛(と)んだら，飛(と)ぶなら or 飛(と)ぶのなら
元気(げんき)な：元気(げんき)だと，元気(げんき)なら，元気(げんき)だったら，元気(げんき)なら or 元気(げんき)なのなら or 元気(げんき)なのだったら or 元気(げんき)なんだったら

2- 歩(ある)く：歩(ある)けば | 寝(ね)る：寝(ね)れば | 頑張(がんば)る：頑張(がんば)れば | 来(く)る：来(く)れば | 泳(およ)ぐ：泳(およ)げば

3- 運転(うんてん)しなければ | 長(なが)くなければ | 本(ほん)じゃなければ

4- *On opening the door, the dog went in. | When I opened the door, the dog went in.*

5- *If he isn't tall, then I won't make him my boyfriend (I wouldn't go out with him if he weren't tall).*

6- *If you dislike the class, go out into the corridor.*

7- *If you are going to school, give my regards to the teacher.*

8- *Excuse me, whom should I make my order to?*

9- *If I were you, I wouldn't do that.*

10- *I would like to go to Greece. | Then go this summer.*

Lesson 57

1- どんなことを考えている／ますか？

2- この物をテーブルの上に置いてください

3- の and こと

4- 私は彼に行くことを命じた

5- 手塚のマンガを読んだことがない

6- The first sentence says either *Mika has never drunk sake* or *Mika has never had the experience of drinking sake*, whereas the second one says either *There are no occasions when Mika drinks sake* or *Mika never drinks sake*.

7- 私は小説を翻訳することになった

8- The first sentence says *Mika herself decided to drink sake* and the second one says *It was decided that Mika would drink sake*, that is, someone unrelated to Mika decided something that affected her, probably against her will.

9- *It is just that I want that handbag!* The nuance of もん is of excuse or even tantrum.

10- 1: 酒を飲むものですか！ │ 2: 酒を飲むもんですか！ │ 3: 酒を飲むもんか！ │ 4: 酒を飲むか！

Lesson 58

1- The three expressions indicating "only" are だけ, しか and ばかり.

a) だけ: Indicates the meaning of "only" in a neutral form.

b) しか: Has a negative nuance, similar to "nothing but." The verb in a sentence with しか must always be conjugated in the negative.

c) ばかり: Adds a nuance of "excess" to the idea of "only."

2- 小説だけを読む │ 小説しか読まない

3- *I not only like women, I also like money.*

4- *Yamamoto does nothing but play videogames (and I think he does it excessively).*

5- テレビを消したばかりだ │ テレビを消したところだ

6- *Which is the most interesting moment in the movie?*

7- 今、映画を見るところだ

8- Now, I have just seen a movie: 今、映画を見たところだ
Now, I'm watching a movie: 今、映画を見ているところだ

9- バイクが壊れたせいで、行けなかった

10- *By the way, are the cats that were in the city / town well?*

Lesson 59

"Translation" of the Kansai dialect conversation in page 141.

● 浩二さん、来られなかった？

● はい、なんばの方で仕事があったので...

解答

● 残念(ざんねん)だね！それじゃ、ビール買(か)っとこうか？
● だめ、だめ！お酒(さけ)飲(の)めないよ
● 本当(ほんとう)に? なんでなの? 変(へん)だね！
● コーラでいいよ。すごくうまいもん
● しょうがないな！じゃ、おごるぞ
● ありがとう！いくらだろう、これ？

Exercises

1- Kansai-ben is the most used Japanese dialect after the standard Japanese spoken in the area of Tokyo. It is used in the 近畿(きんき) region, which includes the prefectures of 京都(きょうと), 大阪(おおさか), 兵庫(ひょうご), 奈良(なら), 和歌山(わかやま), 滋賀(しが) and 三重(みえ). The main cities in the region are 大阪(おおさか), 京都(きょうと) and 神戸(こうべ), among others. The main sub dialects of 関西弁(かんさいべん) are 大阪弁(おおさかべん), 京都弁(きょうとべん) and 神戸弁(こうべべん).

2- ぼちぼちでんなぁ.

Within Japan itself, there are several clichés about the Kansai-ben or, rather, about the people who speak in the dialect of Kansai. Among them, the most predominant are the economic (they say people in Kansai like amassing and hoarding money with stinginess), the criminal (they say there is high yakuza activity and much organized crime in Osaka), and comedy (Osaka is the capital of 漫才(まんざい), a kind of comedy performance very popular in Japan). Therefore, in novels, manga, movies and TV series, the yakuza, comedians and merchants usually speak in Kansai-ben as an "unspoken rule."

3- 疲(つか)れる仕事(しごと)はとても嫌(いや)だな *I really hate tiring jobs.*

4- 梅田(うめだ)は人(ひと)がとても多(おお)いので、歩(ある)けないぞ *Because there are many people in Umeda, you can't walk.*

5- 光彦(みつひこ)はんがまだおらへんさかいに、行(い)ってはあかんで

6- To the dialect of Aichi, spoken in the area around the city of Nagoya.

7- *When you are in Rome, do as the Romans do.*

8- A 四字熟語(よじじゅくご) is a kind of compact proverb, generally borrowed many centuries ago from China, consisting of four kanji characters. **Example:** 一石二鳥(いっせきにちょう) : *To kill two birds with one stone.*

9- **Modern Japanese:** 私(わたし)は織田(おだ)さん(様(さま))のところへ行かないのです。

   English: *I'm not going to the place where Mr. Oda (is).*

10- 北海道弁(ほっかいどうべん) exists to a certain point, since it is basically a variation of the dialect of Tokyo, which is nowadays standard Japanese. It hardly varies from standard Japanese, except for a few small characteristics that have been filtered into the language used by the inhabitants of the island of Hokkaidō through the influence of the Tōhoku dialect. For example, the usage of the end-of-the-sentence particle へ, or some words like こっこ *(son)* or めんこい *(handsome / beautiful)*, typical of 東北弁.

Lesson 60

1- 踊る:踊られる｜招く:招かれる｜食べる:食べられる｜払う:払われる

2- 健は先生にほめられた

3- Literally, *I was cried by Rina (and that meant a problem for me)*. A more appropriate translation would be: *Rina cried (and I didn't like it)*.

4- 踊る:踊らせる｜招く:招かせる｜食べる:食べさせる｜払う:払わせる

5- 編集者は作家を温泉へ行かせた

6- In two ways: 1) *The teacher let me draw a comic book* or 2) *The teacher made me draw a comic book*. Depending on the context, it can have one meaning or the other.

7- 踊る:踊らせられる｜招く:招かせられる｜食べる:食べさせられる｜払う:払わせられる

8- *I was forced by her to buy a ring.*

9- *Write a composition, each of you, on Japan.*

10- *It was because there were readers, that this book could be done.*

Appendix II: Grammar index

Throughout the 60 lessons which make up the three volumes of the *Japanese in MangaLand* series, we have studied all kinds of grammatical constructions. Now is the time to provide you with an index where they will all be listed.

What do we use this appendix for?

You will probably want to review a specific grammatical form some day, and at that moment you might not remember the lesson where it was explained. This index has been planned so that you can have an exhaustive guide of all studied constructions, as well as a tables with the basic verb conjugations which, no doubt, will help you distinguish one conjugation from another at a glance (see the next page).

How to use the list of grammatical forms

Now go to page 173 and look at the list: there are several columns in it. The first column contains a number 4 or 3 : these numbers indicate whether you need to master that grammatical form if you want to pass levels 4 (elementary) and 3 (basic), respectively, of the 日本語 能力 試験, Japanese-Language Proficiency Test (see the INTRODUCTION for more information). You can use the list as a guide to check whether you have mastered the grammatical forms required for the exam.

In the second column you have the grammatical forms, following the order of the kana *a-ka-sa-ta-na-ha-ma-ya-ra-wa-n* and *a-i-u-e-o* (see a complete explanation on how this works in the third appendix of *Japanese in MangaLand*, vol.2). Next, you have the number of the lesson where this construction was explained, and, last of all, you have a brief explanation about its function or meaning, by way of a reminder.

Note: The indication "Vr" means "Verbal root" and indicates a verb conjugated in the -*masu* form without the final ます. Example: 書く *(to write)* ⇒ 書きます (-*masu* form) ⇒ 書きます (verbal root) (L.31).

General table of basic conjugations

	Simple F.	Meaning	-masu f.	Past	Negative	Negative past	-te form	-ō form	Potential	Imperat.	-ba cond.	Passive	Causative
Group 1 Invariable	教える (おしえる)	to teach	教えます	教えた	教えない	教えなかった	教えて	教えよう	教えられる	教えろ	教えれば	教えられる	教えさせる
	見る (みる)	to see	見ます	見た	見ない	見なかった	見て	見よう	見られる	見ろ	見れば	見られる	見させる
Group 2 Variable	貸す (かす)	to lend	貸します	貸した	貸さない	貸さなかった	貸して	貸そう	貸せる	貸せ	貸せば	貸される	貸させる
	待つ (まつ)	to wait	待ちます	待った	待たない	待たなかった	待って	待とう	待てる	待て	待てば	待たれる	待たせる
	買う (かう)	to buy	買います	買った	買わない	買わなかった	買って	買おう	買える	買え	買えば	買われる	買わせる
	帰る (かえる)	to return	帰ります	帰った	帰らない	帰らなかった	帰って	帰ろう	帰れる	帰れ	帰れば	帰られる	帰らせる
	書く (かく)	to write	書きます	書いた	書かない	書かなかった	書いて	書こう	書ける	書け	書けば	書かれる	書かせる
	急ぐ (いそぐ)	to hurry	急ぎます	急いだ	急がない	急がなかった	急いで	急ごう	急げる	急げ	急げば	急がれる	急がせる
	遊ぶ (あそぶ)	to play	遊びます	遊んだ	遊ばない	遊ばなかった	遊んで	遊ぼう	遊べる	遊べ	遊べば	遊ばれる	遊ばせる
	飲む (のむ)	to drink	飲みます	飲んだ	飲まない	飲まなかった	飲んで	飲もう	飲める	飲め	飲めば	飲まれる	飲ませる
	死ぬ (しぬ)	to die	死にます	死んだ	死なない	死ななかった	死んで	死のう	死ねる	死ね	死ねば	死なれる	死なせる
Group 3 Irregular	する	to do	します	した	しない	しなかった	して	しよう	できる	しろ	すれば	される	させる
	来る (くる)	to come	来ます	来た	来ない	来なかった	来て	来よう	来れる	来い	来れば	来られる	来させる

Guide: -masu form (see L.19 for this form and its past, negative, and past negative variations), simple form (L.20), negative (L.20), past (L.20), past negative (L.20), -te form (L.24 / 35), -ō form (L.34), potential (L.32), -ba conditional (L.56), passive (L.56), causative (L.60). We have omitted some forms, because they are simple variations of these.

文型集

List of grammatical forms

Appendix III: Vocabulary index

In this third and last appendix we offer a systematic list of all the words that have appeared in this book, with their respective translation, as well as all the vocabulary needed for the initial levels (4 and 3) of the Japanese Proficiency Test.

Ready for the official test

One of the ideas behind the creation of this method is that, besides being a tool to learn Japanese at a basic level, it can also be used as a guide or handbook to prepare the student to pass levels 4 (elementary) and 3 (basic) of the 日本語 能力 試験, the Japanese-Language Proficiency Test, (see the INTRODUCTION, for more information). Before many of the words in this index you will see a little 4 or 3: these numbers indicate levels 4 and 3, respectively, for the test. In this list you will find all the words which, according to official standards, can appear in the questions in these levels. Therefore, if you study all the words marked with 4, you will master all the vocabulary needed to pass level 4. And the same goes for level 3, of course.

Besides those specified in this list, the other words considered for level 4 are: numbers (L.5), days of the week, days of the month, and months (L.6), the various *kosoa-do* (L.9 and L.34), and, last of all, everyday expressions (L.4 and L.27), all of which can be found in the first book of the *Japanese in MangaLand* series.

Order of the kana

In *Japanese in MangaLand 2*, we already saw how the words are ordered in Japanese dictionaries and in the vocabulary appendix of this book, so we will assume that you know how to look for the words in this index. The kana follow this order: *a-ka-sa-ta-na-ha-ma-ya-ra-wa-n*, and thus, for example, the た line goes after さ and before な. Within each line, the order to follow is *a-i-u-e-o*. That is, within the か co-lumn, we first have か, then き, followed by く, then け, and finally こ.

How to use this index

Take a look now at each of the columns in the vocabulary appendix. In the first column you have the hiragana version of each of the terms, and then its "usual" version in kanji, hiragana or katakana, as appropriate. Next, in brackets, you are given its morphological category (see below), the lesson where it first appeared, and sometimes the lesson where this term has an important role. If "JiM1" or "JiM2" is indicated, this means the word appeared in the first or second volumes, respectively, of the series. If nothing is indicated, it means the word has not appeared in the series, but it is essential to pass levels 4 or 3 of the Japanese-Language Proficiency Test. To conclude, in the last column, you will find the English translation of each word.

Morphological categories

N:	nouns
V:	verbs
V1:	verbs ending in -*eru* or -*iru* from group 1
V2:	verbs ending in -*eru* or -*iru* from group 2
Virr:	verbs with an irregular conjugation
Vn:	nouns that become verbs when adding する
iAdj:	-*i* adjectives
naAdj:	-*na* adjectives
Adv:	adverbs
Ph:	phrases, set phrases
PN:	pronouns
C:	counters
T:	toponyms, geographical proper nouns

- The sign "|" separates the different meanings that one word can have.
- The sign "–KANSAI–" means that the word belongs to the Kansai dialect.

あ A

4	あいすくりーむ	アイスクリーム	(N)	47	ice-cream
3	あいだ	間	(N)	48	between (space or time)
	あいち	愛知	(T)	48, 59	Aichi (prefecture)
	あいつ	あいつ	(PN)	46, 53	that guy
	あいぬ	アイヌ	(N)	59	Ainu
4	あう	会う	(V)	JiM2	to meet, to see
3	あう	合う	(V)		to fit | to agree
4	あおい	青い	(iAdj)	JiM1	blue
	あおもり	青森	(T)	59	Aomori (prefecture, city)
4	あかい	赤い	(iAdj)	JiM1	red
	あかご	赤児	(N)	57	baby (archaic)
3	あかちゃん	赤ちゃん	(N)	57	baby
3	あがる	上がる	(V2)	JiM1	to go up, to rise
4	あかるい	明るい	(iAdj)	46	clear, bright
	あかん	あかん	(Adv)	59	(prohibition) —KANSAI—
3	あかんぼう	赤ん坊	(N)	57	baby
4	あき	秋	(N)	JiM1	autumn, fall
	あきた	秋田	(T)	59	Akita (prefecture, city)
	あきらめる	諦める	(V1)	49	to give up, to resign oneself to
4	あく	開く	(V)	JiM1	to be opened
3	あく	空く	(V)	JiM2	to be empty
3	あげる	あげる	(V1)	48	to give
4	あける	開ける	(V1)	JiM2	to open
4	あげる	上げる	(V1)	JiM1	to go up
	あげる	揚げる	(V1)	47	to deep-fry
4	あさ	朝	(N)	JiM1	morning
4	あさごはん	朝ご飯	(N)	47	breakfast
4	あさって	あさって	(Adv)	JiM2	the day after tomorrow
3	あさねぼう	朝寝坊	(Vn)		to oversleep
4	あし	足	(N)	56	foot | leg
3	あじ	味	(N)	JiM1	taste, flavor
	あじがうすい	味が薄い	(Ph)	47	bland
	あしくび	足首	(N)	51	ankle
4	あした	明日	(Adv)	JiM1	tomorrow
3	あす	明日	(Adv)		tomorrow (formal)
4	あそぶ	遊ぶ	(V)	JiM1	to play | to have a good time
4	あたたかい	暖かい	(iAdj)	JiM1	warm, hot
4	あたま	頭	(N)	JiM1	head
4	あたらしい	新しい	(iAdj)	JiM1	new
	〜あたり	〜当たり	(Adv)	47	per...
4	あつい	厚い	(iAdj)	46	thick
4	あつい	暑い	(iAdj)	48	warm (atmosphere)
4	あつい	熱い	(iAdj)	47	hot (thing)
3	あつまる	集まる	(V2)	JiM2	to be gathered
3	あつめる	集める	(V1)	JiM2	to gather
4	あと	後	(Adv)	48	after
	あな	穴	(N)	55	hole
	あなご	アナゴ	(N)	47	eel
4	あなた	貴方	(PN)	JiM1	you
4	あに	兄	(N)	60	elder brother
4	あね	姉	(N)	JiM1	elder sister
4	あぱーと	アパート	(N)	JiM1	apartment
4	あびる	浴びる	(V1)		to pour water | to take a shower
4	あぶない	危ない	(iAdj)	JiM1	dangerous
	あぶら	油	(N)	47	oil
	あほな	アホな	(naAdj)	48	stupid
4	あまい	甘い	(iAdj)	47	sweet | naive
4	あまり	あまり	(Adv)	48	not much

4	あめ	雨	(N)	JiM1	rain
	あめがふる	雨が降る	(Ph)	48	to rain
	あやうい	危うい	(iAdj)	58	dangerous
3	あやまる	謝る	(V2)	48	to apologize
4	あらう	洗う	(V)	JiM1	to wash, to clean
4	ある	ある	(V2)	JiM1	there is, there are
4	あるく	歩く	(V)	JiM1	to walk
	あるつはいまーびょう	アルツハイマー病	(N)	51	Alzheimer's disease
3	あるばいと	アルバイト	(N)		part-time job
	あれるぎー	アレルギー	(N)	51	allergy
	あんこ	あんこ	(N)	47	bean paste
3	あんしんな	安心な	(naAdj)	46	reassuring
3	あんぜんな	安全な	(naAdj)	48	safe
3	あんない	案内	(Vn)	47	guide

い   I

4	いい	いい	(iAdj)	JiM1	good
	いいきになる	いい気になる	(Ph)	53	to get smart
4	いう	言う	(V)	JiM1	to say
4	いえ	家	(N)	JiM1	house
	いえん	胃炎	(N)	51	gastritis
	いか	いか	(N)	47	squid
3	いか	以下	(Adv)		below
3	いがい	以外	(Adv)		except
	いかいよう	胃潰瘍	(N)	51	gastric ulcer
3	いかが	いかが	(Adv)	JiM2	how about?
3	いがく	医学	(N)	JiM2	Medicine (studies)
3	いきる	生きる	(V1)	JiM2	to live
4	いく	行く	(V)	JiM1	to go
4	いくつ	いくつ	(Adv)	JiM2	who many?
4	いくら	いくら	(Adv)	JiM1	how much (money)?
4	いけ	池	(N)	JiM2	pond
3	いけん	意見	(N)	50	opinion
3	いし	石	(N)		stone, rock
3	いじめる	いじめる	(V1)	57	to bully, to pick on, to abuse
4	いしゃ	医者	(N)	49, 51	doctor
3	いじょう	以上	(Adv)	60	more than | end
4	いす	いす	(N)	JiM1	chair
4	いそがしい	忙しい	(iAdj)	JiM2	busy
3	いそぐ	急ぐ	(V)	JiM1	to hurry
	いたい	痛い	(iAdj)	48, 51	painful
3	いたす	致す	(V)	52	to do (kenjōgo)
	いただきます	いただきます	(Ph)	47	"Bon appétit!"
3	いただく	いただく	(V)	JiM2	to receive
	いたみ	痛み	(N)	50, 51	pain
	いたみどめ	痛み止め	(N)	51	pain-killer
	いためる	炒める	(V1)	47	to stir fry
	いちご	いちご	(N)	47	strawberry
4	いちにち	一日	(N)	JiM2	one day
	いちば	市場	(N)	55	market
4	いちばん	一番	(Adv)	54	the first
4	いつ	いつ	(Adv)	JiM1	when?
4	いつか	いつか	(Adv)	JiM2	some day
3	いっしょけんめい	一所懸命	(Adv)		with all one's might
4	いっしょに	一緒に	(Adv)	JiM2	together with | with
3	いっぱい	いっぱい	(Adv)	48	a lot
4	いつも	いつも	(Adv)	JiM2	always
3	いと	糸	(N)		thread
3	いない	以内	(Adv)		inside

3	うれしい	うれしい	(iAdj)		glad, happy
4	うわぎ	上着	(N)		coat
	うわさ	噂	(N)	50	rumor
3	うん	うん	(Adv)	55	yes (colloquial)
	うんせい	運勢	(N)	55	luck, fortune
3	うんてん	運転	(Vn)	JiM1	driving
3	うんてんしゅ	運転手	(N)	JiM2	driver
3	うんどう	運動	(Vn)	48	to exercise

え E

4	え	絵	(N)	JiM2	drawing, illustration
4	えいが	映画	(N)	JiM1	movie
4	えいがかん	映画館	(N)	JiM2	cinema
4	えいご	英語	(N)	JiM1	English (language)
4	ええ	ええ	(Adj)	59	good, well −KANSAI−
4	ええ	ええ	(Ph)		yes
4	えき	駅	(N)	JiM2	train station
3	えすかれーたー	エスカレーター	(N)		escalator
3	えだ	枝	(N)		branch
	えっち	エッチ	(Vn)	53	to have sex
	えっちな	エッチな	(naAdj)	53	hot, sexual
	えどじだい	江戸時代	(N)	55	Edo period (1603-1867)
3	えはがき	絵葉書	(N)	55	postcard
4	えび	海老	(N)	47	prawn
	えひめ	愛媛	(T)	60	Ehime (prefecture)
	えべれすと	エベレスト	(T)	54	Everest
	えま	絵馬	(N)	55	*ema* votive tablet
	えらい	えらい	(Adv)	59	very −KANSAI−
	えらぶ	選ぶ	(V)	49	to choose
	えれべーた	エレベータ	(N)	JiM2	elevator
4	えん	円	(N)	JiM1	yen
4	えんそく	遠足	(N)	46	excursion
4	えんぴつ	えんぴつ	(N)	JiM1	pencil
3	えんりょ	遠慮	(Vn)		reserve

お O

4	おいしい	おいしい	(iAdj)	47	good, delicious
	おいでやす	おいでやす	(Ph)	59	Welcome −KYOTO−
	おうえん	応援	(Vn)	51	cheering | reinforcement
	おおあめ	大雨	(N)	49	heavy rain
3	おおい	多い	(iAdj)	46	many
4	おおきい	大きい	(iAdj)	JiM1	big
	おおきに	おおきに	(Ph)	59	thank you −KANSAI−
	おおさか	大阪	(T)	59	Osaka (prefecture, city)
4	おおぜい	大勢	(N)	JiM2	many people
3	おーとばい	オートバイ	(N)		motorcycle
3	おーばー	オーバー	(Vn)		to exceed
	おか	丘	(N)	55	hill
4	おかあさん	お母さん	(N)	56	mother
	おかげ(で)	お陰(で)	(Adv)	58	thanks to
4	おかし	お菓子	(N)	JiM2	candy, cookie
3	おかしい	おかしい	(iAdj)	58	odd, strange
4	おかね	お金	(N)	JiM1	money
	おかわり	おかわり	(N)	47	another serving (of food)
	おきなわ	沖縄	(T)	59	Okinawa (prefecture, island)
4	おきる	起きる	(V1)	JiM1	to get up
4	おく	置く	(V)	JiM2	to put, to place
4	おくさん	奥さん	(N)	JiM1	wife (somebody else's)
	おこう	お香	(N)	55	incense

	おこのみやき	お好み焼き	(N)	47	Japanese "omelette"
	おごる	おごる	(V2)	59	to treat
	おこる	起こる	(V2)	57	to happen
4	おさけ	お酒	(N)	47	*sake*
4	おさら	お皿	(N)	47	plate
4	おじ	叔父	(N)	50	uncle
4	おしえる	教える	(V1)	JiM1	to teach
	おしぼり	おしぼり	(N)	47	wet towel
4	おす	押す	(V)	55	to press | to push
	おすすめ	おすすめ	(N)	47	recommendation
4	おそい	遅い	(iAdj)		late
	おそろしい	恐ろしい	(iAdj)	46	terrible, frightful
	おたく	お宅	(N)	52	your house
4	おちゃ	お茶	(N)	47	tea
	おっしゃる	おっしゃる	(Virr)	48, 52	to say (*sonkeigo*)
	おっす	おっす	(Ph)	53	Hello!
4	おてあらい	お手洗い	(N)		toilet, rest room
3	おてら	お寺	(N)	55	Buddhist temple
	おでん	おでん	(N)	47	*oden* hotchpotch
4	おとうさん	お父さん	(N)	JiM1	father
4	おとうと	弟	(N)	JiM1	younger brother
4	おとこ	男	(N)	50	man
	おどし	脅し	(N)	53	threat
4	おととい	おととい	(Adv)		the day before yesterday
4	おととし	おととし	(Adv)		two years ago
4	おとな	大人	(N)	55	adult
	おなくなりになる	お亡くなりになる	(V2)	52	to die (*sonkeigo*)
4	おなじ	同じ	(Adv)	47, 54	the same
	おに	鬼	(N)	49	ogre
4	おにいさん	お兄さん	(N)	JiM1	elder brother
	おにぎり	おにぎり	(N)	47	stuffed rice ball
4	おねえさん	お姉さん	(N)	48	elder sister
4	おば	叔母	(N)	JiM1	aunt
4	おはし	お箸	(N)	47	chopsticks
4	おふろ	お風呂	(N)	JiM1	bath (Japanese style)
4	おべんとう	お弁当	(N)		box lunch
	おぼうさん	お坊さん	(N)	55	Buddhist monk
4	おぼえる	覚える	(V1)	60	to remember
	おまもり	お守り	(N)	55	amulet
	おまわりさん	お巡りさん	(N)	51	policeman, officer
	おみくじ	おみくじ	(N)	55	fortunes
3	おみまい	お見舞い	(Vn)		a visit to a sick person
3	おみやげ	お土産	(N)	JiM2	souvenir
	おむれつ	オムレツ	(N)	47	omelette
4	おもい	重い	(iAdj)	JiM1	heavy
3	おもいだす	思い出す	(V)	JiM2	to remember
	おもいのこす	思い残す	(V)	48	to regret (after dying)
3	おもう	思う	(V)	JiM2	to think, to believe
4	おもしろい	面白い	(iAdj)	JiM1	interesting | funny
3	おもちゃ	おもちゃ	(N)	JiM2	toy
3	おもて	表	(N)		the front (side)
	おもろい	おもろい	(iAdj)	59	interesting −Kansai−
	おや	親	(N)	59	father
	おやこどん	親子丼	(N)	46, 47	*oyakodon*
	おやつ	おやつ	(N)	47	afternoon tea, snack
3	おゆ	お湯	(N)	JiM2	hot water
4	およぐ	泳ぐ	(V)	JiM2	to swim
3	おりる	下りる	(V2)	JiM2	to come down (from a place)
4	おりる	降りる	(V2)	JiM1	to fall down, to get off (of stg.)
3	おる	おる	(V2)	52	to be (*kenjōgo*)

3	おれい	お礼	(N)		gratitude
3	おれる	折れる	(V1)	JiM2	to be folded
	おれんじ	オレンジ	(N)	47	orange
4	おわる	終わる	(V2)	JiM1	to finish
4	おんがく	音楽	(N)	JiM2	music
	おんせん	温泉	(N)	60	hot spring
4	おんな	女	(N)	JiM1	woman

か KA

3	かーてん	カーテン	(N)		curtain
4	～かい	～回	(C)		(counter for times)
4	～かい	～階	(C)	JiM1	(counter for floors)
	かい	貝	(N)	47	clam, shell
	かいかん	開館	(Vn)	55	museum opening time
	かいが	絵画	(N)	55	painting
	かいがん	海岸	(N)	55	seaside
	かいけつ	解決	(Vn)	56	solution
4	がいこく	外国	(N)		foreign country
4	がいこくじん	外国人	(N)		foreign person
	がいしゃ	ガイシャ	(N)	51	victim (jargon)
4	かいしゃ	会社	(N)	48	company
3	かいじょう	会場	(N)	JiM2	a site
	がいじん	外人	(N)	47	foreigner
4	かいだん	階段	(N)	JiM2	stairs
4	かいもの	買い物	(N)	JiM2	shopping
3	かいわ	会話	(Vn)	50	conversation
4	かう	買う	(V)	JiM1	to buy
4	かえす	返す	(V)	JiM2	to return, to give back
	かえる	蛙	(N)	56	frog
4	かえる	帰る	(V2)	JiM1	to return (home)
3	かえる	変える	(V1)	JiM2	to change
4	かお	顔	(N)	JiM1	face
	かかり	係り	(N)	51	in charge
4	かかる	かかる	(V2)	JiM2	to take (time)
4	かかる	かかる	(V2)	JiM2	to be hung
	かがく	化学	(N)	54	chemistry
3	かがく	科学	(N)		science
3	かがみ	鏡	(N)		mirror
	がき	がき	(N)	49, 53	brat, kid
	かきとめ	書留	(N)	55	registered mail
4	かぎ	鍵	(N)	JiM2	key
4	かく	書く	(V)	JiM1	to write
	かく	描く	(V)	60	to draw
	かくす	隠す	(V)	50	to hide
4	がくせい	学生	(N)	JiM1	student
4	かける	かける	(V1)	JiM2	to hang, to put
4	かさ	傘	(N)		umbrella
3	かざる	飾る	(V2)		to decorate
	かざん	火山	(N)	55	volcano
3	かじ	火事	(N)		fire
4	かす	貸す	(V)	JiM1	to lend
4	かぜ	風	(N)	JiM1	wind
4	かぜ	風邪	(N)	51	a cold
	かぜをひく	風邪を引く	(Ph)	48, 51	to catch a cold
4	かぞく	家族	(N)	JiM1	family
3	がそりん	ガソリン	(N)		gasoline
4	かた	方	(N)	52	person (formal)
	かたいれ	肩入れ	(N)	50	support
3	かたち	形	(N)		form, shape

	かんじる	感じる	(V1)	57	to feel
	かんせつ	関節	(N)	51	joint
	かんぜんな	完全な	(naAdj)	58	complete
	かんぞう	肝臓	(N)	51	liver
3	かんたんな	簡単な	(naAdj)	JiM2	simple, easy
	かんとう	関東	(T)	59	Kantō (region)
	かんない	館内	(N)	55	inside the museum
3	がんばる	頑張る	(V2)	JiM1	to make an effort
	かんぺきな	完璧な	(naAdj)	46	perfect

き KI

3	き	気	(N)	JiM1	spirit | steam
4	き	木	(N)	JiM1	tree
4	きいろい	黄色い	(iAdj)	JiM1	yellow
	きうい	キウイ	(N)	47	kiwi
4	きえる	消える	(V1)	JiM2	to be put out, to disappear
	ぎおん	祇園	(T)	55	Gion (in Kyoto)
3	きかい	機会	(N)		opportunity
3	きかい	機械	(N)	JiM2	machine
	きがん	祈願	(Vn)	55	prayer
	きかんしえん	気管支炎	(N)	51	bronchitis
	きかんしゃ	機関車	(N)	58	locomotive
	きぐ	器具	(N)	47	tool
	きく	効く	(V)	51	to take effect
4	きく	聞く	(V)	JiM1	to hear, to listen to
3	きけんな	危険な	(naAdj)	JiM1	dangerous
3	きこえる	聞こえる	(V1)	JiM2	can hear (unconsciously)
	きさま	貴様	(PN)	53	you (threatening)
	きじ	記事	(N)	52	newspaper article
3	ぎじゅつ	技術	(N)		technology
	きす	キス	(Vn)	48	kiss
	きず	傷	(N)	46	wound
	きずつける	傷付ける	(V1)	46	to hurt
	ぎせいしゃ	犠牲者	(N)	60	victim
3	きぜつ	気絶	(Vn)	JiM2	fainting
3	きそく	規則	(N)		rule
	きた	キタ	(T)	59	nickname for Umeda
4	きた	北	(N)	JiM1	north
4	ぎたー	ギター	(N)	JiM2	guitar
4	きたない	汚い	(iAdj)		dirty
	きち	吉	(N)	55	good luck
4	きっさてん	喫茶店	(N)	JiM1	coffee shop
4	きって	切手	(N)	55	stamp
3	きっと	きっと	(Adv)	54	surely
	きつね	きつね	(N)	54	fox
4	きっぷ	切符	(N)	JiM2	ticket
3	きぬ	絹	(N)		silk
	きねんび	記念日	(N)	55	memorial day
4	きのう	機能	(N)	58	capacity, function
3	きびしい	厳しい	(iAdj)	49	strict, severe
3	きぶん	気分	(N)	JiM2	mood | health
	きぶんがわるい	気分が悪い	(Ph)	51	to feel bad
	きぼう	希望	(N)	52	a hope, a desire
3	きまる	決まる	(V2)	JiM2	to be decided
3	きみ	君	(PN)	JiM1	you
	きむち	キムチ	(N)	48	*kimchi* (spicy pickled veggies)
3	きめる	決める	(V1)	JiM2	to decide
3	きもち	気持ち	(N)		feeling
3	きもの	着物	(N)	JiM2	kimono

4	くに	国	(N)	54	country
	くにばんごう	国番号	(N)	55	telephone country code
3	くび	首	(N)	48	neck | head
3	くも	雲	(N)	JiM1	cloud
4	くもる	曇る	(V2)	JiM1	to become cloudy
4	くらい	暗い	(iAdj)	JiM1	dark
	ぐらす	グラス	(N)	47	glass
4	くらす	クラス	(N)	54	class
3	くらべる	比べる	(V1)		to compare
4	ぐらむ	グラム	(N)	47	gram
4	くる	来る	(Virr)	JiM1	to come
4	くるま	車	(N)	JiM1	car
3	くれる	くれる	(V)	JiM1	somebody gives
4	くろい	黒い	(iAdj)	JiM1	black
	くわしい	詳しい	(iAdj)	51	detailed

け KE

	げい	ゲイ	(N)	57	gay, homosexual
3	けいかく	計画	(Vn)	52	plan, report
3	けいかん	警官	(N)	50	police
3	けいけん	経験	(N)		experience
	けいご	敬語	(N)	52	honorifics
3	けいざい	経済	(N)	JiM2	economy
3	けいさつ	警察	(N)	51	police force
	けいさつかん	警察官	(N)	51	police officer
	けいじ	刑事	(N)	51	police detective
	けいせい	形成	(Vn)	46	formation
	けいたいでんわ	携帯電話	(N)	55	cell phone
	げいのう	芸能	(N)	58	performing arts
4	けーき	ケーキ	(N)	47	cake
	げーせん	ゲーセン	(N)	48	game arcade
3	けが	怪我	(Vn)	51	injury
	げかい	外科医	(N)	51	surgeon
	けがにん	怪我人	(N)	51	injured
	げきじょう	劇場	(N)	55	theater
4	けさ	今朝	(Adv)		this morning
3	けしき	景色	(N)	46	landscape
3	げしゅく	下宿	(Vn)		lodging
4	けす	消す	(V)	JiM2	to put out, to turn off, to erase
	けちゃっぷ	ケチャップ	(N)	47	ketchup
	けつあつ	血圧	(N)	51	blood pressure
	けつえき	血液	(N)	51	blood
	けっか	結果	(N)	51	result
	けっかん	血管	(N)	51	blood vessel
4	けっこう	結構	(Adv)	48	quite | good
4	けっこん	結婚	(Vn)	JiM1	marriage, wedding
3	けっして	決して	(Adv)		by no means
	けったいな	けったいな	(naAdj)	59	strange | funny −KANSAI−
	げっぷ	げっぷ	(Vn)	48	burp
	げり	下痢	(N)	51	diarrhea
	けん	県	(N)	51	prefecture
3	げんいん	原因	(N)	56	cause, reason
3	けんか	喧嘩	(Vn)		fight
4	げんかん	玄関	(N)		entrance (of a house)
4	げんきな	元気な	(naAdj)	JiM1	healthy, vigorous
3	けんきゅう	研究	(Vn)		research
	けんきゅうしゃ	研究者	(N)	46	researcher
	けんさ	検査	(Vn)	51	medical examination
	けんじゅう	拳銃	(N)	51	gun

	けんじょうご	謙譲語	(N)	52	language of modesty
	げんぞう	現像	(Vn)	55	(photograph) developing
3	けんぶつ	見物	(Vn)		sight-seeing

こ KO

4	～こ	～個	(C)	JiM1	(counter for small things)
3	こ	子	(N)	JiM1	child
	こいつ	こいつ	(PN)	53	this guy
	ごう	郷	(N)	59	village
	こうあん	公案	(N)	55	*kōan*, Zen saying
4	こうえん	公園	(N)	55	park
	こうかい	後悔	(Vn)	49	repentance
3	こうがい	郊外	(N)		suburbs, outskirts
	ごうかく	合格	(Vn)	46	passing an examination
3	こうぎ	講義	(Vn)		conference
3	こうぎょう	工業	(N)		industry
	こうくうびん	航空便	(N)	55	air mail
	こうけつあつ	高血圧	(N)	51	high blood pressure
3	こうこう	高校	(N)	58	senior high school
	こうしゅうでんわ	公衆電話	(N)	55	public telephone
3	こうじょう	工場	(N)		factory
	こうたく	光沢	(N)	55	glossy (photograph)
4	こうちゃ	紅茶	(N)	47	black tea
3	こうちょう	校長	(N)		headmaster, principal
3	こうつう	交通	(N)	51	traffic
	ごうとう	強盗	(Vn)	49	theft
	こうはん	後半	(N)	54	second part
4	こうばん	交番	(N)	51	police box
	こうべ	神戸	(T)	59	Kōbe
	こうほ	候補	(N)	50	candidate
3	こうむいん	公務員	(N)		public servant
4	こえ	声	(N)	JiM2	voice
4	こーと	コート	(N)	JiM2	coat
4	こーひー	コーヒー	(N)	47	coffee
	こーら	コーラ	(N)	47	cola
	こかん	股間	(N)	59	crotch
	こきゅう	呼吸	(Vn)	51	breath
3	こくさい	国際	(N)	JiM2	international
	こくさいでんわ	国際電話	(N)	55	international phone
	こくはく	告白	(Vn)	49	confession, declaration
	こくりつ	国立	(N)	55	national
	こご	古語	(N)	59	classical Japanese
4	ごご	午後	(Adv)		afternoon
3	こころ	心	(N)	49	heart	soul
3	こしょう	こしょう	(N)	47	pepper
3	こしょう	故障	(Vn)		breakdown, trouble
4	ごぜん	午前	(Adv)		morning
	こそ	こそ	(Adv)	60	(emphasizer)
3	ごぞんじ	ご存知	(N)	52	to know (*sonkeigo*)
4	こたえ	答え	(N)	58	answer
3	ごちそうさま	ご馳走様	(Ph)	47	"It was delicious!"
	こっこ	こっこ	(N)	59	egg, son, daughter (Tōhoku)
	こっせつ	骨折	(N)	51	bone fracture
	ごっつい	ごっつい	(Adv)	59	very, very much —Kansai—
	こづつみ	小包	(N)	55	(postal) parcel
4	こっぷ	コップ	(N)	47	glass
3	こと	事	(PN)	50, 57	thing (intangible)
4	ことし	今年	(Adv)	55	this year
4	ことば	言葉	(N)		word

4	こども	子ども	(N)	55	child
	ことわざ	諺	(N)	59	saying, proverb
4	ごはん	ご飯	(N)	47	boiled rice | meal
	ごま	ごま	(N)	47	sesame
	こまいぬ	狛犬	(N)	55	statue of watchdog
3	こまかい	細かい	(iAdj)		fine | detailed
4	こまる	困る	(V2)	JiM2	to be in trouble
3	ごみ	ゴミ	(N)	56	garbage
3	こむ	込む	(V)		to be crowded
3	こめ	米	(N)	47	raw rice
	こら	こら	(Ph)	53	Hey! (threat)
3	ごらんになる	ご覧になる	(V2)	52	to see (sonkeigo)
	ごりら	ゴリラ	(N)	54	gorilla
	これくとこーる	コレクトコール	(N)	55	collect call
3	こわい	怖い	(iAdj)	JiM1	scary
3	こわす	壊す	(V)	JiM1	to break
3	こわれる	壊れる	(V1)	JiM2	to be broken
4	こんげつ	今月	(Adv)		this month
3	こんさーと	コンサート	(N)		concert
4	こんしゅう	今週	(Adv)	58	this week
3	こんど	今度	(Adv)	JiM2	next time
4	こんばん	今晩	(Adv)		tonight
	こんぶ	昆布	(N)	47	konbu seaweed
3	こんや	今夜	(Adv)	JiM2	tonight

さ SA

	さいあい	最愛	(Adv)	54	the most loved
	さいあく	最悪	(Adv)	54	the worst
	さいきょう	最強	(Adv)	54	the strongest
3	さいきん	最近	(Adv)	54	lately
3	さいご	最後	(Adv)	54	the last one
	さいこう	最高	(Adv)	54	the best
	さいしゅう	最終	(Adv)	54	the last | the final
3	さいしょ	最初	(Adv)	54	the beginning
	さいしょう	最小	(Adv)	54	the smallest
	さいしょくしゅぎ	菜食主義	(N)	48	vegetarianism
	さいしん	最新	(Adv)	54	the newest
	さいせい	再生	(Vn)	55	playback (of a video)
	さいせんばこ	賽銭箱	(N)	55	offertory box
	さいだい	最大	(Adv)	54	the largest
	さいたま	埼玉	(T)	48, 59	Saitama (prefecture, city)
	さいてい	最低	(Adv)	54	the lowest | pathetic
	さいてき	最適	(Adv)	54	the most appropriate, the ideal
	さいはっこう	再発行	(Vn)	51	reissue
3	さいふ	財布	(N)	51	wallet
	さいりょう	最良	(Adv)	54	the best
	ざいりょう	材料	(N)	47	ingredient
3	さがす	探す	(V)	JiM2	to search
4	さかな	魚	(N)	47	fish
3	さがる	下がる	(V2)	JiM2	to go down, to hang down
3	さかんな	盛んな	(naAdj)		flourishing, prosperous
4	さき	先	(Adv)		ahead, beyond
4	さく	咲く	(V)	49	to flower
4	さくしゃ	作者	(N)	JiM2	author
	さくぶん	作文	(N)	60	composition
4	さくら	桜	(N)	JiM1	cherry tree | cherry blossom
	さくらんぼ	さくらんぼ	(N)	47	cherry
	さけ	さけ (鮭)	(N)	47	salmon
3	さげる	下げる	(V1)	JiM2	to lower

3	さしあげる	差し上げる	(V1)	JiM2	to give (formal)
	さしみ	刺身	(N)	47	*sashimi*
4	さす	さす	(V)		to open an umbrella | to pierce
	ざぜん	座禅	(Vn)	55	sitting to meditate Zen style
4	〜さつ	〜冊	(C)		(counter for books)
4	さっか	作家	(N)	60	author, novelist
4	さっかー	サッカー	(N)	JiM2	soccer
3	さっき	さっき	(Adv)	58	a little while ago
4	ざっし	雑誌	(N)	JiM1	magazine
	さっそく	早速	(Adv)	51	quickly
4	さとう	砂糖	(N)	47	sugar
	さとり	悟り	(N)	55	enlightment
3	さびしい	寂しい	(iAdj)		sad, lonely
	ざまみろ	ざまみろ	(Ph)	53	Serves you right!
4	さむい	寒い	(iAdj)	JiM1	cold
	さらだ	サラダ	(N)	47	salad
	さる	猿	(N)	59	monkey
3	さわぐ	騒ぐ	(V)		to be boisterous
3	さわる	触る	(V2)		to touch
	さんか	参加	(Vn)	46	to take part
	さんきゃく	三脚	(N)	55	tripod
3	さんだる	サンダル	(N)		sandal
3	さんどいっち	サンドイッチ	(N)	54	sandwich
3	ざんねんな	残念な	(naAdj)	59	to be a pity
4	さんぽ	散歩	(Vn)	JiM2	a walk

し SHI

	し	市	(N)	51	city
3	じ	字	(N)		character, letter
3	しあい	試合	(N)	JiM2	match | tournament
	しいたけ	しいたけ	(N)	47	*shiitake* mushroom
	しえき	使役	(N)	60	causative mood
4	しお	塩	(N)	46, 47	salt
	しおからい	塩辛い	(iAdj)	47	salty
	しか	しか	(Adv)	58	only
	しかい	歯科医	(N)	49, 51	dentist
3	しかたがない	仕方がない	(Ph)	53	It can't be helped
3	しかる	しかる	(V2)	50	to scold
4	じかん	時間	(N)	JiM2	time
	しきゅう	至急	(Adv)	51	urgently
	しけい	死刑	(Vn)	60	death penalty
3	しけん	試験	(N)	JiM1	exam
	じけん	事件	(N)	50	case, event
3	じこ	事故	(N)	JiM2	accident
	しこく	四国	(T)	54	Shikoku
	じごく	地獄	(N)	54	hell
4	しごと	仕事	(N)	JiM1	work
	じさつ	自殺	(Vn)	49	suicide
4	じしょ	辞書	(N)	JiM2	dictionary
3	じしん	地震	(N)	JiM1	earthquake
4	しずかな	静かな	(naAdj)	JiM1	quiet, silent
4	した	下	(Adv)	JiM1	under
3	じだい	時代	(N)		period, era
	したがう	従う	(V)	59	to obey
3	したぎ	下着	(N)	JiM2	underwear
3	したく	支度	(Vn)		preparations
	しっとう	執刀	(Vn)	52	surgery, operation
3	しっぱい	失敗	(Vn)	49	failure
4	しつもん	質問	(Vn)	52	question

3	しつれいな	失礼な	(Adv.na)	JiM2	rude
	しで	四手	(N)	55	*shide*, bits of paper in zigzag
3	じてん	辞典	(N)	59	dictionary
4	じてんしゃ	自転車	(N)	JiM1	bicycle
	しどう	指導	(Vn)	60	guide
4	じどうしゃ	自動車	(N)	JiM2	car
	しないでんわ	市内電話	(N)	55	local call
3	しなもの	品物	(N)		an article, goods
4	しぬ	死ぬ	(V)	JiM1	to die
	しのうこうしょう	士農工商	(N)	59	feudal caste system
	しのび	忍び	(N)	59	stealth
	しばい	芝居	(N)	56	theatre play
3	しばらく	しばらく	(Adv)		a while
	じびいんこうかい	耳鼻咽喉科医	(N)	51	otolaryngologist
4	じぶん	自分	(N)		oneself
3	しま	島	(N)	55	island
4	しまる	閉まる	(V2)	JiM2	to be shut
3	じむしょ	事務所	(N)		office
4	しめる	締める	(V1)	JiM2	to fasten
4	しめる	閉める	(V1)	JiM2	to shut
	しゃあない	しゃあない	(Ph)	59	It can't be helped –Kansai–
	しゃいん	社員	(N)	60	employee
3	しゃかい	社会	(N)		society
	じゃがいも	じゃがいも	(N)	47	potato
	しやくしょ	市役所	(N)	55	city hall
	しゃけ	しゃけ (鮭)	(N)	47	salmon
4	しゃしん	写真	(N)	50	photography
3	しゃちょう	社長	(N)	JiM1	president, director (company)
4	しゃつ	シャツ	(N)	JiM2	shirt
	しゃったー	シャッター	(N)	55	shutter (camera)
	しゃぶしゃぶ	しゃぶしゃぶ	(N)	47	*shabushabu* stew
3	じゃま	邪魔	(Vn)	57	nuisance, obstacle
3	じゃむ	ジャム	(N)		jam
3	じゆう	自由	(N)		freedom
	じゅう	銃	(N)	51	gun
	〜じゅう	〜中	(Ph)	58	all throughout...
3	しゅうかん	習慣	(N)		habit
3	じゅうしょ	住所	(N)	51, 55	mail address
4	じゅーす	ジュース	(N)	47	juice
	しゅうちゅう	集中	(Vn)	58	concentration
3	じゅうどう	柔道	(N)	46	judo
3	じゅうぶんな	十分な	(naAdj)		enough
	しゅうまい	シュウマイ	(N)	47	*shūmai* dumpling
	しゅうまつ	週末	(N)	48	weekend
	しゅうり	修理	(Vn)	48	repair
4	じゅぎょう	授業	(N)	JiM2	class
	じゅく	塾	(N)	46	cram school
4	しゅくだい	宿題	(N)	JiM2	homework
	しゅじゅつ	手術	(Vn)	51	surgery, operation
	しゅっけつ	出血	(N)	51	hemorrhage
	しゅつじょう	出場	(Vn)	56	participation
3	しゅっせき	出席	(Vn)		attendance
3	しゅっぱつ	出発	(Vn)	JiM1	departure, starting
3	しゅみ	趣味	(N)	JiM2	hobby
	じゅんさ	巡査	(N)	51	policeman, officer
3	じゅんび	準備	(Vn)		preparation
	〜しょう	〜章	(C)	54	(counter for chapters)
	しょうが	しょうが	(N)	47	ginger
3	しょうかい	紹介	(Vn)		introduction
3	しょうがつ	正月	(N)		New Year

す SU

3	たりる	足りる	(V1)		to be enough
4	だれ	誰	(Adv)	JiM1	who?
	だんご	団子	(N)	47	*dango* sweets
4	たんじょうび	誕生日	(N)		birthday
4	だんす	ダンス	(N)		dance
3	だんせい	男性	(N)	60	man
4	だんだん	だんだん	(Adv)		gradually
3	だんぼう	暖房	(N)	JiM2	heating

ち CHI

3	ち	血	(N)	51	blood
4	ちいさい	小さい	(iAdj)	JiM1	small
	ちーず	チーズ	(N)	47, 55	cheese
	ちーむ	チーム	(N)	60	team
4	ちかい	近い	(iAdj)	JiM1	close, near
4	ちがう	違う	(V)	JiM1	to be wrong
4	ちかてつ	地下鉄	(N)	JiM2	subway (train)
3	ちから	力	(N)	JiM1	strength
4	ちず	地図	(N)	50	map
4	ちち	父	(N)	JiM1	father
	ちちおや	父親	(N)	56	father
3	ちっとも	ちっとも	(Adv)		(not) at all
	ちば	千葉	(T)	59	Chiba
	ちび	ちび	(N)	53	kid | midget
	ちゃーはん	チャーハン	(N)	47	fried rice
4	ちゃいろな	茶色な	(naAdj)		brown
	ちゃう	ちゃう	(Ph)	59	You're wrong —Kansai—
	ちゃか	チャカ	(N)	51	gun (vulgar)
	ちゃり	チャリ	(N)	53	bicycle (vulgar)
4	ちゃわん	茶碗	(N)	47	bowl
3	ちゅうい	注意	(Vn)	JiM2	caution
3	ちゅうがっこう	中学校	(N)		junior high school
	ちゅうし	中止	(Vn)	56	cancellation
	ちゅうじえん	中耳炎	(N)	51	inflammation of the ear
3	ちゅうしゃ	注射	(Vn)	51	injection
3	ちゅうしゃじょう	駐車場	(N)		parking
	ちゅうしょく	昼食	(N)	47	lunch
	ちゅうもん	注文	(Vn)	47	order (restaurant)
	〜ちょう	〜町	(N)	51	city / town of...
	ちょう	腸	(N)	51	intestines
	ちょう〜	超〜	(Adv)	53	super–
	ちょうこく	彫刻	(N)	55	sculpture
	ちょうし	調子	(N)	54	state, condition
	ちょうしょく	朝食	(N)	47	breakfast
	ちょうだい	頂戴	(Vn)	56	obtain, receive
4	ちょうど	丁度	(Adv)		precisely
	〜ちょうめ	〜丁目	(N)	51	a city block...
	ちょくぜん	直前	(Adv)	57	just before
4	ちょこれーと	チョコレート	(N)	47	chocolate
4	ちょっと	ちょっと	(Adv)	51, 54	a little
3	ちり	地理	(N)		geography

つ TSU

	つあー	ツアー	(N)	55	tour
	つい	つい	(Adv)	48	suddenly
	ついか	追加	(Vn)	47	addition, sum
4	つかう	使う	(V)	JiM2	to use
3	つかまえる	捕まえる	(V1)	JiM2	to catch
4	つかれる	疲れる	(V1)	JiM1	to be tired

な　NA

4	なつ	夏	(N)	JiM1	summer
	なっとう	納豆	(N)	47	*nattō* fermented beans
4	なつやすみ	夏休み	(N)	48	summer holidays
4	など	など	(Adv)		and so forth
	なぷきん	ナプキン	(N)	47	napkin
	なべ	鍋	(N)	47	pot
4	なまえ	名前	(N)	JiM1	name
	なめる	なめる	(V1)	53	to make a fool of | to lick
	なら	奈良	(T)	55	Nara (prefecture, city)
4	ならう	習う	(V)	48	to learn
4	ならぶ	並ぶ	(V)		to be in a row, to form in line
4	ならべる	並べる	(V1)		to arrange, to put side by side
3	なる	鳴る	(V2)		to sound, to ring
3	なるべく	なるべく	(Adv)		as possible
3	なるほど	なるほど	(Ph)		I see, indeed
3	なれる	慣れる	(V1)		to get used to
	なんば	なんば	(T)	59	Nanba (in Osaka)
	なんぱ	ナンパ	(Vn)	48, 53	to pick up on, to hit on
	なんぼ	なんぼ	(Ph)	59	how much is it? —KANSAI—

に NI

3	におい	匂い	(N)	JiM2	smell
	におう	仁王	(N)	55	Niō statues
3	にがい	苦い	(iAdj)	47	bitter
4	にぎやかな	賑やかな	(naAdj)		lively, merry
	にぎりずし	握り寿司	(N)	47	*nigiri* sushi
	にぎる	握る	(V2)	47	to clasp
4	にく	肉	(N)	47	meat
3	にげる	逃げる	(V1)	JiM2	to escape
	にごる	濁る	(V2)	49	to become muddy, cloudy
4	にし	西	(Adv)	JiM1	west
3	にっき	日記	(N)		diary
	にっしゃびょう	日射病	(N)	51	sunstroke
	にほんしゅ	日本酒	(N)	47	*sake*
4	にもつ	荷物	(N)	JiM2	luggage
3	にゅういん	入院	(Vn)	48, 51	hospitalization
3	にゅうがく	入学	(Vn)	58	entrance into a school
	にゅうじょう	入場	(Vn)	55	entrance
4	にゅーす	ニュース	(N)		news
	にょう	尿	(N)	51	urine
	にょらい	如来	(N)	55	statue of a Buddha
	にら	にら	(N)	47	scallion
3	にる	似る	(V1)	JiM2	to look like
	にる	煮る	(V1)	47	to boil
4	にわ	庭	(N)	55	garden
3	にんぎょう	人形	(N)	JiM2	doll
	にんじゃ	忍者	(N)	59	ninja
	にんじん	にんじん	(N)	47	carrot
	にんにく	にんにく	(N)	47	garlic

ぬ NU

	～ぬき	～抜き	(Adv)	47	without...
4	ぬぐ	脱ぐ	(V)	JiM2	to take off, to undress
	ぬく	抜く	(V)	49	to pull out
3	ぬすむ	盗む	(V)	51	to steal
3	ぬる	塗る	(V2)		to paint
3	ぬれる	ぬれる	(V1)		to get wet

ひ HI

4	ぴあの	ピアノ	(N)		piano
3	ひえる	冷える	(V1)	JiM2	to grow cold, to cool (down)
	びえん	鼻炎	(N)	51	rhinitis
	ひがいしゃ	被害者	(N)	51	victim
	ひかく	比較	(Vn)	54	comparison
4	ひがし	東	(Adv)	JiM1	east
4	～ひき	～匹	(C)	58	(counter for small animals)
3	ひきだし	引き出し	(N)		drawer
	ひきのばす	引き伸ばす	(V)	55	to enlarge (photo)
4	ひく	引く	(V)	JiM2	to draw, to pull | to look up
4	ひくい	低い	(iAdj)	JiM1	low
3	ひげ	ひげ	(N)	JiM1	beard
4	ひこうき	飛行機	(N)	JiM2	airplane
3	ひさしぶり	久しぶり	(Ph)		"It's been a long time!"
3	びじゅつかん	美術館	(N)	55	art museum
3	ひじょうに	非常に	(Adv)	49	very, extremely
	ぴすとる	ピストル	(N)	51	gun
4	ひだり	左	(N)	JiM1	left
3	びっくり	ビックリ	(Vn)	60	surprise
3	ひっこす	引っ越す	(V)		to move (to)
	ひっこむ	引っ込む	(V)	53	to withdraw, to retire
	ひつじにく	羊肉	(N)	47	mutton
	ひったくる	ひったくる	(V2)	51	to snatch
3	ひつような	必要な	(naAdj)	JiM1	necessary
4	ひと	人	(N)	JiM1	person | people
3	ひどい	ひどい	(iAdj)	50, 53	horrible, terrible
	びびる	びびる	(V2)	53	to be scared stiff
	びびんば	ビビンバ	(N)	56	*bibimbap* (Korean dish)
	ひふ	皮膚	(N)	51	skin
4	ひまな	暇な	(naAdj)		to have spare time
	ひみつ	秘密	(N)	60	secret
	ひゃくとうばん	110番	(Ph)	51	#110 (police/ambulance)
4	びょういん	病院	(N)	51	hospital
4	びょうき	病気	(N)	51	sickness
3	ひらく	開く	(V)		to open
3	びる	ビル	(N)	56	building
4	ひる	昼	(N)	JiM1	noon
4	ひるごはん	昼ご飯	(N)	47	lunch
4	ひろい	広い	(iAdj)	JiM2	wide
3	ひろう	拾う	(V)		to pick up
	びん	瓶	(N)	47	bottle
	ひんけつ	貧血	(N)	51	anemia
4	ぴんぽん	ピンポン	(N)		ping-pong

ふ　FU

	ふ	府	(N)	51	prefecture (Osaka or Kyoto)
	ふぁすとふーど	ファストフード	(N)	47	fast food
	ふぁっくす	ファックス	(N)	46	fax
	ぶいさいん	Vサイン	(N)	55	victory sign
4	ふぃるむ	フィルム	(N)	55	roll of film
4	ふうとう	封筒	(N)	55	envelope
	ふうみりょう	風味料	(N)	47	seasoning
4	ぷーる	プール	(N)	56	swimming pool
3	ふえる	増える	(V1)	JiM2	to increase, to rise
4	ふぉーく	フォーク	(N)	47	fork
3	ふかい	深い	(iAdj)		deep
	ふきん	付近	(N)	51	environs, neighborhood
4	ふく	吹く	(V)		to blow
4	ふく	服	(N)	JiM2	clothes

ほ　HO

4	ほう	方	(Adv)	54	a way
	ぼう	棒	(N)	60	stick
3	ぼうえき	貿易	(N)		trade
	ほうげん	方言	(N)	59	dialect
	ほうこう	方向	(N)	55	direction
4	ぼうし	帽子	(N)	53	hat
	ぼうず	坊主	(N)	55	Buddhist monk
3	ほうそう	放送	(Vn)		broadcasting
	ほうたい	包帯	(N)	51	bandage
	ほうちょう	包丁	(N)	48	kitchen knife
	ほうべん	方便	(N)	59	means, instrument
3	ほうりつ	法律	(N)		law
4	ぼーるぺん	ボールペン	(N)		pen
	ほかす	ほかす	(V)	59	to throw away —KANSAI—
3	ぼく	僕	(PN)	JiM1	I
4	ぽけっと	ポケット	(N)		pocket
	ほけん	保険	(N)	51	insurance
	ぼさつ	菩薩	(N)	55	*Boddhisattva*
	ほし	ホシ	(N)	51	suspect (jargon)
3	ほし	星	(N)	JiM1	star, planet
4	ほしい	欲しい	(iAdj)	JiM2	to want, to wish
	ぽすと	ポスト	(N)	55	mailbox
4	ほそい	細い	(iAdj)		fine, slender
	ほたる	蛍	(N)	56	firefly
4	ぼたん	ボタン	(N)		button
	ぼちぼち	ぼちぼち	(Adv)	59	so so —KANSAI—
	ほっかいどう	北海道	(T)	47, 59	Hokkaidō (prefecture)
4	ほてる	ホテル	(N)	JiM2	hotel
3	ほど	ほど	(Adv)	58	approximately
	ほとけ	仏	(N)	59	Buddha
3	ほとんど	ほとんど	(Adv)		almost, for the most part
	ほな	ほな	(Ph)	59	well, then —KANSAI—
	ほね	骨	(N)	51	bone
3	ほめる	ほめる	(V1)	60	to praise
4	ほん	本	(N)	JiM1	book
4	～ほん	～本	(C)	JiM1	(counter for slender objects)
	ほん～	本～	(Ph)	51	this...
	ほんげつ	本月	(N)	51	this month
	ほんこう	本校	(N)	51	this school
	ほんじつ	本日	(N)	51	this day (today)
	ほんしゃ	本社	(N)	51	this company
4	ほんだな	本棚	(N)		bookshelf
4	ほんとうに	本当に	(Adv)	JiM2	really
	ほんぶ	本部	(N)	51	headquarters
	ほんまに	ほんまに	(Adv)	59	really, truly —KANSAI—
3	ほんやく	翻訳	(Vn)	JiM2	translation

ま　MA

4	～まい	～枚	(C)	55	(counter for flat things)
4	まい～	毎～	(Adv)	50	each...
4	まいど	毎度	(Ph)	59	Hello —KANSAI—
4	まいにち	毎日	(Adv)	56	every day
3	まいる	参る	(V2)	52	to come / go *(kenjōgo)*
4	まえ	前	(Adv)	48	before
4	まがる	曲がる	(V2)	55	to turn, to bend
	まきずし	巻き寿司	(N)	47	*makizushi* sushi
	まく	巻く	(V)	47	to roll
	まぐろ	まぐろ	(N)	47	tuna

3	まける	負ける	(V1)	53	to lose
	まじ	マジ	(Adv)	53	seriously, in earnest
3	まじめな	真面目な	(naAdj)	48	serious, earnest
3	まず	まず	(Adv)		first of all
4	まずい	まずい	(iAdj)	54	bad (taste)
4	まだ	まだ	(Adv)	JiM1	still
4	また	また	(Adv)		again
3	または	または	(Adv)		either... or
4	まち	町	(N)	JiM2	town
3	まちがえる	間違える	(V1)	JiM2	to make a mistake
4	まつ	松	(N)		pine tree
4	まつ	待つ	(V)	JiM2	to wait
4	まっすぐ	まっすぐ	(Adv)	55	straight ahead
4	まっち	マッチ	(N)		match
	まっちゃ	抹茶	(N)	47	green tea
3	まつり	祭り	(N)	55	festival
4	まど	窓	(N)	JiM2	window
	まなぶ	学ぶ	(V)	57	to learn
3	まにあう	間に合う	(V)	JiM2	to be in time
	まねく	招く	(V)	60	to invite
	まやく	麻薬	(N)	50	drug
	まよう	迷う	(V)	48	to get lost | to hesitate
	まよねーず	マヨネーズ	(N)	47	mayonnaise
	まらそん	マラソン	(N)	46	marathon
4	まるい	丸い	(iAdj)		round
	まるで	まるで	(Adv)	54	just like
3	まわり	周り	(N)		the surroundings
3	まわる	回る	(V2)	JiM1	to go round
3	まんが	漫画	(N)	JiM1	comic book
	まんかい	満開	(Vn)	49	full bloom
	まんざい	漫才	(N)	59	*manzai* comic performance
3	まんなか	真ん中	(Adv)		in the middle

み MI

3	みえる	見える	(V1)	JiM2	can see (unconsciously)
	みおぼえ	見覚え	(N)	53	recollection
4	みがく	磨く	(V)	48	to polish
4	みかん	みかん	(N)	47	mandarin
4	みぎ	右	(Adv)	JiM1	right
	みぎがわ	右側	(Adv)	55	to the right
	みさき	岬	(N)	55	cape
4	みじかい	短い	(iAdj)		short
4	みず	水	(N)	47	water
3	みずうみ	湖	(N)	55	lake
	みずから	自ら	(Adv)	52	oneself | in person
	みずぶそく	水不足	(N)	56	drought
4	みせ	店	(N)	JiM2	shop
4	みせる	見せる	(V1)	JiM2	to show
3	みそ	味噌	(N)	47	*miso* fermented paste
	みそしる	味噌汁	(N)	47	*miso* soup
4	みち	道	(N)	JiM1	road
3	みつかる	見つかる	(V2)	JiM2	to find
3	みつける	見つける	(V1)	JiM2	to find
	みどころ	見所	(N)	55	place worth seeing
3	みどり	緑	(N)		green
4	みなさん	皆さん	(PN)		all of you
3	みなと	港	(N)	55	harbor
	みなみ	ミナミ	(T)	59	nickname for Nanba
4	みなみ	南	(Adv)	JiM1	south

	みまもる	見守る	(V2)	50	to protect, to watch
4	みみ	耳	(N)	JiM1	ear
	みゃくはく	脈拍	(N)	51	pulse
	みゅんへん	ミュンヘン	(T)	50	Munich (city in Germany)
	みょうおう	明王	(N)	55	Myōō Buddhist guardians
	みょうな	妙な	(Adv.na)	49	strange
	みりん	みりん	(N)	47	sweet sake
4	みる	見る	(V1)	JiM1	to see, to look
4	みるく	ミルク	(N)		milk
4	みんな	皆	(PN)		everybody

む MU

	むかい	向かい	(Adv)	55	the opposite side
3	むかえる	迎える	(V1)	JiM2	to go to meet
3	むかし	昔	(Adv)	59	long ago
	むかつく	むかつく	(V)	53	to get angry
	むこ	婿	(N)	50	son-in-law
4	むこう	向こう	(Adv)		the other side, over there
3	むし	虫	(N)		insect
	むす	蒸す	(V)	47	to steam
4	むずかしい	難しい	(iAdj)	JiM2	difficult
3	むすこ	息子	(N)	JiM1	son
3	むすめ	娘	(N)	JiM1	daughter
	むだん	無断	(Adv)	48	without permission
	むね	胸	(N)	47	breast
3	むら	村	(N)	59	village
3	むりな	無理な	(naAdj)	51	impossible
	むりやりに	むりやりに	(Adv)	60	by force, unwillingly

め ME

4	め	目	(N)	JiM1	eye
	めいじじだい	明治時代	(N)	59	Meiji period (1868-1912)
	めいじる	命じる	(V1)	57	to command
	めいれい	命令	(Vn)	50	command
	めいわく	迷惑	(Vn)	46	trouble
	めーかー	メーカー	(N)	51	manufacturer | brand
4	めーとる	メートル	(N)		meter
4	めがね	眼鏡	(N)	JiM1	glasses
3	めしあがる	召し上がる	(V2)	47, 52	to eat (sonkeigo)
3	めずらしい	珍しい	(iAdj)		unusual, uncommon
	めっちゃ	めっちゃ	(Adv)	53, 59	very, very much –Kansai–
	めにゅー	メニュー	(N)	47	menu
	めろん	メロン	(N)	47	melon
	めんきょ	免許	(N)	49	license, certificate
	めんどう	面倒	(N)	56	trouble, bother
	めんどうをみる	面倒を見る	(Ph)	56	to take care of someone

も MO

4	もう	もう	(Adv)		already
	もうかる	儲かる	(V2)	59	to earn money
3	もうしあげる	申し上げる	(V1)	52	to say to a superior (kenjōgo)
3	もうす	申す	(V)	52	to say (kenjōgo)
	もうちょうえん	盲腸炎	(N)	51	appendicitis
	もくげきしゃ	目撃者	(N)	51	witness
3	もし	もし	(Adv)	56	if
4	もしもし	もしもし	(Ph)	55	Hello? (telephone)
	もち	餅	(N)	47	mashed rice paste
	もちかえり	持ち帰り	(N)	47	take home, "to go"
4	もちろん	もちろん	(Adv)		of course

	ゆうびんばんごう	郵便番号	(N)	55	zip code
4	ゆうべ	昨夜	(Adv)	58	last night
4	ゆうめいな	有名な	(naAdj)	52	famous
4	ゆき	雪	(N)	JiM1	snow
3	ゆしゅつ	輸出	(Vn)		exportation
4	ゆたかな	豊かな	(Adv.na)	56	rich, plentiful
	ゆでる	ゆでる	(V1)	47	to boil
3	ゆび	指	(N)	JiM1	finger
3	ゆびわ	指輪	(N)	51	ring
3	ゆめ	夢	(N)		dream
3	ゆれる	揺れる	(V1)		to shake, to sway

よ YO

3	よう	用	(N)		use, affairs
3	ようい	用意	(Vn)	52	preparation
3	ようじ	用事	(N)		affairs
	ようちえん	幼稚園	(N)	57	kindergarten
4	ようふく	洋服	(N)		clothes (Western style)
	よーぐると	ヨーグルト	(N)	47	yogurt
4	よく	よく	(Adv)	48	very much | often | well
4	よこ	横	(Adv)		beside
	よこになる	横になる	(Ph)	51	to lie down
	よこはま	横浜	(T)	59	Yokohama (city)
3	よごれる	汚れる	(V1)	JiM2	to become dirty
	よじじゅくご	四字熟語	(N)	59	four-kanji sayings
3	よしゅう	予習	(Vn)		preparation of lessons
3	よてい	予定	(N)	JiM2	expectation
4	よぶ	呼ぶ	(V)	JiM1	to call, to summon
4	よむ	読む	(V)	JiM1	to read
3	よやく	予約	(Vn)	JiM2	booking, reservation
3	よる	寄る	(V2)	49	to come near, to call on
4	よる	夜	(N)	JiM1	night
3	よろこぶ	喜ぶ	(V)		to be glad
3	よろしい	よろしい	(iAdj)	52	good (formal)
	よろしくつたえる	よろしく伝える	(Ph)	56	to give regards
3	よわい	弱い	(iAdj)	JiM1	weak

ら RA

	らーめん	ラーメン	(N)	47	*rāmen* Chinese noodles
4	らいしゅう	来週	(Adv)	JiM2	next week
4	らいねん	来年	(Adv)	JiM2	next year
	らいばる	ライバル	(N)	60	rival
4	らじお	ラジオ	(N)		radio
	らじこん	ラジコン	(N)	60	radio-controlled device
	らす・べがす	ラス・べガス	(T)	50	Las Vegas (city)
	らぶらぶ	ラブラブ	(Vn)	58	loving, make out

り RI

	りーぐ	リーグ	(N)	60	league
	りこん	離婚	(Vn)	58	divorce
4	りっぱな	立派な	(naAdj)		splendid, worthy
3	りゆう	理由	(N)	50	cause, reason
4	りゅうがく	留学	(Vn)	JiM2	studying abroad
	りゅーまち	リューマチ	(N)	51	rheumatism
	りゅっく	リュック	(N)	51	backpack
3	りよう	利用	(Vn)		use
	りょう	料	(N)	55	price
4	りょうしん	両親	(N)		parents
3	りょうほう	両方	(Adv)		both